SHATTERED NORMS
A punk's journey to the boardroom

("A dark humoured story of Defiance, Transformation, and Achievement")

Simon Mennell

Copyright © 2025 by Simon Mennell

All rights reserved.

No part of this book may be reproduced or used in any way; electronic, mechanical, photocopying, recording, scanning, or otherwise—without the publisher's express written consent. This book is prohibited from being copied, posted online, or distributed in any other way without the copyright owner's permission except for the use of quotations in a book review.

First paperback edition March 2025

DISCLAIMER

This book is a memoir based on the personal experiences and recollections of the author. While every effort has been made to present events accurately, certain names, locations, and identifying details have been changed to respect privacy, and some conversations have been reconstructed based on memory.

The views and opinions expressed in this book are solely those of the author and do not reflect those of any individuals, organizations, or entities mentioned. This book is not intended to provide professional, legal, medical, or financial advice. Readers seeking guidance on any related issues should consult qualified professionals.

The author and publisher disclaim any liability for any outcomes resulting from the use of the information presented in this book.

DEDICATION

To

Dottie, Winan, Rory, Ailsa and of course, my siblings, Carole, Nick and Lisa. Thank you for inspiring me, grounding me, and filling my life with love and laughter.

TABLE OF CONTENTS

DEDICATION iv

CHAPTER 1 *Arrival* 1

CHAPTER 2 *The Milk Monitors Guide to Musical Mayhem* 11

CHAPTER 3 *The Unexpected Arrival of Family* 26

CHAPTER 4 *The Cold Day* 32

CHAPTER 5 *The Black Frying Pan* 37

CHAPTER 6 *The Culinary Awakening* 44

CHAPTER 7 *My doggy companion* 48

CHAPTER 8 *The Rubber House bounces back* 54

CHAPTER 9 *A Beacon of Kindness* 58

CHAPTER 10 *Brotherhood in the Church Lads Brigade* 65

CHAPTER 11 *Skiing to Anarchy in the Classroom* 73

CHAPTER 12 *Chemistry and Catastrophes* 83

CHAPTER 13 *The Winter of Discontent and Shocking Revelations* 90

CHAPTER 14 *The Rise of The Shove* 95

CHAPTER 15 *Rolf on Saturday* 105

CHAPTER 16 *Memories of Grandad* 111

CHAPTER 17 *Sweet Times and Coming of Age* 116

CHAPTER 18 *Night Shifts and Seaside Trips* 125

CHAPTER 19 *Shaking the foundations of the village* 139

CHAPTER 20 *Entering the Digital Age* 143

CHAPTER 21 *The Misadventures of Trevor the "Slopa"* 148

CHAPTER 22 *Rising Through the Ranks* 154

CHAPTER 23 *A Defining Moment* 163

CHAPTER 24 *Getting Maui'd and the Mysteriously Sober Stag Night* 169

CHAPTER 25 *The HR Transition and the Lion City* 180

CHAPTER 26 *The Idiosyncrasies of Global Media Organisation* 194

CHAPTER 27 *Did Someone Mention Fraud?* 203

CHAPTER 28 *The Day the World Changed* 212

CHAPTER 29 *A Dark Time in Singapore* 221

CHAPTER 30 *Our family grows.* 235

CHAPTER 31 *The Challenge of SARS* 257

CHAPTER 32 *The Z Chronicles and the panty stealer* .. 266

CHAPTER 33 *Thailand and the Ladyboy* 278

CHAPTER 34 *The Move Back to the UK* 285

CHAPTER 35 *A New Home in Aldbury* 297

CHAPTER 36 *The Relocation of a Major European Publication* 310

CHAPTER 37 *Dubai to Jersey* 325

CHAPTER 38 *To the Home of Golf* 354

CHAPTER 39 *A Solo Return to Dubai* 362

CHAPTER 40 *Holidays with Rory and Ailsa* 369

CHAPTER 41 *Back into the Fray, My Friends* 383

CHAPTER 42 *New Beginnings in Qatar* 391

CHAPTER 43 *The journey home* 406

CHAPTER 44 *Life Lessons and Reflections* 411

CHAPTER 1
Arrival

I arrived in this world in the summer of 1965, a tiny bundle of life who could have easily been mistaken for a cartoon character rather than a baby. I was born in the quaint village of Westow, home to the maternity hospital that served families from the surrounding countryside. They say a child doesn't develop memories until around the age of four, but I can tell you this—every time I smell disinfectant, I'm reminded of my arrival into the world.

My parents lived in the village of Osbaldwick, just outside the boundary of York. My entrance into life was anything but typical. In an era when coal fires filled homes with their distinct scent and everyone knew each other's business, my arrival became the talk of the village. The small community was tightly knit, a tapestry of familiar faces and shared experiences. Yet, my debut played out like an unexpected drama.

I was born a "blue baby," and Westow wasn't equipped to handle such emergencies. As a result, I was whisked away to

Scarborough Hospital for an emergency blood transfusion—a critical procedure in an era when medical practices were still evolving. I can only imagine the worried faces of my family, the frantic nurses racing down the hallways, and the sharp, sterile scent of antiseptic filling the air. Talk about starting life with a bang! Honestly, who knew my very first day would involve a race against time and medical jargon worthy of a textbook?

My sister's first impression of me was anything but warm. "Can he go back?" she asked my father, stamping her feet on the floor. "Boys stink!" Her disappointment was evident to everyone around her—she had clearly been hoping for a sister. It seems she had her own ideas about what life with a sibling should be like, and here I was, shattering her dreams of shared secrets and tea parties.

To smooth things over—and perhaps quell some of her budding resentment—my parents made a surprising concession: they let her name me. "Simon Templar!" she declared, inspired by the charismatic character from The Saint, who was all the rage at the time. And just like that, I became Simon—a name that carried both charm and an air of mystery, though I dare say I lacked the suave demeanour to match.

I was also given the middle names Charles Geoffrey—Charles after my grandfather, who had passed away just before I was born, and Geoffrey after my father. If you had added The Right Honourable before my name, you might have mistaken me for aristocracy. As if my early years weren't already spiralling in unexpected directions, I was soon introduced to pyloric stenosis—a hereditary condition that, in those days, often led to creative, if not questionable, treatments. The remedy? A spoonful of brandy! Yes, you read that right. Back then, the medical community relied on a mix of folk remedies and half-understood science, and this was their solution for me.

Today, it's a straightforward minor operation, but in the 1960s, infants were treated in ways that seem shocking by modern standards. Not that I remember any of it—thankfully. My life was just beginning, and I was far more interested in the curious shapes and sounds of the world than my emerging medical history. It was a time when simple solutions often took precedence over thorough examinations—a period tinged with naivety yet marked by resilience.

The plot thickened when, at just 18 months old, doctors discovered a cyst lurking behind my left eye. Out it came—

along with my eye, though only temporarily. It was a classic "let's remove the cyst and keep the eye" situation. However, the procedure left me with a lazy eye for a few years, an unfortunate accessory paired with some rather dreadful plastic NHS glasses. Those contraptions were an embarrassment to any toddler—especially considering the designer-rimmed options kids have today.

My attempts to adjust to life with a patch over my right eye were, unknowingly, the start of my comedy routine. I stumbled through the world half-blinded, turning everyday moments into episodes of slapstick hilarity. Children, as you might know, can be startlingly cruel. And while I love a good joke as much as the next person, the laughs were often at my expense—thanks to those unfortunate spectacles. Thankfully, I wasn't alone; several classmates sported the same NHS wonders.

A few years later, I found myself back in the hospital, embarking on an adventure that would leave lasting impressions on both me and my sister—though for entirely different reasons. I was whisked into a room, the spotlight on my not-so-private parts—let's just say my "wedding tackle" was in the line of fire. My sister and mother trailed behind the doctor, who looked less like a medical professional and more like a man preparing for a Netflix special.

With a single glance, he made the fateful decision to execute what can only be described as a half-hearted circumcision—one that left me howling in pain while my sister stood frozen, horrified by the live spectacle of What Not to Do in a Hospital. The botched job left me caught somewhere between a Roundhead and a Cavalier. And my sister?

Well, let's just say she walked away with a lifetime supply of therapy sessions—and an equally tough time explaining to her classmates why her brother had the most interesting excuses for skipping swimming lessons.

And speaking of spectacles, I quickly became quite skilled at breaking them. It didn't take long for me to master the art of disaster, wielding my clumsiness like a badge of honour. Whenever I inevitably cracked the lenses or snapped the hinges, my mother's solution wasn't to buy a shiny new pair—oh no! Her ingenious remedy? An Elastoplast. Yes, a simple adhesive plaster—one of those skin-coloured ones—slathered over the broken hinge before sending me back out into the world.

Nothing says childhood resilience quite like sporting a plastered pair of glasses with misplaced pride. My humble eyewear became a spectacle (pun intended), a constant reminder that sometimes, life is about making do with what you have—even if what you have looks like it survived a natural disaster.

My mother's name is Dorothy, but I and a few others call her "Dottie"—and I can assure you, no one in history has ever been more aptly named. Bonkers doesn't even begin to do her justice.

Home life wasn't exactly a walk in the park. My parents had a volatile relationship that could easily rival any soap opera. My mother had a gift for making her voice carry through walls, her passionate monologues echoing like theatrical performances. My father, a placid soul, took the shouting without response, while my mother had an unparalleled talent for creating drama. Her Oscar-worthy performance? Fake fainting—at any opportunity. It became the stuff of legend, traumatizing me and my sister well into adulthood.

My poor sister and I found ourselves caught in the storm, navigating the choppy waters of parental tension. You could hear my mother's shouts from a mile away, her frustrations spilling over like a boiling kettle. Years later, we discovered from our neighbours that my mother's antics had been a regular talking point in the village.

As I witnessed this tumultuous atmosphere, I had no idea that the chaos would come to define much of my childhood.

Speaking of chaos—if my father went out without my mother, she would often disappear for days on end, leaving my older sister—just eight years old at the time—in charge. Imagine the weight of that responsibility! My sister, brave and resourceful in the ways of survival, would dash around the house, doing her best to keep me entertained while quietly wondering where our mother had gone.

In the midst of all this madness, there was Auntie Helen—a wonderful soul who lived just a few doors down and whom we still hold fondly in our thoughts. She wasn't our real auntie, of course. Back in those days, close neighbours were all called "auntie" and "uncle." Auntie Helen would come to our rescue, a whirlwind of love and support, sweeping in during our mother's absences. With warmth and calm, she ensured we never felt alone or hungry.

Auntie Helen played an unsung role in our lives, filling the void whenever Mum disappeared. I can still hear her laughter, her reassuring voice making us feel safe even when the world around us seemed to be crumbling.

During one of my mother's mad episodes, she announced one morning—right after Dad had left for work—"You're not going to school today, Carole. We are moving house. NOW!"

My sister and I, confused, asked about Dad—was he coming with us? Mother's response was swift and final: "No."

It was a terrible situation for any child, especially since Dad had no idea about Dottie's sudden decision. As it turned out, she had been planning this move in secret for quite some time. The impact on my sister was far greater than on me; she had to leave her school, start fresh at a new one where she knew no one, and—just to add to the chaos—my mother registered her under her middle name.

With minimal belongings, Mother quickly counted out three forks, three knives, three plates, and three cups, and off we went—to a council house in Stockton-on-the-Forest, where we knew no one. My poor sister struggled to settle in. We had gone from a lovely semi-detached home to an unfamiliar place, and to make things worse, our father had no idea where we had been taken.

After a few weeks, my sister began to miss her friends in Osbaldwick. Determined to maintain some sense of normality, she took matters into her own hands. I can still picture her riding her bike down the back lanes, making treks to Osbaldwick to meet up with her old friends—navigating the long, winding country paths that led back to our former home. It must have felt like a labyrinth to her, but she rode with a fierce determination, unwilling to let go of the life she had known.

Within a few months, we moved back to Osbaldwick, and with that, some form of normality returned.

Unfortunately, even darker days were yet to come. My mother was a complex woman who faced severe mental challenges of her own. It was as though life had tossed her into a circus where she juggled numerous ailments. She was also quite a selfish person, and often, we—her children—came second to her.

My uncle, her brother, often called her "the princess" because she had shown the same tendencies in her youth. Still, her struggles made her less available to us, leading to confusion and resentment in later life. Yet, she was our mother, and we loved her, so we generally accepted what life had dealt us.

Overall, the early parts of my childhood were a delicate mix of chaos and stability. My parents often embraced the rhythm of life, frequently heading out to dance the night away while my sister and I were left to our own devices. Despite the whirlwind of their social life, we always maintained a strong family unit during events like weddings, birthdays, and holidays, creating a tapestry of memories that balanced wild nights with cherished moments spent together.

This harmonious routine continued right up until I hit the rebellious age of 15. Family gatherings became arenas for laughter and camaraderie, with my parents' lively dance moves often setting the stage for unforgettable antics. It was a time when family bonding shone bright amidst the chaos—whether we were tearing up the dance floor or navigating the joys and trials of growing up together.

Little did we know that soon, the dance floor would become a distant memory as life pulled us in different directions.

Buckle up—things were about to get interesting!

CHAPTER 2
The Milk Monitors Guide to Musical Mayhem

Growing up in Osbaldwick and attending the village county primary school was a defining chapter of my childhood, filled with both laughter and its fair share of anxiety. School wasn't far from our house—a short and rather uneventful walk, unless, of course, my mates decided to drag their feet or kick a football around the street like they were playing in the World Cup. I didn't really bother trying to stay clean in those days, even though my mother would shout as I left the house, "Don't you dare get dirty!" Not that she would have noticed if I had—most of her comments were more for show than anything else. I also had this massive leather satchel that I carried around, though I don't think it had much in it.

My grandparents would often visit us, especially if Dottie had gone on one of her walkabouts, and they would regularly come to the school gates to pick me up. I had this awful habit of running away from them when they came. One day, I ran out of the school gates, expecting to see them waiting. But this time, no one was there. I remember running home, only to find my grandparents sitting and watching TV. They said they were sick of coming to pick me up since I would just run away and head home alone. Feeling utterly wronged, I grabbed my bag, threw it across the room, and stormed off, shouting, "Sod the lot of you!"

Happy days. One bright spot in my life was my grandparents—such happy memories. Whenever they were around, we knew we'd get something nice to eat because my Nana would cook for us. But more than the walk home, it was the cast of characters waiting inside the school that made my stomach churn and my heart race.

There was our headmaster, Mr. Feasby—a formidable chap if ever there was one. He carried an aura of authority that demanded respect, not unlike a mad wizard looming over a group of hapless students, ready to cast spells of terror—or rather, what felt like a daily dose of dread. His obsession with music was legendary. Every day began with assembly. I can still hear the clang of the bell summoning us to his lair—the school hall—where a mix of excitement and sheer terror bubbled in our young hearts.

He was a strict disciplinarian who took his role very seriously—or, on reflection, more likely a sadist. So serious, in fact, that he felt compelled to deliver personal critiques while we sang.

Picture this: rows of children attempting to sing pointless songs and hymns while he strolled past, scrutinizing every tone. It was a bizarre mix of charming and terrifying, especially when he would stop mid-song to knock someone on the head—a sort of musical rude awakening.

"Grunter, you're a grunter, boy!" he would bellow, singling out the victims of his wrath. My good friend David had, unfortunately, received this title more times than anyone should, his undying enthusiasm leading him to belt out the high notes with a fervour akin to a cat in a fire. To this day, I can still hear the awful sound coming from his mouth.

As the years rolled by, we learned that school was occasionally a masterclass in controlled chaos. One day, my friend Paul and I found ourselves banished from class and sent to Mr. Feasby's office—the reason remains a mystery, though undoubtedly some minor infraction.

As we stood outside his door, we heard a faint humming as he walked down the corridor toward us. It was as if he were conducting a symphony in his head, his invisible baton moving with the music. He opened the door and walked in without a word, seemingly lost in his own private concert, before suddenly bellowing, "Come on in!"

He wanted to know our crime. Paul explained, oblivious to the storm brewing, while my gaze fell on a pile of books on his desk. Then, Mr. Feasby reached behind the desk. In his hand was the cane—his trusty instrument of justice.

There was a beat. I saw it all before it happened. He whacked a book off his desk; it fell to the floor with a resounding thud. "Smith, pick that up now, boy!" he roared. Before I could react, Paul had bent over to scoop up the offending volume.

A swift, brutal swish and a sharp crack across his buttocks—Paul let out a yelp. I looked at him, thinking to myself that I wasn't going to fall for that trick. So, I held out my hand, a small grin playing on my lips, bracing for the inevitable.

A loud crack, and it was done.

"Get out! Get back to class and don't come back!" Mr. Feasby boomed, his fury finally spent. I caught Paul's eye as we made our way back to the classroom, exchanging amused glances. Somehow, we had managed to turn a minor infraction into an unforgettable piece of school folklore.

I have to give credit where it's due, though—Mr. Feasby did introduce me to the world of music, and for that, I owe him a reluctant nod of gratitude. One particular assembly in my final year of primary school stands out. A big music concert was coming up at Huntington Secondary School, with several local primary schools participating.

By this time, Mr. Feasby had somewhat turned his critical gaze away from me, possibly out of sheer exhaustion from hearing my enthusiastic yet slightly off-key contributions. He held auditions for various instruments, particularly the drums—an instrument that seemed almost mystical, something I felt I could actually play.

After what felt like an eternity of raising my hand—so persistently that even a game show host would have been impressed—Mr. Feasby finally decided to give me a chance. I nervously approached the drum kit, thinking, This could be my moment in the sun... or the moment a slipper gets hurled at me with precision.

In that instant, the old headmaster, his eagle eyes peering through thick, black-rimmed spectacles, discovered that I actually had some rhythm. As I struck the drums, the echoes filled the hall, and to his surprise, not only did I keep time, but I added a flair even he hadn't expected. Suddenly, I was thrust into the "in gang," a title I wore like a badge of honour among my peers. The kid who had once been just another anonymous face in the crowd was now a musical aficionado—or at least, I was in my own mind.

But the grand saga of Osbaldwick Primary wouldn't be complete without another force of nature lurking within its walls: the infamous Miss Curry. If Mr. Feasby was a baton-wielding, crazed conductor, then Miss Curry was the mad scientist of the educational realm—a pyrotechnic presence capable of sending shivers down anyone's spine.

She reeked of cigarettes, the stench clinging to the air like an unwelcome guest, and her hair often resembled a bird's nest caught in a strong wind. She always seemed to wear a string of pearls—her signature look back in those days—along with thick brown stockings that would have made Nora Batty proud. If you were foolish enough to make eye contact with her when she was in one of those moods, you might as well have been signing up for a rollercoaster ride you never wanted to take.

Miss Curry had a peculiar habit of slapping legs—yes, legs! It was almost like a twisted rite of passage. She'd scurry down the aisle of desks like a hawk hunting its prey, her hand suddenly emerging from the shadows to deliver a swift and shocking warning.

Her other party trick? Shaking the living daylights out of her victims. And as if that weren't enough, she'd punctuate the shaking with an almost obsessive chant: "You'll jolly well listen to me!"—repeating it over and over. Ironically, no one ever remembered anything she actually wanted them to listen to. Maybe the shouting made it seem legitimate to her—who knows? One thing was certain: she was an absolute nutcase. In today's world, she'd probably be locked up.

You could almost rate your luck on a scale from "blessed" to "will never walk straight again." Any minor infraction—whispering in class, misplacing a pencil, giggling, or even sneezing—was enough to set her off. I quickly learned to perfect the art of silence, operating with the precision of an undercover agent.

Even at a young age, we quickly figured out that two roles reigned supreme among the ranks of children: the illustrious head server and the coveted milk monitor. Within this hierarchy of responsibility, both positions carried their own unique allure—along with a sprinkle of mischief, as was customary for any bunch of Yorkshire kids. Some might argue that being a prefect was the ultimate goal, but most of us knew better. A prefect was simply a brown-noser—the type who'd probably turn in their own mother for running in the corridors.

The head server was, without question, the gold standard of student roles. A dignified badge of honour, it promised not only preferential treatment at lunchtime but also a lofty perch from which to survey the sea of hungry peers clamouring for their daily sustenance. From the frontlines of the dining hall, head servers wielded their spatulas like sceptres, serving up portions while exchanging winks and nods with the side servers. It was a coveted throne—one that sparked envy in the hearts of many. The perks were undeniable: almost royal access to extra food, the added responsibility of helping to distribute meals, and the undeniable glow of admiration from fellow students.

Then there was the role of the milk monitor—a position that, while perhaps not as glamorous, commanded its fair share of reverence and potential kickbacks.

The job wasn't just about collecting and counting milk bottles. No, being a milk monitor meant becoming a stalwart hero, braving the harsh winter elements to retrieve the nectar of the gods—those tiny glass bottles of milk—across frostbitten playgrounds.

Each morning, the promise of milk hung heavy in the cold air, beckoning us with its chilled allure. The very thought of stepping outside, bundled up in coats and gloves—some of the kids wearing oversized hand-me-downs—sent a thrill through us, like dauntless explorers setting sail for uncharted waters. But this trek wasn't without its hazards. With every snowy step across the playground, we risked slipping on treacherous patches of ice that could send our precious cargo crashing to the ground—especially if the caretaker hadn't yet been out to spread the salt.

Then came the glorious moment when those milk bottles would arrive—crates stacked high, each little bottle glimmering like a trophy, waiting to be claimed from the unrelenting cold. Milk monitors clambered for their class's share of the nectar, eager to fulfill their sacred duty.

As a milk monitor, you were entrusted with a responsibility that measured your worth—a mission demanding bravery, coordination, and an almost reckless enthusiasm. With delighted shouts, we'd gather together, hefting the crates triumphantly and shuffling back across the blustery playground, frozen fingers clenching glass that held pure magic inside.

But the true thrill of being a milk monitor lay in the prospects of acquiring spare bottles—those divine treasures left unattended, waiting for us to uncover. If a classmate was absent due to illness or if sheer luck was on our side, we'd find ourselves in the enviable position of scoring extra rations. Just picture it: a small horde of those little bottles, bolting down the corridors like a stampede of white gold, as word spread like wildfire among our peers. Bottle retrieval became an art form—a dance of stealth and cunning that we executed with flawless precision.

Ah, but all good things must come to an end, and the enchanting era of milk for all was soon threatened by storm clouds gathering on the horizon in the late '70s. Enter Thatcher, the Milk Snatcher—a figure destined to go down in history for her infamous policy changes that stripped schools of free milk, sending shivers down the spines of many.

The dark day she became a sworn milk-snatching villain marked the end of an era. Parents and children alike mourned the loss of this cherished ritual—the simple pleasure of those little glass bottles of milk, a special treat that had brightened our chilly days. The echoes of laughter from snowy adventures were soon replaced with grumbles and groans, as children felt the sting of that unwelcome decision.

Years later, we would find ourselves reminiscing about the glory days of carrying milk across frozen playgrounds, our imaginations running wild. No longer would children enjoy their daily ration of chilled inspiration. But for a fleeting moment in time, we had known unadulterated joy beneath the winter sun—sipped from tiny bottles we affectionately deemed the nectar of the gods.

Looking back on those days, it's hard not to appreciate how the smallest moments—whether it was securing the head server's spot in the dining hall or embarking on daring milk-retrieval missions—became woven into the fabric of our lives. They prepared us for the greater struggles and triumphs that lay ahead, shaping us in ways we never realised at the time. These were little victories worth celebrating.

Another unforgettable memory of Osbaldwick School was the legend himself—Mr. Birdsall, the caretaker. To us, he was a tower of a man, ex-military, with arms thick as tree trunks and covered in tattoos. He was rarely seen without his Alsatian dog by his side. Every lunchtime, he would stand near the main entrance, leaning casually against the wall, waiting. And like clockwork, we would attack.

It didn't matter how many of us tried—five, ten, twenty—he was simply too strong. He swatted us away with ease, delivering playful karate chops to the backs of our necks as we charged at him, laughing and shouting. Today, in an age of rules, restrictions, and woke oversight, I imagine he'd be in trouble for this. But back then, fun was more important than feelings.

I wouldn't trade those days for anything, and I feel a pang of sadness for the children who will never know that kind of carefree, rough-and-tumble joy.

My childhood at Osbaldwick Primary School was an epic tale of hilarity and chaos, where music, madness, and a love for Yorkshire collided into one unforgettable experience. Navigating the strict corridors of authority shaped me in ways I couldn't yet appreciate, but as the years passed, I came to recognize their impact.

Looking back, it's impossible to ignore the feelings of neglect that often lingered in the air. My dear old dad, on occasion, would be stirred by guilt over our circumstances. In an effort to lift my spirits and create moments of happiness, he established a cherished ritual: every birthday, he treated me to something special—a day filled with promises of joy and wonder.

One such tradition led us to London's Toy Shop in Heworth, a place that stood as a beacon of childhood magic. Walking into that shop felt like stepping into another world. The sights and sounds wrapped around me, inviting me to explore every corner. The aisles overflowed with treasures beyond imagination, but it was the upstairs area that truly stole my heart.

There, in that whimsical paradise, rows upon rows of gleaming pedal cars shimmered under the soft glow of overhead lights. At that moment, I felt as though I had discovered the greatest treasure trove on Earth.

I still remember the thrill of that very first year I visited, around the age of six, when my dad surprised me with an E-Type Jaguar pedal car. Picture it: pure white, its sleek lines reminiscent of the real thing—and it was mine! I can still see the way the sunlight glinted off its surface, making my awe and excitement soar.

Back then, the streets were much quieter. We could play football and create our own adventures without the chaos of heavy traffic. With my dad's encouragement, I pedalled my shiny new car up and down the pavement, the wind rushing through my hair as I zoomed along. I revelled in the experience, pretending to flick imaginary cigarette ash out of the window—just like my dad used to do. I felt like a superstar, cruising through the neighbourhood with absolute pride.

The following year brought another wonderful surprise—an American army jeep, painted a deep green with a bold white star emblazoned on the bonnet. Every time I climbed into that jeep, a sense of bravery and adventure enveloped me, as if I were a soldier embarking on a top-secret reconnaissance mission. My imagination ran wild as I drove through the streets, fully immersed in the role that the toy allowed me to play.

The last pedal car I received as a birthday treat was a dumper truck, equipped with a lifting bucket on the front. I remember feeling an overwhelming sense of accomplishment as I maneuvered the truck, weighed down with toys and treasures, happily pedalling it around the neighbourhood. My childhood joy felt complete as I navigated the hills and valleys of the pavement, feeling like a master builder on a grand construction site.

These experiences and gifts helped fill the void that my neglected childhood often left behind. My father's efforts, though not always perfect, shone through during these moments, giving me cherished memories that would last a lifetime. They represented simple pleasures—a contrast to the complexities of our home life—where the laughter and excitement of playing with my new toys became the highlights of my youth.

In the years that followed, I have struggled with those dark days, but I have also carried those cherished moments in my heart. Each pedal stroke I took in those little cars served as a reminder that life, despite its challenges, could still offer pockets of delight, laughter, and the warmth of family bonds. And so, with the small echoes of joy from my childhood, I realised that sometimes the simplest experiences can form the most enduring legacies of love and happiness.

CHAPTER 3
The Unexpected Arrival of Family

When I was about six years old, our family life was fraught with chaos and unpredictability, a theme that was all too common during those formative years. One of my mother's many ill-fated trips found my sister and me dragged down the street to the number 11 bus stop, heading to an undisclosed location. We were accustomed to her impulsive nature, but this time felt particularly charged. It wasn't long before we discovered we were being taken to one of my dad's girlfriends' houses—a woman named Margaret, who had become a regular fixture in his life.

As we arrived at Margaret's home, I remember my mother's sharp knock on the door, ringing with authority. The door opened, and Margaret greeted us with a hesitant, "Oh, hello." Before she could say another word, Mother unceremoniously pushed us inside the house with a force that felt less like a loving maternal gesture and more like an eviction from her life. "You've got my husband; you may as well have his kids too," she declared, her voice laced with an edge I had not heard before. It was one of those surreal moments I would later look back on—a hazy memory that felt more like a scene from a soap opera than real life, a snapshot of the strange family dynamics we were forced to navigate.

Margaret greeted us with a hint of confusion but quickly worked to ease the situation, shifting the atmosphere from tense to welcoming. She asked if we wanted anything to eat, and my stomach growled at the mere thought. As usual, my mother had neglected to feed us before her frantic trip, leaving us hungry.

After a brief phone call to Dad, we overheard her say, "She just showed up, dropped off Carole and Simon, and took off. What should I do?" Once she hung up, Margaret reassured us that he would come to pick us up later, then headed to the kitchen to prepare lunch.

What I remember most vividly about that day was the meal Margaret brought back: two plates of eggs and chips—a simple dish. But the real highlight was the presentation—the tomatoes were cut in a fanciful zig-zag pattern, a culinary flourish that left my sister and me in awe. It looked so elegant compared to the meals we typically had at home that we could barely contain our smiles. In that moment, we were convinced Margaret was the best cook in the world, and we savoured every bite.

Eventually, Dad arrived to collect us, and as we returned home, my mother put us through an interrogation about what had happened, likely hoping for some terrible story about our day. However, my sister and I eagerly recounted our adventures. We spoke of how wonderful it had been at Margaret's, complete with our tale of the elusive zig-zag tomato.

For weeks afterward, my mother attempted to replicate the dish—an effort that often teetered between slapstick comedy and culinary disaster. Every time a tomato appeared on our plate; she would present it in the same zig-zag fashion. Unfortunately, her attempts usually made it look as though Jack the Ripper had been at work rather than a skilled chef.

My life continued to have both good and bad times, though it seemed to be heading toward worse than good. Dad and Margaret eventually moved into a house in Stamford Bridge as their relationship developed, though Dad still spent half his time living in Osbaldwick.

When Dad was staying at Stamford Bridge, Sundays were supposed to be my day with him. But more often than not, he wouldn't show up. I'd be dressed and waiting for hours, while my mother almost seemed to take joy in telling me he didn't care and wasn't coming. It was usually because Margaret had thrown a fit as he was about to leave, so he would stay with her to avoid the drama. Other times, he would come for just a few minutes before driving away, leaving me chasing after the car, calling his name with tears streaming down my face.

I can't imagine what Dad must have been going through at that point—did he put his child first, or rush back to Stamford Bridge to keep the peace?

Over the years, our interactions with Margaret continued, each encounter adding to a complex patchwork of relationships filled with unspoken understanding, awkward moments, and, more often than not, equally erratic behaviour from both our mum and Margaret. Dad certainly knew how to pick them!

One specific memory stands out in my mind. I was about ten years old, sitting beside my sister as we watched TV in Osbaldwick—one of those rare occasions when the electricity was actually working. Suddenly, there was a knock at the door.

Dottie jumped up to answer it, and there stood Margaret, cradling a newborn baby in her arms.

"Is Geoff home?" she asked, delivering one of those gut-punch revelations. We stood there, wide-eyed in shock, as she introduced us to our new half-brother.

"This is Nick," she said with a wry smile—the latest addition to our already complicated family tree. The weight of it all hung heavy in the air, especially since our dad was still married to our mother.

The reality hit us—Dad had become a father again, and our childlike minds struggled to grasp the full implications. It was a moment where innocence collided with a growing awareness of our unconventional family dynamics and the hidden intricacies shaping our world.

A few years later, another half-sibling, Lisa, would join our ever-expanding family, further complicating our structure but also enriching it in ways I would eventually come to understand, accept, and even be grateful for.

It wasn't until years later that Dad and Margaret officially tied the knot—an event that felt oddly reassuring yet carried its own complexities. A large number of family members attended the registry office service in Pocklington, including my sister and me—though Nick and Lisa had been left at home with their grandmother.

Through all these experiences—the laughter, the unexpected surprises, the real hardships, and the shock of new familial connections—a dynamic was forged that would forever shape my understanding of family and relationships. While my childhood was a patchwork of chaos and confusion, Margaret's presence, along with the addition of new siblings, taught me invaluable lessons in resilience, acceptance, and the beauty of forging bonds amid life's unpredictability.

Looking back, I am profoundly grateful for the deep bond that developed between me, Carole, Nick, and Lisa over the years. The shared experiences, laughter, and unwavering support we provided each other created a connection that ultimately surpassed what is typically found between most siblings.

CHAPTER 4

The Cold Day

When I was about seven years old, my childhood took a turn I can still recall with chilling clarity. By then, my mother had started working in Leeds for a debt collection agency, zipping around in a green Austin Morris van that oddly mirrored the unsettling nature of our lives. The van had seen better days, much like my mother, who often disappeared into the hustle of the city, leaving me to navigate the confusion of home life alone.

During the summer holidays, she sometimes took me along, and I remember how the towering buildings in Leeds felt enormous compared to the world I knew. One particular day stands out vividly—cold and surreal. Early that morning, she woke me from my slumber, announcing that we were going somewhere special. She didn't say where, but I trusted that whatever adventure lay ahead would be insignificant compared to the chaos we faced at home.

I was half asleep when she bundled me into the van, still groggy and oblivious to the goosebumps rising on my skin from the chilly air. Dressed in shorts, I was far from prepared for the biting cold, but my mother didn't seem to mind. In a small, almost comical safety measure, I wore a coat with gloves attached by elastic—an attempt to keep me from losing them.

We drove for what felt like hours, the familiar stretch of the main road starkly contrasting with the growing unease building inside me. "Where are we going, Mum?" I asked, but she didn't reply. The steady hum of the engine and the endless road ahead became almost oppressive. Then, as if emerging from a dream, we turned onto a narrow lane, and the scene transformed, revealing a long, tree-lined driveway. Finally, the van rolled to a stop in front of a grand but foreboding Victorian building. The sight unsettled me, though I had yet to grasp the true purpose of that day.

My mother exited the vehicle quickly, walking briskly. To my shock, she came around to my door and pushed me out. "Stay here," she instructed loudly before turning back to the van and driving off without a glance.

I stood there, shivering, confusion wrapping around me like the cold air. A wave of dread washed over me as I realised, I was completely alone outside this enormous building—a place that felt like something out of a ghost story. Fear tightened in my chest, and tears welled in my eyes. I was lost, terrified, and half expecting—no, hoping—she would come back for me.

As I stood there, a nurse emerged. I remember with startling clarity how she approached me, gliding across the ground like an angel. She had brown hair neatly tucked beneath a nurse's hat and wore a warm, reassuring smile that softened my panic. "What are you doing here, little man? Where are your parents?" she asked gently, concern lacing her voice.

I replied, "My mum left me here and told me to wait, then drove off."

That was the moment of realization—my mother had deliberately left me at an asylum for the insane. It's a concept difficult to comprehend today, but at the time, such institutions were a stark reality. I could hardly grasp the severity of the situation, nor did I understand that I had been used as a pawn in my mother's precarious game against my father.

The nurse looked at me with sympathy and quickly ushered me inside. I was taken to a small room with faded floral wallpaper and large white radiators lining the walls. The air was thick with a sense of confinement. Someone handed me a glass of orange juice—a simple gesture, yet I can still recall how it felt like a lifeline, a small moment of comfort amid the chaos. Time blurred around me, and the world beyond those walls felt both distant and unreal.

They asked me questions about my mum and dad. All I could remember was that my dad worked at a garage in York that sold Datsun cars. That was the clue they needed to move forward.

Eventually, my dad arrived to pick me up, and with great relief, I was taken home. But that incident lingered in the shadows of my mind like a dark cloud that refused to dissipate. Even now, the strong smell of disinfectant is a trigger—just a slight whiff takes me straight back to that cold day.

During one of her episodes, my mother had inadvertently thrust me into a tangled web of emotional turmoil, far beyond my ability to understand. I couldn't make sense of her actions or the reasons behind them; all I knew was that we were trapped in a cycle of chaos.

Over the years, the haunting nature of that day seeped into my dreams, interspersing fragments of fear and confusion. It became one of those memories that visited unannounced, lurking in the dark corners of my sleep and leaving me with a discomfort I couldn't shake. The tension between my parents, the erratic behaviour, and the feeling of abandonment echoed through my waking life, shaping my outlook in ways I didn't yet comprehend.

In those early years, I learned a weathered lesson—not all memories are warm and reliable. Some are chilling reminders of the complexities of relationships and familial ties. The shadows of that day became a poignant chapter of my childhood, a constant reminder that life is interwoven with moments that define us, teach us, and sometimes haunt us long after they've passed.

Reflecting on another defining experience from my youth, I recall yet another moment that forced me into fast-track learning. Despite my mother's lack of culinary skills, I was thrust into the world of cooking at the tender age of nine during the school holidays. It was a necessity born from the chaos of our family dynamics. Left to fend for myself with no well-cooked meal in sight, I decided it was high time to learn the basics—and so began my adventure in the kitchen.

CHAPTER 5

The Black Frying Pan

Now, amid my school day antics, one of the most fantastic things about Osbaldwick Primary was the school dinners. Let me tell you, some of the most wholesome food I had ever encountered awaited us in the dining hall. It felt like stepping into a culinary paradise compared to the sparse offerings at home.

Picture this: creamy mashed potatoes, crispy chips, fresh vegetables, and fantastic mains—all topped off with a delicious pudding and custard. We had two side servers and a head server, who dished out the food from serving trays to the others at the table. The side server would always ask, "Who wants the lurgy?" referring to the custard skin. Someone would always take it.

Food at school was a real sanctuary for me. My mother, God bless her, was arguably the worst cook in the history of mankind—she could burn a cup of tea without even trying.

She had this black frying pan in the kitchen that was permanently on the stove, and she cooked everything in it. The handle was coated in a thick layer of burnt gunk which, if studied properly, might have held the cure for cancer, given the sheer number of bacteria it harboured. I remember her constantly cooking sausages and gravy in it. To be honest, I didn't realise a sausage was supposed to have some moisture until I was about twelve and had them at a mate's house. My mum's sausages could have been used as a weapon—they were that hard.

You always knew dinner was ready when the smell of burnt food drifted through the house. Vegetables were boiled for hours, stripped of any goodness, and drained of all flavour. Everything she made was either burnt or tasteless, which was rather ironic, considering my Nana—Dottie's mum—was a fantastic cook. Clearly, none of that skill had passed down to my mum.

In fairness, though, she could bake a decent cake. Her jam tarts, rice cremola cakes, and butterfly buns weren't half bad. Nearly always burnt, mind you, but at least not to the point of resembling the surface of Mercury like her other dishes.

There were so many stories about my mother's culinary skills, I could quite literally fill a book with them. Another memory involving the infamous "black frying pan" was when my mother would leave food in it for days after cooking. I recall walking into the kitchen one day and finding mince still sitting in the pan. You could tell it had been there for a few days, as it had developed a thick skin and even gathered a layer of dust. I couldn't eat mince for years without gagging, haunted by that image burnt into my memory.

School holidays were always a time for fun, although, with my mother constantly at work, I had to find ways to fill the time and figure out how I would eat. Thankfully, my uncle Albert was around for parts of the summer. He was a sales representative for a medical products company and would drive around farms and rural areas in the north of England. I would travel in the back of the car with him, while my absolute legend of a grandad—"Kojak," as I nicknamed him—rode shotgun. We went all over the place and always stopped somewhere nice for lunch.

My grandad would call me every morning during school time since I was always alone, as my mother had already left for work. He would insist that I recite my times tables and name all the capitals of the world before I went to school. Occasionally, my dad would stop by on his way to work and give me a lift. By this time, I was in my final year of primary school.

One terrible day, my grandad didn't call. I tried ringing him, but he didn't answer. When my dad arrived, I told him, and thankfully, he rushed straight over to my grandad's house. He'd fallen and was hurt—I think I likely saved his life that day. Once he was feeling better, we were back to our usual routine. I was always excellent at geography and maths at school, which was entirely down to his influence.

As my sister entered her teenage years, around fourteen, she began to venture further from our chaotic home life, often spending hours away with her boyfriend, Russ. This left me alone more often, wandering the quiet rooms of the house while my mother carried on as if everything were normal. However, in her infinite wisdom—or perhaps misplaced frustration—my mother devised a solution that was both amusing and mortifying: she made my sister take me along with her and her friends on their outings. This arrangement also allowed my mum to slip away for her own trips to the Derwent Arms.

The result was a motley crew of misfits, clad in the bell-bottomed fashions typical of the '70s. My sister and her friends paraded through the streets, each of them embodying the spirit of teenage rebellion, laughter, and carefree excitement. As we walked, they listened to the radio, losing themselves in tunes from T. Rex, Sweet, and The Rubettes—Sugar Baby Love was the first record I ever bought!

Amidst this whirlwind, my sister and her friends had the brilliant idea to nickname me Mr. Shit, a consequence of being the unwanted little kid tagging along. It's hard to describe how that felt for a young boy trying to find his footing in the chaotic landscape of family life and teenage antics. Picture a small kid trailing behind his sister, soaking up their laughter while being playfully teased—a nickname I never asked for but quickly learned to endure. Within their circle, it became a kind of running joke, a twisted badge of honour. But each time I heard it, a small part of me wished they'd just let me belong without it.

The childhood joys of Saturdays were never complete without a visit to the ABC Cinema in Piccadilly for the Minors, where children gathered in droves to watch an array of films and cartoons. I remember those mornings vividly—the sheer excitement of seeing movies like The Railway Children, Chitty Chitty Bang Bang, and Bedknobs and Broomsticks. Adding to the thrill were the beloved classic cartoons, Looney Tunes and Tom and Jerry, perfectly designed to keep young audiences entertained.

The experience was always marked by the familiar routine of my sister disappearing to the back row with Russ, leaving me to sit in the front, proudly clutching my badge emblazoned with a letter of the alphabet. "Don't you dare look around!" she would hiss as she settled in beside her boyfriend. Not that I had any intention of doing so—my fascination was firmly fixed on the film unfolding before me, not on the teenage antics happening behind me.

Each Saturday should have felt like a celebration, marked by the thrill of collecting the entire alphabet of badges. This became my secret mission—one I pursued with the determination of a young adventurer on a quest for hidden treasure. Armed with a Kiora orange juice and a tub of ice cream, I would step into the ABC Minors, a childhood paradise where escapism reigned supreme. "The lights would dim, but before the film started, we sang the ABC Minor song—'We are the boys and girls well known as minors.'"…….and before long, popcorn was flying through the air as we were whisked away to a world of wonder.

In those moments, despite the teasing and the quirks of my family's dynamics, I found a slice of joy amidst the chaos.

Lost in the flickering images on the screen, I escaped—if only for a little while. Each visit to the ABC Minors became a treasured ritual, punctuating my young life with wonder and nostalgia, even as I navigated the complicated waters of adolescence and sibling rivalry.

While I remained "Mr. Shit" in my sister and her friends' eyes, I began to realize that those experiences planted the seeds of resilience within me. No matter how much they laughed or teased, I learned to absorb it with a little grin—a quiet defiance, a testament to my youthful spirit and my longing to belong.

Those Saturdays at the ABC Minors became more than just outings; they were stepping stones toward finding my own place in the world. Amidst the chaos of our family life, they offered fleeting moments of joy and connection. But childhood is full of turning points, and before long, I would venture out on my own, no longer the little brother trailing behind.

CHAPTER 6
The Culinary Awakening

In our house, like most in those days, we had a rotary telephone—a fascinating device that allowed you to call a number and hear the time of day! There was also a feature called "Dial-a-Disk," where a different song would play each day. You could even buy a lock for the phone to prevent others in the house from using it without permission.

My mother, ever resourceful, had purchased one of these locks to stop us from making calls. The idea was simple: you placed the lock on the first number, preventing the dial from turning further. However, in a stroke of luck for us, she had misunderstood how it worked and locked the zero—the last number on the dial. This meant the phone could still be used as normal, a mistake that proved particularly useful one day.

I fondly recall my first foray into cooking, which involved a nerve-wracking phone call to my dad's partner, Margaret. Nervous but determined, I gripped the receiver and explained that I was hungry and needed her step-by-step guidance to make scrambled eggs on toast. I could hear the mixture of concern and delight in her voice as she carefully talked me through my early kitchen manoeuvres, her warmth shining through even over the phone.

"First, crack two eggs into a bowl," she instructed, her friendly tone instantly easing my nerves. I carefully broke the eggs, watching the golden yolks glisten against the white.

"Now, whisk them up nicely! Add a pinch of salt—but not too much, just enough to bring out the flavour!"

I followed her instructions closely.

"Next, heat a pan on the hob, but make sure it's not too hot, or you'll end up with a burnt mess. Trust me, no one wants that!"

I nodded, even though she couldn't see me, feeling a rush of excitement and trepidation all at once. As I followed her directions to the letter, I melted butter in the pan, watching it sizzle and bubble while a sense of newfound independence washed over me.

"Now comes the fun part—gently pour the eggs into the pan," she advised. "But don't forget to stir! Keep them moving so they don't stick, and keep an eye on them. Remember, we want them creamy, not rubbery.

With her guidance, I learned the importance of patience and control.

"And don't let them sit too long—just as they start to set, take them off the heat. They'll keep cooking in the pan. Make sure to turn the gas off now!"

Finally, I grabbed some bread and popped it under the eye-level grill—no toaster back then—eagerly awaiting the moment I could assemble my creation.

When everything was ready and plated, I took a moment to admire my handiwork: fluffy scrambled eggs sat atop golden toast, glistening with melted butter.

"Well done! A great job, Simon!" Margaret exclaimed over the phone, and I felt a swell of pride—this was a small victory amidst the madness of my life.

From that humble beginning, my culinary explorations expanded. I ventured into making pasta, realizing I didn't need a culinary degree—or a Michelin star—to whip up something delicious. I experimented with tins of soup, each opening revealing a world of warmth, comforting after long days. Even sandwiches became creative masterpieces as I piled on whatever I could scavenge from the fridge.

Cooking quickly became both a necessity and an enjoyable pastime. I sought to infuse flavours and textures into each dish, realising that my time in the kitchen was not just about preparing food but also about finding solace in the rhythm of culinary creation.

Those early experiences nurtured a love for cooking that stayed with me into adulthood. Whether preparing meals for friends or crafting a special dish for my family, cooking became a way of connecting with others—nourishing both their bellies and their souls. Today, I often think back on those early days, remembering the warmth in my stepmother's voice as she guided me through the steps that shaped my growth and independence.

It's funny how something as simple as scrambled eggs can spark a lifelong passion. While my mother's reluctance to cook may have nudged me into the kitchen, it was the journey itself that truly enriched my life, allowing me to create joy and comfort through food. As I stir, sauté, and simmer in my kitchen today, I find solace in those sweet memories—woven into every meal I prepare. Cooking isn't just a skill; it's an expression, a love language that remains a significant part of who I am.

CHAPTER 7
My doggy companion

As time rolled on, Mum and Dad continued their strange relationship, where we would still attend events as a family—even though Dad spent most of his time at Stamford Bridge. Occasionally, he still lived at Osbaldwick.

We frequently visited my dad's brothers, particularly Uncle Les and Auntie Nora's pub in Hull. Uncle Les was a force of nature—a tough, unbreakable man, a veteran of the Burma Railway. His time as a prisoner of war had forged in him a resilience that few possessed. He was a "tough cookie," as they used to say.

Looking back, I realise the pubs on Hessle Road were far rougher and more dangerous than I understood at the time—a world far removed from the warmth of those family visits. During one trip, one of their Alsatian guard dogs had delivered a litter of puppies, and I was gifted one—a scrappy little ball of energy that my mother, surprisingly, agreed to bring home. Perhaps she hoped the puppy would serve as a distraction, something for me to care for in an otherwise chaotic environment.

And so, there I was—a young boy with a furry companion, navigating the mixed emotions that came with my mother's unpredictability. I named him Trex, after my sister's love of Marc Bolan and T. Rex.

There were plenty of difficult moments in my childhood—many of which, in hindsight, were almost comical.

When I was around nine years old, my dad stopped by our house in Osbaldwick on his way back to Stamford Bridge. He walked in only to find that my mother had disappeared once again, leaving me alone with my furry companion. By then, her disappearing acts had become routine.

My older sister had already found her escape, carving out a life beyond the chaos, seeking refuge in friendships that kept her far from home. I, however, was left to navigate the oddities of our family life—my only constant being Trex, my beloved dog.

When Dad arrived and saw me alone in the house, he was understandably upset. It was clear he was concerned not just for my welfare, but for the overall state of our home. Without hesitation, he decided to take me back with him to Stamford Bridge. He changed my clothes, and off we went.

That journey felt monumental. It was more than just a ride to Dad's house—it was an escape from the cold, dark home I had known for far too long.

Upon arriving at my dad's home, which he now shared with his long-term partner, Margaret, I immediately sensed a shift in atmosphere. The house was immaculate—inside and out—free from the chaos and clutter I was so used to. Everything about it felt fresh and inviting. The moment I stepped inside, I was enveloped by a warmth that had always been absent from our own home.

Margaret, whose culinary skills stood in stark contrast to my mother's haphazard meals, graciously offered me something to eat.

"What do you fancy, Simon?" she asked with a kind smile.

I could only grin sheepishly, savouring the thought of properly prepared food. I remember it as if it were yesterday—fish fingers and chips. To me, it was food of the gods.

Every bite was a revelation; the flavour, the care in its preparation—it all reminded me of just how much I had been missing. And yet, it was only fish fingers and chips. Perhaps that was the appeal for Dad as well—an oasis of normalcy after years of enduring chaos.

However, that peaceful reprieve was not meant to last. After about an hour of blissful normalcy and home-cooked food, a sharp knock echoed through the house, shattering the serenity. To my dismay, it was my mother—undoubtedly playing one of her games—demanding that I return with her and accusing Dad and Margaret of kidnapping me. I would later look back on this moment with dark humour; if only I had been so lucky.

Reluctantly, I was escorted back to our cold, dimly lit house, leaving behind what had felt like a small slice of heaven. The weight of disappointment settled heavily in my chest as I stepped once more into the familiar turmoil of my mother's world—a world rife with anxiety, unpredictability, and a darkness that loomed heavier than any storm. At least Trex was happy to see me.

In that brief window of escape, I had glimpsed something different—a life of warmth, stability, and normalcy. Those fleeting moments at Dad's house left an indelible mark, crystallizing in me a deep yearning for security, for something more than the chaos that had always defined my childhood.

That day was yet another painful reminder of the challenges my family faced, but it also became a catalyst for my resolve—to build a life rooted in love, care, and nurturing friendships. It reinforced the idea that while I couldn't change my circumstances, I could strive for something better—both for myself and for the family I would one day create.

In those early years, I learned a hard but invaluable lesson: not all memories are warm and reliable. Some are chilling reminders of the complexities of relationships and familial ties. The shadows of that day became a defining chapter of my childhood, a reminder that life is woven together with moments that shape us, teach us, and sometimes linger long after they have passed.

Trex created a great mystery for my sister and me when I was in my mid-teens. Around that time, my mother had found a new man, Ken, and decided we were moving in with him—immediately. Ken, a fireman at Rowntree's, had a house provided near the factory, so in typical fashion, my mother insisted we sell the house and go.

The real mystery began just before we moved: Trex disappeared. We searched everywhere, asked around the village, but there was no sign of him. My mother offered explanations—perhaps he had run away to die of old age, or maybe the "tinkers" had taken him. With no evidence to the contrary, I had little choice but to accept her story. Yet, given my mother's history, I couldn't shake the feeling that there was something more sinister at play.

Years later, my sister confided in me that one evening, after too many drinks, Mum had admitted to taking Trex to the dog's home.

CHAPTER 8
The Rubber House bounces back

As my cooking skills developed over the years, I grew to appreciate the local culinary delights of Osbaldwick—though not always for the reasons one might expect. Chief among them was the infamous fish and chip shop, which we affectionately (and somewhat sarcastically) referred to as "the Rubber House." The nickname came from its owner, "the rubber man"—a burly Polish man with a notoriously short fuse, making every visit an adventure.

As kids, we eagerly anticipated our trips to the Rubber House, though they often ended in disappointment. The chips were legendary—not for their quality, but for their baffling texture. Rather than crisp and golden, they had the unmistakable chewiness of rubber, proving that not everything fried was delicious. Yet, despite their lacklustre appeal, they remained a staple of our childhood. With few alternatives in the area, we made do.

Back then, York had no McDonald's or Burger King—the first McDonald's wouldn't arrive until well into the 1980s. Our fast-food options were limited to fish and chips or the single KFC on Blossom Street in the city centre, which stood as a lone beacon of indulgence. On the rare Sundays when Dad took me swimming, I'd be treated to a KFC meal afterward. Those barbecue beans, warm and rich, tasted like heaven after a long swim.

Riding our bikes past the Rubber House became a daily ritual—one filled with mischievous fun and outright teasing. As we cruised by the shop's front, we couldn't resist hurling playful taunts about the food he was dishing out, mocking the rubbery chips.

"Hey, Rubber Man, your chips bounce, and they taste like crap!" we'd yell, our voices ringing through the air.

His response was always the same—a booming roar of expletives chasing after us. We'd hear the rattle of his apron as he stormed out from behind the fryer, arms flailing in a mix of fury and hilarity. Looking back, you'd think he would have realised that if he simply ignored us, we'd have stopped. But he never did—so we kept at it!

Those moments were exhilarating—a childhood game of tag mixed with the absurdity of our encounters. The inevitable result? A furious banishment from the chip shop.

"You're barred!" he'd bellow, red-faced with rage.

In hindsight, that was probably for the best. Our digestive systems no doubt thanked us for dodging those questionable meals, and our laughter lingered in the air long after the rubbery chips were left behind.

One fateful Saturday lunchtime, it seemed as if fate itself had taken a mischievous turn. As we gathered nearby, chatting and laughing like the carefree kids we were, we noticed thick smoke billowing from the Rubber House chimney. Shock quickly gave way to excitement as fire engines swarmed the scene, sirens blaring, their bright lights slicing through the afternoon air. We stood together, eyes wide, watching as the temple of terrible fish and chips went up in flames.

Firefighters worked frantically to control the blaze, and with each passing moment, we felt a strange mix of joy, disbelief, and nostalgia. It was as if we were witnessing the grand finale of a story we'd been telling for years—a dramatic conclusion to the place that had, in its own way, shaped our childhood. For all our teasing, we almost mourned its demise, realising that, rubbery chips or not, it had been part of our lives.

Months passed, and we awaited the shop's return with a curious mix of anticipation and dread. When the Rubber House finally reopened, we felt both relief and disappointment; our game of cat and mouse resumed, and, as if by some unshakable twist of fate, the rubbery chips were still there.

As I think back on those days, I realise the Rubber House was more than just a fish and chip shop; it was a symbol of our carefree youth, where laughter and adventure were woven into our childhood memories. Those experiences taught us the value of friendship, humour, and resilience, even in the most unexpected places. As we made our way into adulthood, those lessons remained with me—a lasting reminder of the joy found in the delightful chaos of growing up.

CHAPTER 9
A Beacon of Kindness

Uncle Harold and Auntie Jean were two of the kindest souls I had the privilege of knowing. Harold, my mother's brother, was a gentle giant with a heart that seemed boundless, while Jean possessed a warmth that could brighten even the darkest days. In stark contrast to my mother and her struggles, they embodied selflessness and compassion, becoming beacons of hope and support during our tumultuous childhood.

They lived in a cosy little bungalow in Rawcliffe, which became a sanctuary for my sister and me. Harold worked as a train driver and had a treasure trove of stories, often regaling us with captivating tales from his time behind the controls. He would enthral us with dramatic accounts of being chased by Messerschmitts during the war—adventures that felt larger than life, like something straight out of a film. Then there was his hilarious story of derailing a train full of Smarties at the sidings next to the factory. I couldn't help but chuckle at the mental image of candy-filled chaos spilling across the tracks. Of course, Harold was known for embellishing his stories just a little.

Perhaps the best story was the time Harold had the privilege of driving the iconic Flying Scotsman steam train. The locomotive was on a farewell journey around the country, and Harold was at the wheel—what could possibly go wrong?

The plan for the day was that he would roll into Leeds Station, where a civic reception awaited, with the Lord Mayor and other dignitaries gathered to celebrate its arrival. But, of course, Harold being Harold, he forgot to stop the train. As he thundered into the station, the band played their hearts out, the crowd cheered in eager anticipation—and Harold steamed straight through, oblivious. Realising his blunder, he had to reverse the train back into the station to meet the waiting crowd. Classic Harold—one of the many reasons we loved him dearly.

What truly defined their relationship with us, however, were the delightful summer days spent at their golf course in Ampleforth. Harold and Jean introduced me to the game at a very young age, and it quickly became one of my cherished pastimes. The course itself was stunning, but to say it was uphill and down dale would be an understatement. My first few rounds were filled with laughter, sweat, and the occasional lost ball, yet those moments remain some of my fondest memories.

I also had a knack for finding things on the course while playing, and Harold always had two cans of Coke tucked in his bag—one for him and one for me. Truly happy days!

During warm, sun-drenched summer afternoons, I'd ride on the back of Harold's trusty Honda 90 motorbike, clutching onto him tightly as he navigated the winding country roads. To say Harold was a good and safe rider wouldn't be entirely accurate. The way he took corners on that 90cc bike, I'm sure he imagined himself as the one and only Barry Sheene.

The bike had a wooden box strapped to the back, engraved with the initials HHOB—shouting out Harold Henry Oswald Barnes! An emblem of Harold's pride and a symbol of our shared adventures. The rush of wind in my hair and the thrill of the ride enveloped me in a wave of freedom, setting a beautiful tone for our time together. It also sparked a lifelong love of motorbikes—one that stays with me to this day.

I recall a rare weekend in Blackpool with my mother, Dottie, Uncle Harold, Auntie Jean, and me. We stayed in one of those bed and breakfasts along the front, looking out across the sea. The air was thick with the scent of candy floss, hotdogs, and popcorn, mingled with the constant calls of the bingo announcer, who cheerfully shouted phrases like, "Two fat ladies—eighty-eight!"

Compared to this place, Fawlty Towers would have been a beacon of warm hospitality. The landlady had the demeanour of an escaped guard from a prisoner-of-war camp, running the establishment with unwavering vigour. A very large woman who always wore an apron—usually with a stain on it—she ruled the dining room with military precision.

Harold would often recount, in later years, the rigid evening meal ritual. The landlady would stand in the doorway, holding everyone back until the clock chimed six o'clock. According to him, one evening I'd finally had enough and kicked the waiter on the shin to get through. I have no memory of this, so more than likely, Harold was indulging in his usual exaggeration.

I do, however, remember the landlady—and those perpetually leaking silver teapots. I sometimes wonder if there's a special shop for them, as no matter where you go, they all seem to leak.

Harold and Jean, unable to have children of their own—a tragic blow, as they were the kind of people who truly should have had them—poured all their love and energy into my sister and me. Though their loss was deeply felt, for us, it became an unexpected blessing. They showered us with affection and attention, understanding the challenges we faced and doing everything in their power to provide a nurturing environment.

Auntie Jean's gentle voice, her love of cricket, and Harold's wise stories created a home-like atmosphere that felt safe and welcoming—a stark contrast to the turmoil of our everyday lives.

In many ways, I often felt as though fate had intervened, blessing us with the presence of such extraordinary individuals. It was as if the universe had looked down and said, "You two have a difficult life; I'm sending you the very best to help you." Even though I'm not a particularly religious man, I couldn't help but feel a deep sense of gratitude.

Throughout our lives, Harold and Jean played an important role in my sister's and my upbringing. In later years, Harold suffered from Alzheimer's, which was heartbreaking to witness. It is a cruel disease that takes your loved ones twice—first when their memories fade, and they no longer recognise you, and then again when they pass away. It is a terrible and painful thing to endure for all involved, except, thankfully, for those who suffer from it.

One peculiar thing about this disease is that, on certain days—often when you least expect it—they seem to come back, even if only for a short while. I had one of those days with Harold when I was much older and had children of my own.

I took my son Rory, along with Uncle Harold and Auntie Jean, to the National Railway Museum in York—a fabulous place showcasing a variety of trains, from the great age of steam to the modern electric ones we use today, as well as Japanese and other international trains.

As we walked near one of the steam trains, Harold wasn't really with us—lost in his own world—when suddenly, he started talking about the trains and how they worked. He spoke with such authority that one of the museum guides stopped to listen and even began asking him questions. In that moment, Harold was back—in his element and centre stage. Others gathered around, eager to hear him speak. It was like watching a miracle unfold.

He explained the challenges of maintaining the right steam pressure and how they would scoop up water from trenches as the trains roared down the tracks. His knowledge was captivating, and for anyone present, it was both fascinating and educational.

The smile on Jean's face as she watched was priceless—pure pride in the moment. And then, just as suddenly as he had returned, he was gone. We lost him again as he drifted away, his mind retreating into the fog of the disease. Confused expressions surrounded us until I explained what was happening—that he had the terrible illness.

I look back on that moment not with sadness, but with joy. For a fleeting instant, I had the old Harold back, and Rory got to witness it.

CHAPTER 10
Brotherhood in the Church Lads Brigade

When I was around nine years old, I joined the Church Lads' Brigade (CLB) in Osbaldwick, a group similar to the Boys' Brigade and Scouts but distinctly aligned with the church. Although, as I have previously mentioned, I wouldn't consider myself a religious person, I hold a deep appreciation for those who are. The CLB provided me with a sense of belonging and support during a time when I was searching for connection and purpose.

It was at the CLB that Graham and I came together. He was my best friend and a key person in my life—stable and loyal—until his passing many years later.

The CLB quickly became a significant part of my life, filling my week with excitement and engagement. We met on two evenings each week in the church hall, an old school hall from a century before, which wasn't the warmest place in winter. It didn't matter, though; we soon warmed up with our activities. We played games and honed our skills in football, as well as Starboard and Port—a game that involved running to various walls. We played music and did lots and lots of marching.

I forged friendships that would last for years. The atmosphere was always filled with laughter and joy—those evenings became cherished moments.

In addition to the games, the CLB had an impressive marching band, which piqued my interest immediately. Although my heart belonged to the drums, I wasn't quite big enough to carry one just yet. So, with a mix of determination and a dash of creativity, I chose the bugle as my musical weapon of choice. Its much lighter weight allowed me to take part in the music-making while still feeling connected to the band's unity.

The power of those notes carried through the air as we practised marching and playing together, creating a sense of pride and community that I valued deeply. The bugle was brass, so I would spend hours polishing it with care and pride—I wanted it to gleam in the sunshine.

One of the most memorable experiences of my time with the CLB was our camping trips to Dalby Forest, with its lush greenery, flowing streams, and enchanting woodlands. The scent of wild garlic filled the air—it was heaven. The excitement of gathering with fellow lads, pitching tents, and breathing in the fresh air only heightened the sense of adventure.

There was also a cookhouse where we would gather for our meals. The smell of cooking onions in the air was enough to get your stomach rumbling, along with sausages and burgers—exactly the kind of food an energetic young lad craves. Plastic plates were everywhere, along with those kits you could get with a knife, fork, and spoon all in one, like a Swiss Army knife.

Back in those days, all the tents were made of canvas, not like the modern lightweight ones we have today. Now, for those who have never experienced a canvas tent, let me tell you—they're great until it rains, and someone leans against the side. At that point, you have a leaking tent, which is no fun for anyone.

Camp chores were assigned, and let me tell you, nobody wanted toilet duty. Picture this: primitive facilities in the middle of a forest, and the contents—well, let's just say they went straight into a black bin bag, a smell I can still remember to this day. I managed, through some unknown intervention (possibly my mother's), to avoid that particular task on most trips.

But honestly, the true highlight of those summers was the week-long CLB gathering in the New Forest—a glorious escape to a grand stately home filled with swimming, music, and laughter, where groups from across the UK would come together.

We were all bunked up in rooms of six beds and placed into teams for the entire week. We participated in various activities, as well as some schooling—be it religion, music, or maths. I thrived in the supportive environment fostered by our leaders—John, Ken, and David, to name a few. Each of them played a significant role in shaping my early years, guiding me with care and wisdom. Their encouragement wasn't limited to activities but extended into invaluable life lessons that left lasting impressions.

John was a deeply religious man who would go off and spend months in a monastery to gather his thoughts and focus. These days, we often hear unsettling stories about people working with children in the '70s, but I can thankfully say I never experienced anything of the sort during my time with the CLB. Instead, I was met only with support and care from those who selflessly gave their free time. For that, I will be forever grateful to those kind people.

The uniform we wore had a military-like appearance, striking in black with red stripes. But it was more than just clothing; it represented our shared experiences, a sense of identity, and a moment in time that made us feel proud to belong. Polishing the brass buckles and belts was a chore, but one I enjoyed. Putting it on signified commitment—a badge of honour that bound us together as brothers, united under the banner of the CLB.

Learning to swim was one of those rites of passage that, despite my best efforts, eluded me for far too long during childhood. By the time I was around ten, I still hadn't managed to conquer that feat, much to my growing frustration. My father would take me on occasional Sunday mornings to the Edmond Wilson Baths in York, eager to teach me the basics. But with the added excitement of the water, nerves kicked in, and more often than not, I would flounder in the shallow end while watching other kids glide effortlessly through the pool.

It was during my time with the CLB that I began to see changes. The organisation offered a summer programme where we'd venture to the Archbishop's swimming pool, a school just outside Osbaldwick. It was a charming open-air facility that seemed like a hidden gem in those days. The thrill of those outings grew each week as we gathered with friends and fellow lads, all eager to dive into the fun that awaited.

My parents had given me an inflatable ring to help build my confidence some years earlier. Looking back, that was probably something that delayed my success.

As we arrived at the pool, the laughter of my peers filled the air. The excitement of splashing around and swimming was contagious, and I quickly realised that I wasn't alone in my struggle. There was a shared mission among the kids to encourage one another, forming an unspoken bond that turned the pool into a welcoming environment.

Evenings would begin with supervised swimming lessons, followed by thirty minutes of free play. One evening, Russ arrived and decided to throw me into the deep end to teach me how to swim. Rightly or wrongly, it had the desired effect—I was off, swimming on my own.

My mother, a devoted member of the CLB at this point, also played a key role in supervising the swimming sessions, showing a level of dedication that seemed to bring her a sense of calm. It was as if the structured environment of the brigade provided a stability that positively influenced her demeanour—a bonus that extended to her efforts in helping me learn to swim.

Thanks to Russ's straightforward approach, it wasn't long before I could proudly say that I had mastered the water. Those summer evenings at the Archbishop's swimming pool, surrounded by my brothers from the brigade, etched themselves into my memory. Each time I dove into the deep end, I felt a surge of freedom—a child no longer bound by the fear of floundering, but one who had conquered the water.

Ultimately, this learned skill did more than just open up the world of swimming; it embodied the joys of my childhood, and the influential role played by the Church Lads' Brigade. Their emphasis on teamwork, encouragement, and shared experiences became the cornerstones of my character. This chapter—filled with splashes, laughter, and the scent of summer—reminded me that growth often comes from stepping outside our comfort zones and finding support in those around us.

There was a ritual at the baths involving some of the older kids from nearby Tang Hall, a council estate just outside the village. Once our allotted time in the pool was up, many of them, having hidden behind nearby buildings, would wait for us to leave. As soon as we disappeared, they would sprint towards the water and dive in. A year or two later, the school erected a tall fence to keep them out, though it did little to deter them.

The friendships I forged through the brigade evolved into bonds that extended far beyond our meetings. We became a family—a group of lads navigating the early complexities of life together. Whether mastering tunes on the bugle during practice or sharing stories around campfires on our outings, we found joy in each other's company and learned the value of teamwork, respect, and shared experiences.

Reflecting on my time in the Church Lads' Brigade reminds me that significant moments often arise from unexpected beginnings. While I may not have been a religious man myself, being part of the CLB offered me a different kind of faith—one rooted in growth, friendship, and adventure. It instilled in me a sense of purpose that extended far beyond the church hall. The foundational lessons I learned there remained with me as I ventured further into life, shaping my relationships and attitudes long after those early days.

CHAPTER 11

Skiing to Anarchy in the Classroom

Transitioning to secondary school felt like preparing for battle after a long truce in primary—a whirlwind of emotions marking the end of one era and the thrilling uncertainty of another. If you'd asked me about my feelings on the last day of primary school, I probably would have mumbled something about being a little fish in a big pond, parroting Mr Feasby's stale wisdom.

"You are going from being a big fish in a little pond to a little fish in a big pond," he'd said, his words carrying the weight of some profound revelation. I could practically hear the dramatic orchestral score behind his proclamation, ominously hinting at the challenges ahead. I thought to myself: I'm certainly going to miss this mad musical nutjob.

Stepping into the long corridors of secondary school, I felt a real sense of awe. The buildings formed a sprawling labyrinth filled with older kids who looked like they'd already gone through several cycles of puberty—complete with facial hair and questionable fashion choices that somehow blended school uniform with heavy metal influences. We had a uniform, of course, but the older students had taken some liberties with it. Most were in that phase of tying their ties with absurdly big knots, as if competing for the most ridiculous look.

As a fresh-faced P7 student, I stood in wide-eyed disbelief, searching for my first class while also estimating just how many higher-year students I could sidestep. I quite literally felt like a midget among them.

Then there was the formidable PE teacher, Mr. Wilson—a mountain of a man with a beard that could put any lumberjack to shame. His eccentric enthusiasm for rugby was legendary, and he insisted on referring to it as "rugger." Hearing him bellow, "Let's have a game of rugger, lads!" was both terrifying and oddly amusing.

Most schools in Yorkshire played rugby league, but Mr. Wilson was unwavering in his admiration for the union game, probably because he fancied himself as some sort of rugby oracle. His idea of fun? Forcing students to hurl themselves at each other in the pouring rain, rolling through the mud, while he stood on the sidelines with his arms crossed, an astute expression plastered across his face—no doubt imagining himself coaching a World Cup final.

And then there were the slippers. The man had an alarming habit of throwing them at students like some deranged lunatic in a discount shoe store. I vividly remember one time when he chased me around the gym in a crazed mood because I refused to be the hooker. He must have hurled at least ten slippers at me. I kept thinking, "Where the hell is he getting all these shoes from?!

As luck would have it, my first major adventure as a secondary school student came in the form of a school ski trip to Bulgaria. Now, let's set the scene: Eastern Europe, 1976—grey, cold, and depressingly bleak. Even the people seemed to exist in permanent desaturation, like extras in a black-and-white film, only without the excitement of a gripping plot twist.

But there I was, ready to conquer the slopes with my classmates. As was customary on these trips, we were signed up for daily ski lessons, which sounded thrilling—until I met the ski boots. They were, without a doubt, the most uncomfortable things I had ever put on my feet. Imagine a medieval torture device, something straight out of the Spanish Inquisition, except instead of being strapped to a rack, I had to walk in them.

Upon arriving at the ski resort, I wasn't quite prepared for the peculiarities of my new surroundings. We had originally been booked into a palatial hotel further up the hill, but for reasons unknown, we were moved to a more modest establishment. It was acceptable, though noticeably lacking in grandeur.

As we approached the entrance, a soldier in a heavy grey trench coat stood outside, watching each student file in with an intensity that made me question whether we were checking into a hotel or a low-security prison.

One day, curiosity got the better of me, and I decided to venture up the hill to see what I was missing at the nice hotel. While there, I spotted the lifts and figured, why not take a ride for fun? Now, if you can imagine a 1970s Eastern European hotel lift designed with absolutely no regard for modern health and safety standards—this was it. The lift had no door, just open walls, meaning you had to stand back if you valued your limbs.

Unfortunately, my harmless joyride took a turn for the worse when I found myself trapped inside with a group of Germans who, for reasons best known to them, thought the best course of action was to jump up and down while shouting. I was studying German at school at the time, but my skills weren't yet developed enough to decipher their frantic yells. For all I knew, they could have been reciting poetry or screaming out their last wills and testaments.

Eventually, a maintenance man arrived and manually wound the lift up just enough for me to jump through the gap. Thankfully, I was a lot thinner in those days and managed a swift escape. The overly large Germans, however, were not so lucky. They remained stuck for quite some time—hopefully reconsidering their approach to crisis management.

I spent countless evenings sharing laughs with my mate Graham, who was always my partner-in-crime. The ever-present chill in the air never deterred us from venturing out, even on the day when it was a bone-chilling -30 degrees. One particular afternoon, we decided to trek across a snowy field to the sauna at the next hotel down the valley—a journey that quickly taught us the snow was a lot deeper than it looked.

Now, you must understand, this was our first proper exposure to the concept of nudity in a sauna—the kind of experience that would haunt our teenage minds forever. As we sat there, attempting to acclimatise to the warmth in our budgie smugglers, a group of naked women strolled in as if it were the most natural thing in the world.

Panic set in. Graham and I looked at each other, then at the women, then back at each other. This went on for a few moments, neither of us daring to move. I couldn't tell if I was sweating because of the sauna or because there were three naked women sitting directly behind my head. Prior to this encounter, the only naked women Graham and I had ever seen had staples through them from the pages of Playboy magazines.

That was it. We could hold it together no longer. We sprinted out of the room like lions chasing a gazelle, gleefully cannonballing into the plunge pool. You could almost hear the fizz as we hit the water, howling with laughter. I can still hear the echoes of our squeals mingling with the freezing cold air as we plunged into the icy depths, desperately trying to remind ourselves that the whole experience was meant to be relaxing.

This was truly a holiday of encounters with the opposite sex—a whole new world opening up to me in my early teens. In addition to my school, there was also a school from Derby. The kids in their group were slightly older than us, more like 14 or 15.

There was this rather attractive girl who seemed to take a shine to me. One can't blame her, to be fair—she was only human, after all. Anyway, the romance began brewing within the first two days and blossomed as the week rolled on. It finally reached a crescendo, and we ended up having a quick fumble behind the hotel. Let's just say that when the mercury drops to minus 10, things take a bit of finding.

Anyway, it was all over faster than a honeybee. Let's leave it at that.

One morning, the chairlift loomed—a metal beast against the pristine white expanse of snow. Paul and I, filled with the bravado of youth, approached it with reckless abandon.

"Crouch down!" yelled the instructor. "Skis up!"

Paul, ignoring the warning, remained upright. The chair lurched, and he was thrown forward with violent force, his skis ploughing into the snow. The sudden stop ripped through the quiet of the mountain. His face took the full brunt of the impact. It wasn't pretty, but such mishaps were just another rite of passage in our youthful adventures.

Skiing itself was an adventure worth remembering—or perhaps forgetting, depending on your perspective. With every majestic sweep down the slope, I envisioned myself as Franz Klammer, the legendary Austrian downhill skier. I carved dramatic turns and graceful arcs, growing more confident with each descent, thanks to a few lessons earlier in the week.

Yet, amid my triumphant aspirations, came the moment of truth: I suddenly realized I had yet to master the fundamental art of stopping.

In what felt like slow motion, I hurtled downhill, eyes wide, heart pounding, and shouting, "Oh no!" as I ploughed straight into a group of unsuspecting skiers. Among them stood a woman in a striking leopard-skin jacket—a fashion choice that screamed 1970s flair.

I collided with her, spinning wildly as we both struggled to regain our balance. Somehow, she managed to grab my shoulder and plant her feet firmly on my skis. Together, we continued our chaotic descent, giggling uncontrollably as we flew down the hill in an absurd, tangled duet.

It was a less-than-regal moment. Before we knew it, we'd toppled over in a heap of laughter and flailing limbs, much to the amusement—and shock—of onlookers.

As I lay there, tangled in ski gear and laughter, one thought ran through my mind: How the hell am I ever going to get up again? The thrill of skiing had become hopelessly entwined with the chaos of my adolescence. In the end, though, skiing was not for me. I could never bear the agony of those awful ski boots, and, if I were being honest, I had always despised the cold.

Little did I know that I was not headed for more snowy slopes, but for an entirely different kind of rollercoaster—one that would plunge me straight into the tumultuous world of secondary school, where anarchy was about to reign supreme.

Returning from my one and only ski trip, still riding a wave of teenage exhilaration, I stepped back into school with a newfound confidence. The once-daunting hallways now seemed alive with possibility—ripe for mischief, friendships, and more shenanigans than I could possibly tally. Yet, as much as my school years shaped my adventures, they did not set me on the path I would eventually take. Those decisions would come a little later.

But confidence had its flip side. What began as harmless fun soon spiralled into something more rebellious. As the reign of Mr. Feasby faded into memory, a new spirit infiltrated our veins—punk rock music. The soundtrack of our lives shifted from monotonous school routines to the electric pulse of defiance. Suddenly, our school felt less like an institution and more like a never-ending concert, where every corridor hummed with rebellion, laughter, and the ever-present thrum of bass guitars.

CHAPTER 12
Chemistry and Catastrophes

A h, school days—the golden years of unbridled curiosity and occasional mischief that defined our education. To be honest, I didn't attend as often as I should; there were always far more tempting distractions than school. However, there will always be teachers we remember for a lifetime, for a variety of reasons.

In the bustling halls of Huntington Secondary Modern School, two teachers stood out, each with their own unique brand of madness: Mr Thompson and Mr Parkin, whose lessons were equal parts chaos and creativity.

Mr Thompson, our form tutor and chemistry teacher, was an imposing figure clad in tattered, old suits that looked as though they had belonged to him since the dawn of time. Honestly, I'm not sure what was more terrifying—his wardrobe or his habit of barking rudimentary commands at us, making us feel less like students and more like overgrown puppies.

"Get back in your baskets!" he would bellow with fervour, his way of ordering us back into our seats. The phrase conjured an image of us leaping into dog beds at a moment's notice. It was his rather eccentric method of maintaining order, though it often prompted more laughter and eye-rolling than obedience.

Before we embarked on the day's educational adventures, our form room was nestled within the science labs—a space buzzing with mystery and excitement. I vividly remember those thrilling moments gathered around the lab benches, where the allure of Bunsen burners transformed an ordinary school day into a miniature explosion of creativity. Clearly, health and safety regulations were still a work in progress at that stage.

Once those little flames flickered to life, a sense of comfort washed over us—the thrill of science unfolding before our eyes. Of course, our primary interest often lay in mischievous experiments that frequently teetered on the edge of mayhem.

And then there was Mr Parkin, a small, ginger-haired chap with a beard—our woodwork and metalwork teacher. A true craftsman with a passion for creation and a keen eye for detail, he was a decent bloke who treated us all fairly. I already had a good relationship with him, as he had led the school trip to Bulgaria. He was well-liked among the students, his classroom a haven of sawdust, tools, and the comforting scent of freshly cut wood mingling with the metallic tang of machinery.

Between the whirring machines and the serrated edges of various projects, one could only imagine the adventures that awaited.

A vivid memory from Mr Parkin's class that still makes me chuckle involves a school project where we crafted copper ashtrays. I can't imagine that being allowed these days, but perhaps back then, the idea of teenage smokers with their quaint little ashtrays hadn't quite been deemed inappropriate. Our task was meant to teach us the valuable art of planishing copper and soldering—an experience that felt gloriously rebellious given the context.

As we carefully assembled our pieces, Mr Parkin guided us through the intricacies of soldering, always reminding us of the next crucial step: quenching. This process involved rapidly cooling the newly soldered pieces—a mesmerising transition from scorching to cool, requiring a delicate balance of temperature and technique. And then, of course, came the moment when we plunged our freshly soldered copper ashtrays into the sulfuric acid bath—a step that made me feel like a mad scientist in a wonderfully chaotic laboratory.

Enter Anthony Warrilow—a lad who was more brawn than brains and certainly one of the more entertaining personalities in our class. A big lad with bright ginger hair, Anthony had a heart of gold but wasn't exactly the sharpest tool in the shed.

During one fateful lesson, I remember the commotion building as Anthony busily prepared to quench his ashtray after soldering. Perhaps motivated by youthful glee or sheer confusion, he missed a critical step. Instead of quenching his work, he boldly plunged it straight into the sulfuric acid. The moment it hit, it was as if someone had unleashed chaos upon our workshop.

We all stared, eyes wide, as red-hot acid spewed everywhere like a scene out of a disaster movie. The acid hissed and spat angrily, sending sizzling plumes into the air as it made contact with copper. In a flurry, we watched in horror as pieces of metal and bits of ashtray dissolved before our minds could even register what had happened. The classroom erupted into uproar, teachers dashed in from adjacent rooms, and laughter ricocheted off the walls as we instinctively ducked to avoid the unfolding mayhem.

I can still hear Mr Parkin yelling, "Warrilow, you bloody idiot! What the hell are you doing? Get out of the way!" as he rushed to contain the situation—all while desperately trying to maintain his composure. It was an incredible spectacle, one that solidified itself as a legendary tale among our peers for years to come.

It's funny how we navigated both madness and education within the school walls. With Mr Thompson bellowing commands and Mr Parkin guiding us through inventive mishaps, we found ourselves in a world that balanced responsibility with the thrill of danger.

Through their chaotic instruction and passionate dedication, those teachers inadvertently taught us vital life lessons—lessons about curiosity, the fine line between caution and exploration, and just how much fun could be found in the mess. Looking back now, I realize that the wild experiments, the laughter amidst the chaos—all of it helped shape our understanding of science and craftsmanship in ways that textbooks never could.

In the late '70s and early '80s, teachers could dish out punishments as they saw fit. There was no talk of being woke or considering pupils' feelings back then. I remember one occasion when a teacher punched me multiple times around the head—hard enough to break my nose. Was he arrested or reported to the police? No, that was simply how teachers dealt with pupils.

Looking back, no real harm was done—apart from the broken nose, of course—but discipline and life lessons were part of the package. Everyone can recall a time when a blackboard rubber would go flying into the crowd, launched by an irate teacher. Anyone unlucky enough to be hit would simply lie unconscious on the floor for a while—happy days indeed.

That said, I do believe some teachers were there purely to get their kicks—full-on abusers who should have been locked up. Thankfully, I didn't come across many of those.

Following my flutter with the opposite sex during my Bulgarian holiday, we also had sex education at school. Most of the class already had a solid understanding of the so-called birds and the bees. Mother, of course, was never going to tell me anything about that. Instead, the task fell to my sister's boyfriend, Russ, who would eventually become my brother-in-law.

I felt for him as he awkwardly approached me one day and asked if I had any questions. Wanting to make him feel valued, I decided to humour him and asked what a lesbian was—despite already knowing full well. He nervously answered and then, perhaps in an attempt to avoid further discussion, handed me two Playboy magazines and said, "Everything you need to know is in there."

With great excitement, I stashed them behind my wardrobe for safekeeping. My mother was never known for her detailed cleaning, so I figured they would be safe there. Alas, they were not—she found them within days. Busted.

So, I did what any good snitch would do—I blamed my sister's boyfriend. I can still remember Mother kicking off at him. Poor lad.

CHAPTER 13
The Winter of Discontent and Shocking Revelations

Growing up in the 1970s was an era marked by social change and challenges—the most notable of which was the notorious Winter of Discontent. For many families, this winter was defined by industrial strikes that crippled various sectors, leading to severe power outages, shortages, and mountains of rubbish piling up in the streets.

However, in my household, we had a uniquely complicated relationship with electricity and power—not just because of the national crisis, but because my mother often refused to pay the bills as a way of punishing my father. She claimed she was also paying for the streetlights outside!

Even before the national strikes heightened the discomfort, power outages were already a familiar part of our lives. We sat by candlelight for illumination and relied on the coal fire for warmth. When the lights flickered out, we made do with whatever distractions we could muster. More often than not, that meant heading to a friend's house to watch TV, relishing the warmth of their brightly lit living rooms while ours remained shrouded in darkness.

In contrast, summer brought a liberating sense of freedom. It didn't matter whether we had power at home—outdoors was an escape filled with endless adventure. Mornings stretched into afternoons of football and cricket, set against the backdrop of laughter and cheers from our friends. We played until the streetlights flickered on at dusk—that was the unspoken rule for everyone to head home.

But when those carefree days faded into dark evenings with no power at home, a sense of unease would creep in. My mother often scurried off to the Derwent Arms pub in the village. If my sister was babysitting me, she'd be bribed with a bottle of Babycham or a Cherry B and a bag of crisps as a reward. When she was off with her friends, I was left to my own devices, often sitting outside, perched on the wall with my best mate, Trex. I felt too scared to step back inside the house without electricity—an ominous emptiness lurked in the shadows.

Instead, we found solace outside the Rubber House, where the faint glow of light cast a stark contrast against the darkness.

As the months dragged on, the impact of my mother's choices settled heavily over our home. When she finally mustered the effort to call the electric company and restore the power, I naively envisioned a new dawn—one illuminated with possibilities and comfort. Yet, fate had one final joke in store.

With electricity back, a sense of normality began creeping in. Domestic life resumed, and for a brief moment, it felt as though things might return to how they once were. One fateful evening, after the initial excitement of lights flickering back to life, I excused myself to the toilet.

Our three-bedroom semi-detached house had a quirky layout—the loo was separate from the main bathroom. A charming oddity, or so I thought, until that night delivered an unforgettable lesson in the unpredictability of household life.

I had just finished my business and reached for the flush when disaster struck. Unbeknownst to the family, a leak had been quietly seeping beneath the floorboards, its water creeping towards the junction box below. The moment my hand gripped the metal handle, the universe seemed to conspire against me—a violent surge of electricity ripped through my body, turning my world upside down.

The result was unforgettable. Boom!—I was thrown out of the toilet, crashing against the wall with a jolt that left me breathless. The irony of it all struck hard; after months without electricity, just as we were settling back into normality, I experienced the shock of a lifetime—literally. It would have made a fabulous scene in a Carry-On film, but sadly, this was real life.

That moment became one of the more bewildering tales of my upbringing—a reminder that life is often unpredictable, and that normality can shatter in an instant. The electricity had returned only to greet me like a mischievous prankster toying with an unsuspecting child, adding yet another layer to the already complicated dynamics of our family. For years, we continued with the erratic cycle of power coming and going, an ongoing tug-of-war between stability and uncertainty.

Looking back, those years carried a strange duality—laughter interwoven with intimidation. The tumult of the Winter of Discontent mirrored my own struggles at home, shaping the stories that would stay with me long after the events themselves had faded into memory. They became the unwelcome building blocks of my resilience, lessons drawn from both darkness and light. And as I stepped into adulthood, I carried with me not just the weight of those experiences but also a humorous tale and a newfound respect for both the shadows and the sparks that define a life.

CHAPTER 14
The Rise of The Shove

By now, I had become deeply entwined in the local punk scene. Clad in bondage pants and sporting questionably coloured hair, I joined my friends in our misadventures, feeling untouchable and alive. We would gather in darkened corners, sharing mixtapes filled with infectious riffs and adrenaline-pumping rhythms. The artists I adored—The Damned, The Sex Pistols, Siouxsie and the Banshees, Angelic Upstarts, to name a few—resonated deeply with the transient angst of youth. Their lyrics swirled around me like a battle cry, urging us to take on the world.

York University was a prime venue for bands passing through. By then, my tastes had evolved from my very first concert—where Lindisfarne sang folk songs—to pogoing in the student union as The Skids and The Damned belted out their anthems.

This electrifying eruption of creativity spilled over into our lessons as well. With teachers struggling to maintain order while attempting to rehash age-old topics, our punk rock ethos seeped into the classroom like ink staining paper. Instead of adhering to traditional academic solemnity, we sought humour in what should have been serious subjects. Imagine our teacher trying to explain quadratic equations while someone in the back row posed the ultimate question every student ponders—"When are we getting out of here to start a band?"

Ultimately, it was in those chaotic classroom moments that I learned a valuable lesson about life and acceptance. I realised that secondary school was not merely a minefield of authority and discipline but a vibrant tapestry of personalities, where humour bridged the divide between teacher and student. Whether it was inadvertently cracking jokes during history, sneaking hilariously subversive drawings into our coursework, or simply playing truant instead of attending class, I found solidarity with my classmates—an unspoken bond that made the learning experience richer than any textbook ever could.

Punk rock wasn't just a genre of music; it was a lifestyle that seeped into every corner of my burgeoning identity. To paraphrase one of the great punk anthems, it was both a feeling and a revolution—one that pulsed through my veins and electrified my very being. Those rebellious notes blared through our hearts, reminding us that we were young, wild, and free. Each time the bell rang, signalling the end of class, we'd tumble into the hallway, fuelling our defiance with laughter and leaving a trail of chaos in our wake.

As my time in secondary school unfolded, so did my journey of self-discovery, shaped by anarchy, music, and unforgettable moments. It was an era when skiing mishaps effortlessly morphed into skateboarding stunts, and mischief reigned supreme—when laughter echoed louder than even our most unruly escapades. With each passing day, I became further entwined with the loose threads of rebellion, a proud member of the punkiest gang on the block, all while navigating the uncharted waters of impending adulthood. I was no longer just a little fish; I was becoming a force of nature, ready to make waves.

At the time, I had my own drum kit at home—much to the delight of my neighbours—as I pounded away to the Buzzcocks, belting out classics like Orgasm Addict.

One seemingly ordinary night, I stepped into the De Grey Rooms, a small but lively venue in the heart of York, where the pulse of local music beat strong. The air was thick with anticipation, the low hum of chatter mingling with the scent of drinks and youthful exuberance. As the band set up on stage, I could sense the excitement crackling through the crowd—a shared understanding that we were about to witness something unforgettable. Little did I know; my life was about to take a remarkable turn.

It was there, amidst the vibrant chaos of guitars and amplifiers, that I met Lewis—or Straw, as he was widely known—standing at the bar. He was impossible to miss, with his shock of straw-coloured, spiky hair that seemed to have its own gravitational pull.

Approaching me with a grin that hinted at mischief, he introduced himself with an air of casual confidence.

"I play guitar in a band called The Shove," he said, his enthusiasm contagious.

"Interesting. I play the drums," I replied.

His eyes lit up. "We're looking for a drummer. You interested?"

Most would have paused to consider the weight of such an invitation, but my mind was already racing with possibilities. Here I was, basking in the glow of music, and suddenly, an opportunity to be part of something bigger was right in front of me.

Without hesitation, I grinned. "Absolutely! When and where do we practice?"

From that moment on, I was thrust into the whirlwind that was The Shove, forging lifelong friendships that could never be broken. Along with Straw, we had 'Mad Mick' Turl on bass guitar and Steve Colo on vocals—we were The Shove!

Our chemistry was immediate. Straw and the rest of the band brought an electrifying energy to our practices, blending our unique styles into a raw, exhilarating sonic concoction. Each jam session became an explosion of creativity, filled with laughter, experimentation, and the occasional flubbed note—but those imperfections only added to our charm. Though I say so myself, I was a bloody good drummer back in those days—probably too good to be playing punk—but that was my world, and nothing would stop me!

Before long, we found ourselves playing packed gigs across Yorkshire, the energy reverberating through every venue we entered. As we tore through our setlist, I could feel the audience's excitement propelling us forward like a powerful wave. Our sound struck a chord with so many—a no-nonsense blend of punk rock infused with an urgency that could ignite a room. We amassed a large following of dedicated 'nutters.' We weren't the best, but we were the best entertainers.

Our name became synonymous with football, the pogo, gritty lyrics, and a fresh take on punk that people couldn't resist. It wasn't always smooth sailing—we played the Arts Centre to sell-out crowds and once launched into two songs before realising Mick was still upstairs in the green room. Then again, given he wasn't exactly the best bass player at the time, we could barely tell whether he was there or not! He spent a large portion of every gig surfing across the crowd. What he lacked in pure talent, he more than made up for with sheer madness.

As we honed our skills, we ventured into Pollen Studios on the outskirts of York. I had my bondage pants on, and we wore these red and black striped jumpers—a bit like the one Freddy Krueger wore in the horror films. It's fair to say we didn't exactly look like The Beatles!

We weren't entirely sure what we planned to do that evening, but we thought, let's lay down some tracks and see what happens. We only had enough money for four hours of studio time, so we needed to record fast.

The studio had a central control area where the engineer, Dick Sefton, sat. To the right was a small room for my drums, and at the far end of the studio were the guitar and vocal setups.

"Right-o, boys, off you go," said Dick, and we launched into our song, "Pigs." We knew we needed to record four songs. Then, once we had finished and started mixing them with Dick, we realised we had to create a record. That was when the Rough and Ready record label was born, and we were about to be unleashed on the world.

The EP featured tracks such as "Raise the Roof Tonight," "Violence," "Pigs" (not about farming), and the anthem we became known for, "The Nutters of York"—a song about standing on the terraces, following our beloved York City Football Club.

With four songs that spoke to our collective experiences, hopes, and defiance, we captured the essence of who we were in raw, unapologetic form. Those songs didn't just touch our lives; they invaded jukeboxes in pubs across York, becoming anthems for the young and restless.

The thrill of walking into a pub and hearing ourselves on the jukebox—or hearing one of our tracks played alongside classic artists on John Peel's Radio One—was, to put it simply, surreal.

The night we got the call that we'd be featured on his show, we celebrated as if we had just won the lottery, dancing wildly in the living room of our small rehearsal space.

It was my last year at school, and suddenly, I was like a celebrity—kids running up to me saying, "Hey, I heard you on the radio last night!" Amazing!

Our songwriting process was a cauldron of creative chaos—every detail intentional, yet nothing left to chance. We were like mad scientists in a lab, crafting musical potions designed to evoke emotions or provoke thoughts.

Our lyrics had a storytelling quality, blending raw emotion with sharp commentary on the world around us, while Straw and I laid down the rhythm that drove our narratives forward. The synergy between us fuelled our songwriting, leading to tracks that not only tore through speakers but also forged a real connection with our growing following.

As word spread, our fanbase exploded, capturing the hearts of fellow punks and music lovers across the region. People connected with our music—it became their escape, a soundtrack to their rebellious spirit. With each new gig, our following swelled. I'd often look out into the crowd and see familiar faces cheering us on—a beautiful, chaotic tapestry of supporters, bound together by a shared love for our art.

The momentum truly began to solidify when we were invited to support established bands, including Theatre of Hate. Opening for them felt monumental; there we were—a group of enthusiastic kids with a wild dream, sharing the stage with seasoned musicians. The electric atmosphere added a new edge to our performances, turning nerves into adrenaline as we fed off the crowd's energy. It was a whirlwind of excitement—a heady mix of anticipation and the raw thrill of performing.

As we took the stage that night, I had to admit—I felt like a rock star. The surroundings blurred into the background, and all that mattered was the pounding rhythm of the drums and the sound of our collective voices cutting through the air. And when we finished our set, the roar of the crowd, chanting "Shove! Shove! Shove!" over and over, echoed back at us like a wave, sending shivers down my spine.

The end of The Shove felt like saying goodbye to a part of ourselves—a youthful energy we'd never quite recapture but would always cherish. Then time moved on, carrying us through family, careers, and personal growth.

A few years later, we found a new rhythm in Three Billion Things—a calmer sound, yet somehow, we managed to build a fresh following, people who connected with our new style of music. The gigs around the York area held a different energy, a bittersweet harmony between our past and present.

But the dream of a new life in Singapore beckoned, ending that chapter for me, while Lewis and Mick continued on the Yorkshire folk scene with a mellower sound.

With a touch of irony, The Shove are more famous now than we ever were in the '80s. We've ended up on three compilation albums alongside The Ramones, The Damned, and the likes—played on radio stations. Who would have thought that back then!

Being part of The Shove was a transformative experience. Together, we captured moments through notes and words, creating a shared diary of our lives. We weren't just a band—we were a movement, a family, challenging perceptions, fostering camaraderie, and evolving as artists.

The connection we forged through our music became something lasting. More importantly, it created a friendship—a brotherhood that has endured for more than four decades.

CHAPTER 15
Rolf on Saturday

In the early 1980s, Rolf on Saturday became a staple of British children's television, captivating audiences with its vibrant mix of entertainment and creativity. Hosted by the charismatic Rolf Harris, the show blended art demonstrations, music, and sketches, embodying the lively spirit of Saturday mornings. His infectious enthusiasm, coupled with his natural ability to engage children, made him a beloved figure across the nation.

When the announcement came that Rolf on Saturday would be filming an episode at Huntington School, a wave of excitement swept through the halls. The idea of a television production arriving on our doorstep sent us into a frenzy of anticipation. The prospect of appearing on TV was thrilling in itself, but the chance to meet Rolf Harris—a figure we had watched and admired on screen—felt almost unreal.

As the day approached, the energy in the school began to shift. Teachers and staff were abuzz as the TV crews transformed the school hall into a vibrant stage, complete with colourful backdrops and props. A sense of anticipation hung in the air as students whispered eagerly about the chance to see the filming live. Since the programme mainly featured junior school children, very few of us actually had the opportunity to take part.

On the day of the shoot, we skulked around, trying to catch glimpses of the action from behind the scenes. The crew arrived early, bringing with them an array of machinery and equipment that looked as if it belonged in a sci-fi film. There were massive cameras, tripods, sound equipment, and an entire team of technicians bustling about. The atmosphere was electric as the producers coordinated with the talent, ensuring everything was ready for the shoot.

As they set up, I found myself fascinated by the canteen wagons providing food for the crew and celebrities. The tantalising aromas wafting through the air made my mouth water as I imagined the delicious meals prepared for those on set. I couldn't help but wonder what it must be like to indulge in such treats regularly rather than settling for the occasional fish and chips from the local chippy. The thought of glamorous canteen meals—where chefs crafted mouth-watering lunches for the stars—only added to the magic of the day.

As filming began, we watched Rolf interact with the children, welcoming their energy and laughter as they joined in the antics on camera. He painted, sang, and performed sketches that had everyone in stitches. The joy radiating from the set was infectious, and as I stood alongside my friends, we felt a swell of pride knowing that Huntington School was part of such a lively and exciting production.

We watched, wide-eyed, as directors barked instructions and cameras captured the magic. Rolf's playful energy and ability to connect with everyone around him created an atmosphere brimming with enthusiasm. It was fascinating to witness firsthand how a television show came to life—the sheer hard work and coordination required to bring laughter and creativity into homes across the UK.

As filming wrapped up, we were elated. The show had been a celebration of creativity and joy—moments I wished could remain frozen in nostalgia forever. Yet, in time, the joy of that experience would become entangled with the darker revelations surrounding Rolf Harris.

Years later, the fallout from his actions would tarnish the joy of many childhood memories. In 2014, he was convicted of multiple counts of sexual abuse spanning years, shaking the foundations of trust among those who had once admired him.

As the shockwaves of his crimes rippled across the nation, I couldn't help but revisit that day at Huntington School—once filled with innocent laughter and excitement, now overshadowed by the sinister turn his life had taken.

Had he used his charm and persona to manipulate and coerce? The unsettling thought lingered, casting a pall over the cherished memories of our time in his presence. I often wondered if anyone had sensed the darkness lurking beneath his jovial façade. It was a painful reminder of how often we overlook the warning signs in those we idolize, leaving us to wrestle with the conflict between fond nostalgia and the ugly truths that later emerge.

As I continued to reflect on that day, I found myself grappling with the complexities of childhood memories. The joy of shared laughter and the excitement of the filming now mingled with the sour aftertaste of betrayal. The contrast was striking—how could one person's warmth and creativity have coexisted with such profound darkness?

Yet beyond the shadows and uncertainty, I recognized that my time at Huntington School—basking in the laughter of my peers and witnessing the light-hearted magic of Rolf on Saturday—had created something real: a sense of community and happiness.

Ultimately, those precious memories taught me something enduring about trust and vulnerability. In a world filled with disillusionment, I reminded myself that joy could still thrive, even amidst darkness. The laughter we shared that day should not be erased by the actions of a man whose true character was revealed much later.

We were just kids, and in the end, it was those fleeting moments of joy and creativity that would continue to light our paths, even in the face of adversity.

Harris was, in the end, nothing more than a dirty old man.

I recall the last day of secondary school when a particularly unpleasant teacher approached me and declared that I would amount to nothing in life—likely ending up in jail.

Years later, after finding success in my career, I was invited back to Huntington to give a talk on human resources and business to a group of students. After the presentation and Q&A, I made my way down the steps, and who should be waiting at the bottom but that very same teacher?

To his credit, he apologised, admitting he had been wrong about me. I pointed out that, at the time, he might not have been entirely mistaken—I was a bit of a lad back then. But in the end, I was the one who thanked him. His words had fuelled my determination to prove him wrong, and for that, I was grateful.

"So really," I said with a grin, "you were my inspiration!"

CHAPTER 16
Memories of Grandad

Growing up, I spent a great deal of time with my grandfather, the man we affectionately called Kojak. He was my paternal grandfather and a key figure in my early life. I would never know my maternal grandfather, who was killed by a drunk driver while cycling home just three months before I was born. That tragic loss only deepened my bond with Kojak, who became a steady presence in the chaos of my childhood—a comforting anchor in an uncertain world.

Kojak had a gift for making the ordinary extraordinary. With nothing more than a newspaper, he could create paper hats, shields, and swords, each one sparking joy in my eyes. With a flick of his wrist and a few deft folds, he transformed scraps into treasures that fuelled my imagination. Together, we embarked on grand adventures, me fully kitted out in my paper armour, feeling every bit the knight ready to conquer the world.

Sunday afternoons were always a treat—tinned salmon sandwiches followed by a tin of mandarin oranges with Carnation milk. Pure bliss for the taste buds.

One of our favourite spots was Rowntree's Park, just a short walk from my grandfather's house. The park featured a large pond teeming with life, and Grandad would take me there to search for tadpoles. Armed with a net and the boundless enthusiasm of childhood, I felt like a naturalist on a noble quest. Kojak would carefully tie a piece of string around a jam jar to keep our captured tadpoles contained, sharing his wisdom about nature with every catch. He taught me that you didn't need expensive things to enjoy life; often, the greatest fun came from creating something out of nothing— a lesson easily forgotten in today's materialistic world.

During those trips, he seamlessly blended learning with play. With his patient guidance, I absorbed knowledge while being completely enchanted by his stories and presence. Those afternoons in the park formed the bedrock of my childhood memories—a time when love and laughter flowed freely.

However, the joyful interlude of my youth came crashing down when I was fourteen; Kojak fell seriously ill. The weight of the news was crushing, and my heart sank at the prospect of losing another significant figure in my life. I still remember the urgency of that day as my family rushed to the hospital, a tense silence filling the air.

Stepping inside the sterile hospital room, I can still hear the dreadful rattling sound he made as he struggled to breathe—a haunting echo that clings to my memory to this day. Even now, when I close my eyes, that sound returns with painful clarity, accompanied by the overwhelming rush of emotions I felt in that moment. It seemed unbearably unfair that I was about to lose a grandfather who had given me so much love and wisdom.

When the inevitable day came, his funeral was a harrowing affair. Surrounded by relatives, I felt a deep, aching sadness, mingled with confusion at the gatherings that followed. People began sifting through his possessions, their hands filling bags as they sorted through items that had once formed the fabric of his life. What the hell is happening here? I thought in disbelief, struggling to process the unsettling scene unfolding before me. Frankly, I was disgusted.

I can still picture a relative with a carrier bag, stripping the ornaments from his piano while I stood frozen, unable to comprehend the heartlessness of it all. The sight left me feeling hollow and furious. Waves of anger surged through me—I felt as though I was watching my grandfather's life being dismantled piece by piece, an added indignity on top of our collective grief.

Overcome with frustration, I ran out of the house, suffocated by the insensitivity unfolding inside. There stood my dear cousin Kevin, his expression mirroring my own disgust. As our eyes met, I realised I wasn't alone in grappling with the cruel finality of it all.

Later, my uncle approached me, seemingly aware of my grief. "Do you want anything from inside?" he asked. With an earnest heart, I replied, "Just make sure I have a photo of my grandad." That simple request felt like an anchor amid the chaos.

To this day, that photograph hangs proudly on the wall of my home office—a testament to the love and wisdom my grandfather imparted. It embodies my fondest memories of him, reminding me of the warmth, laughter, and life lessons he shared during those formative years.

As the old saying goes, you can choose your friends, but not your family. The complexities of family life often cloud relationships, yet this experience taught me the true value of appreciation and the importance of honouring those who leave a lasting mark on our lives.

Kojak's legacy continues to inspire me, a constant reminder to focus on love and kindness, even amid chaos and uncertainty. Ultimately, he showed me that while family dynamics can be complicated, the bonds forged through love will always endure.

CHAPTER 17
Sweet Times and Coming of Age

A t just sixteen years old, I stepped into the vibrant world of Rowntree's in York, where the delightful aroma of chocolate and sugar infused the very air we breathed. Thousands of workers busily crafted the iconic treats we adored—Kit Kats, Aero bars, Black Magic, Drifter bars, After Eights, Smarties, Polos, and Fruit Gums. The factory was a wonderland for the senses, with colourful packaging whirling in every direction and laughter blending with the rhythmic whir and clank of machinery. It was the beginning of my working life—a sweet start, indeed.

Initially, I landed a job in the packing and store warehouses, working behind the scenes to help ensure all those delightful creations made their way out into the world. My first two years, until the age of eighteen, involved rotating through private accounts and collecting tickets from production runs. This meant I was constantly on the move, darting around the factory to ensure everything was accounted for. Little did I know that some of the most exciting moments would come from my encounters on the various floors of this candy-coated behemoth—with the opposite sex.

I remember one of my first days vividly, stepping out to deliver a parcel to the infamous 12 Store's back landing, where we loaded cargo for the train. The atmosphere buzzed with energy as I manoeuvred through the bustling warehouse, pushing the package on a buggy. However, at that moment, I stumbled upon a chaotic scene that would be etched into my memory forever.

On that fateful journey, I encountered the notorious Charlton Brothers—two boisterous figures, both barely five feet tall, known not just for their antics but for their harmless (and sometimes not-so-harmless) mischief. Both seemed to have perpetually high blood pressure, dashing around like lunatics while shouting at each other. They were, however, the kings of jesters, capable of turning even the most mundane day into a riot of laughter and mayhem.

Amid their merry mischief stood Madeline, a veteran of the packing and store operation, who had become something of a local legend herself. Madeline, an older woman with a flair for colourful makeup, always sported bold lipstick and enough blush to rival a pantomime dame—complete with theatrical gestures and effortless charm. While she had her own loyal assembly line, the boys had their sights set on a bit of nonsense that day.

As I approached the back landing, I saw the brothers stumble upon Madeline. In a burst of youthful theatrics, they seized her and lifted her jumper, revealing her sagging chest with loud shouts of, "Aye, young 'un, what do you think of these?"

I can still picture the moment—the shock of seeing the infamous Charlton Brothers in their element and the startled expression on Madeline's face, with a hint of amusement, of course. It was Madeline, after all.

To say I was taken aback would be an understatement. Utterly aghast and unable to process the sheer absurdity of the moment, I did the only thing a sixteen-year-old in a panic could do: I dropped the parcel from my hands and bolted down the warehouse, my cheeks burning hotter than the chocolate melting elsewhere.

The peculiar scene played out behind me, laughter echoing off the warehouse walls as I stumbled away, thinking to myself that they'd seen better days! That moment is indelibly stamped in my memory—a chaotic slice of life that perfectly captured the spirited essence of Rowntree's factory in those days. A time when people joked, and no one seemed too easily offended.

Looking back, I can't help but chuckle at how that bizarre incident taught me about the unpredictability of working life, especially in such a lively environment. The factory wasn't just filled with sweet creations but with hilarious characters who turned each day into an adventure worth remembering. While I initially thought I was merely rotating parcels, I soon realised I was stepping into a world brimming with laughter, mischief, and, of course, the delicious aroma of chocolate wafting through the air.

Young people today, raised in a world of woke culture and cotton wool protection, would never believe it—nor likely survive it. The Charlton boys would be fired within minutes of their first prank. It's a shame, really, as work back then was so much fun, and people didn't take life too seriously.

This was the beginning of my journey at Rowntree's—a place where I would learn much about leadership, communication, and the dynamics of a thriving workplace. Here, youthful exuberance blended with the artistry of confectionery, creating lasting memories amidst the sweet chaos of everyday life.

For the next two years, I attended day-release at college, studying management, accounting, and other essential skills that would shape my career.

By the time I reached eighteen, the bustling world of Rowntree's had become a cornerstone of my existence. But I could feel an inevitable shift approaching—the fast track to a shift rotation. My journey from a wide-eyed newbie to a seasoned worker had unfolded within those chocolate-scented walls. CF1 Store, the nerve centre of the distribution operation, buzzed with activity, and I was about to ascend further into its thriving chaos.

As I embraced my eighteenth birthday, the day carried a duality that made it both memorable and slightly bittersweet. I was stepping into adulthood—a milestone often celebrated with carefree exuberance—yet it was also tinged with the inevitability of change. It was a day I wouldn't soon forget, filled with the anticipation of new beginnings yet shadowed by reflections on those who had become part of my daily life.

That afternoon, I encountered Ann Smith, just as I had most days over the past two years. A vivacious presence in the office, she reminded me of a younger version of Madeline, with her infectious laughter and sparkling eyes. Ann knew how to have a good time, and, as fate would have it, she had a surprise waiting for me. With a sly, almost mischievous smile, she handed me a brown envelope—my birthday present—the anticipation lingering in the air.

As I peeled it open, I was greeted by an unexpected surprise—a suspender belt. I blinked in confusion, taken aback.

"What the hell am I supposed to do with this?" I found myself asking.

Her response came in a dry, teasing tone as she leaned over and whispered into my ear, "Bring them round to my house tonight, and I'll get into them for you."

A mixture of disbelief, fear, and amusement washed over me. Ann was not shy about enjoying life, and her cheeky proposition sent my adrenaline racing with both excitement and confusion. At that moment, I recalled the words of the great Ron Fisher some months earlier: "Little Annie, that girl could get milk out of an iron bar."

The sweat on my brow was starting to flow! I was tempted and had tentatively agreed to an eight-thirty meet-up. However, I received a call from a friend who said, "Anne is walking around with a clipboard and your name on it, stating 8:30."

At that point, I backed out of what could have been a very enjoyable evening—well, certainly an educational one.

The atmosphere was charged with unspoken possibilities—a moment that encapsulated the essence of a more carefree time. And yet, a whisper of adulthood loomed around the edges. Laughter echoed through the air, and I wondered if this was my initiation into the unscripted world of grown-up tomfoolery.

In the midst of the birthday revelry, I was unexpectedly summoned to Bob Pulleyn's office—the authoritative figure who ruled over distribution day-to-day operations with a no-nonsense demeanour. As I stepped over the threshold, the air felt thick with purpose.

He pointed to the wall adorned with various staff names, and there it was—my name etched among the greats on one of the shift sheets.

It was a small yet significant acknowledgment, and a wave of disappointment surged within me, knowing that the easy days were now over—no more chatting up the girls on the Drifter line.

"Congratulations! You're about to join the best shift in the department," he told me. Those words acted as a subtle enforcer of motivation, solidifying all the hard work that had led me to this very moment.

I asked when, hoping for a few weeks to get my head around the idea. He said, "Monday night—enjoy it."

Reluctantly, I was ready to immerse myself in the challenges that came with the territory, knowing that behind those shift doors lay a tribe of great guys who were ready to welcome me into their fold—as well as subject me to initiation and pranks.

As I left Bob's office, the joy of my birthday celebrations, intertwined with the weight of change, left me both exhilarated and contemplative. I felt as though I was on the cusp of a new chapter—one that encapsulated the youthful spirit of mischief Ann embodied, alongside the dawning responsibilities of adulthood and the exciting prospects of my future within Rowntree's.

My eighteenth birthday became a turning point—a coming-of-age moment wrapped in chocolate-scented memories. It was funny how one day could be filled with playful banter and unexpected surprises, all while standing at the precipice of a journey that promised not just work, but the building blocks of my newfound identity.

The shift rotations loomed ahead, bringing with them new experiences and friendships—ones that would keep that cheeky spirit alive with every challenge and adventure that awaited.

CHAPTER 18
Night Shifts and Seaside Trips

Stepping into my first night shift at Rowntree's on the fabled 12 Store back landing felt like entering the realm of shadows—a different world filled with the hum of machinery and the intoxicating scent of chocolate wafting through the air, even in the wee hours of the night. At eighteen, I had now been initiated into the workforce, and after the standard rigmarole of training, I found myself at the helm of a fleetingly quiet night shift.

The first order of business upon turning eighteen was to learn how to operate machinery—heavy-duty forklifts and loading equipment that felt like toys compared to the responsibilities I was now expected to shoulder. Loading trucks in the dark was a rite of passage, one that promised a whirlwind of excitement and a touch of trepidation. On that foreboding back landing, the night felt both exhilarating and slightly eerie, especially with only the glow of safety lights casting shadows against the cold metal of waiting trains.

In that moment of solitude amidst the busy loading operation, I quickly realised how intimidating it could be to navigate such a dimly lit environment, surrounded by the hulking forms of machinery and the distant sound of rolling wheels. It was a place that demanded focus, and there I was, braving the depths of night with a mix of bravado and slight unease.

As the hours ticked away, I settled into a rhythm, methodically loading the trains. But just as I began to embrace the stillness of my surroundings, it happened. My heart nearly leapt out of my chest as Harry, a notorious prankster and beloved character among the crew, jumped off the top of one of the trains right in front of me. He landed with a dramatic thud, shouting some nonsensical phrase that completely shattered the night's silence.

Let me tell you, it scared the living daylights out of me! The sudden shock jolted through my body like a shot of adrenaline, and I nearly fumbled my load. "Harry! You total twat!" I shouted, half-frightened and half-amused, as he erupted into laughter. Moments like these were a reminder of the team spirit and light-heartedness that filled the otherwise serious work environment, breaking the monotony of night shift hours.

As the weeks progressed, I transitioned between shifts—days, nights, afternoons, and early mornings—each one a rollercoaster of routine and spontaneous moments that shaped my experience. The day shifts were spent back in the main factory, a chance to reconnect with all those lovely ladies in manufacturing and, of course, to arrange Friday nights out on the town.

Rowntree's had a theatre, and back in those days, they would show 15-minute bursts of a film at lunchtime. It started on a Monday, and by the end of the week, you'd seen the whole film.

A quirky setup meant that night shifts would start with a bone-shaking two hours of adrenaline as everyone rushed to finish everything at the beginning. After that wild flurry of productivity came a quieter spell, marked by a temporary lull that often resulted in some well-earned downtime. Packing and Store was seen throughout the factory as a plum job, and only the best people got to be there.

Yet, there was a pattern: five hours of sleep between shifts always felt too short—like a fleeting wink of night before being thrust back into the day. When I finally returned to the warehouse for the last hour, it felt like a clock ticking down to a mad finale—us scrambling to catch up as fatigue clashed with a final burst of residual energy. It boiled over into a frenzy, fuelled by teamwork and punchy banter, revealing the resilience born from the sheer absurdity of our nightly encounters.

Each shift brought its own stories—some riveting, others downright comical—the kind that would go down in Rowntree's lore. And through it all, I learned to navigate both the physical demands of the job and the unpredictable nature of working with characters like Harry. The back landing became my stage—not just for the nighttime loading, but for the entertaining episodes that unfolded under the pale moonlight.

As I reminisced about those early nights, I came to appreciate the unexpected joy hidden within the grind and the bonds forged under the weight of hard labour. My journey into adulthood was suddenly marked by laughter, midnight antics, and the satisfied murmurs of my fellow workers—each of them making the nighttime chaos feel like just another part of life. It was a journey laced with sweetness, both in spirit and in the long hours spent among the endless rows of tempting chocolates and candies.

And then, it was that time of year again—the annual trip to Bridlington, a tradition that had become legendary among our shift in Packing and Store. Organized by Gerry, a larger-than-life character with a knack for crafting unforgettable escapades, the trips always promised a day filled with fun, laughter, and just the right amount of mayhem. With excitement building, we were ready to drink as much as we could and throw caution to the wind.

Each year, the plan was gloriously simple: depart at 9 a.m., stop halfway for a hearty breakfast at a hotel, and then hit the pubs in Bridlington by lunchtime. It was a ritual designed to rev up our spirits in the best possible way—a chance to escape the confines of work and lose ourselves in the seaside revelry.

Gerry was our ringleader, waving the flag of freedom as he orchestrated the day like a maestro conducting a raucous symphony. A fabulous guy, taken from us far too soon in later years, his passing sent shockwaves through us all.

As the bus rolled out of York, we settled in for the two-hour journey, already buzzing with excitement. The chatter was infectious—a harmonious mix of banter, laughter, and playful ribbing filled the air. Five-card brag was the game of choice, and the main challenge was not to lose all your money before even reaching Bridlington.

Waiting until the breakfast stop felt nearly impossible. A full English feast fuelled us for the day ahead, lining our stomachs—as we were always told—for the mammoth drinking session that awaited.

Once we finally arrived in Bridlington, the atmosphere was electric. The salty sea breeze danced against our skin, while the rhythmic crashing of waves provided the perfect soundtrack for our adventure. It felt like a Jolly Boys' Outing—practically a scene straight out of Only Fools and Horses.

With barely a moment to pause, we hit the first pub by lunchtime, and the drinking commenced with gusto. Pints flowed like water, the clinking of glasses mingling with our boisterous laughter.

We were lucky to have a tight-knit crew—colleagues who were just as eager to revel in a day free of responsibility. Then there was Sid, the elder statesman of the group and the life of the party, who had somehow turned chatting up old ladies into an Olympic sport. The legend of Sid running around with his pants down from previous years had cemented itself in Rowntree's lore, and as he geared up to outdo himself once again, we couldn't help but cheer him on

Alan, on the other hand, was the wild card—a man given the nickname Psycho, and for good reason. A fellow worker known for his off-the-wall antics and questionable decisions, he had applied to be a Chargehand more times than I'd had hot dinners, yet he never quite made the cut.

Despite this, Alan brought an infectious energy that could set the whole room aflame. His unpredictable nature made him both the star of the show and a magnet for chaos. His motivations—sometimes skirting dangerously into sex pest territory—created a mix of amusing yet occasionally cringe-worthy moments. He smoked a pipe, chewing on it noisily while making strange sounds. A true legend.

Ironically, a few years later, Psycho finally landed the promotion he had so desperately sought. It didn't end well. He was, to put it bluntly, a disaster.

I still vividly remember the day it all came crashing down. As I walked through the warehouse, I heard a loud commotion on the back landing. Following the crowd of cheering workers, I arrived at the scene just in time to witness pure anarchy—Alan tied to a pole, a small fire crackling beneath him, while his so-called team danced around him, whooping and making war cries straight out of an old cowboy film. Clearly, they had reached their limit with Alan as their leader.

Back in Bridlington, on one of these infamous trips, Keith and I—after an afternoon of dedicated drinking—decided it would be a brilliant idea to get tattoos. Fueled by liquid courage, we stumbled into a tattoo parlor and made our selections.

Looking back, it's highly unlikely that any respectable tattoo artist today would ink two blokes who had consumed as much beer as we had. But back then, no questions were asked. I opted for a Geisha Girl—thankfully dodging the skull and crossbones I had previously considered. The experience was painful and cost me a mere £5. Little did I know that years later, I would spend thousands trying to have that same tattoo removed—a process that was significantly more painful than getting it in the first place!

As the day morphed into night, our adventures only escalated. We moved from the pubs to the nightclubs, where pounding music and flashing lights set the stage for an evening of unchecked revelry. The dance floor became our kingdom, and the chaos unfolded with even greater intensity.

Silly dares turned into legendary moments, laughter echoed through the club, and keeping a straight face became impossible—especially when Alan attempted the latest dance moves. His efforts usually ended in slips, trips, and a tangle of limbs on the floor, sending us all into fits of uncontrollable laughter.

But amidst the revelry, there was something deeper—the unbreakable bond of brotherhood. We weren't just out for a good time; we were making memories that would last a lifetime.

The nighttime adventures stretched on until the first light of dawn, signalling the inevitable call for the bus. After hours of dancing, mingling, and making questionable choices, we staggered back to the waiting vehicle, souvenirs of the night clinging to our clothes, our voices hoarse from laughter and song.

By the time the bus rumbled home at 4 a.m., exhaustion had finally caught up with us. Some drifted into sleep, while others sat in quiet reflection, replaying the night's escapades. We knew that once we stepped back onto the factory floor, old rivalries and daily routines would resume. But for now, Bridlington remained with us—like the lingering scent of sunscreen on sunburnt skin—reminding us of the wild adventures, the camaraderie, and the bonds forged in laughter and recklessness.

In reflection, Gerry's annual trip to Bridlington wasn't just a day at the seaside—it had become a rite of passage, a celebration of youthful spirit, and, perhaps, just a touch of chaos. Each year felt like unlocking a treasure chest of wild stories—laughter, antics, and unforgettable memories that carried us through the ups and downs of life and work. No matter what the year had thrown at us, we always looked forward to these adventures, knowing that amidst the thrill and mayhem, friendships flourished. We were part of something bigger—a story woven with mischief and camaraderie, one that whispered joy to our hearts long after the sun had set on the seaside.

As with most large factories, some characters became notorious, their reputations growing with each whispered tale. In the dimly lit corners of Rowntree's 12 Store—where the steady rhythm of stocking shelves and loading trucks was the heartbeat of the place—one figure was known to all: Brian, affectionately dubbed "Slippery Fingers." His job was simple—collect stock and transport it to the employee sales shop, where workers could buy products and factory rejects at discounted prices.

At first, his nickname might have seemed innocent, almost playful. But those in the know understood the truth behind it. Fingers had a knack for, shall we say, unexpected acquisitions—on an industrial scale.

As the shifts wore on and fatigue gnawed at our minds, it became impossible to ignore Brian's uncanny ability to waltz into the stores—seemingly harmless, yet always up to something. He moved with an effortless air of nonchalance, his sleight of hand as smooth as a seasoned magician's. With an unassuming demeanour, he'd casually stroll through the aisles, his eyes darting like a performer surveying his stage, waiting for the perfect moment to execute his next trick.

One day, I remember it distinctly. While the rest of us tore through the day's grind—loading trucks, checking inventory, packing orders—there was Fingers, slipping into the back like a shadow, embodying the very essence of stealth. With a practiced glance, he would scout the stock that wasn't meant for him—the chocolates, the little snacks, the goods momentarily misplaced... or so it seemed.

With a nimble flick of his wrist, he would snatch up a packet of beloved sweets as effortlessly as a magician pulling a handkerchief from a hat. Before we knew it, he'd be strolling past the loading area, his impressive haul casually tucked under his arm or mysteriously concealed behind his back. Fingers was the wizard of the warehouse, and most of the time, we were too busy spinning piles of chocolate-covered parcels to notice the vanishing act happening right under our noses.

"Just keeping things balanced, lads!" he'd call out, grinning with mischief as he nimbly made his way towards the exit, delightful treats meant for retail vanishing like smoke. It was all in good fun—harmless, really—unless, of course, you were the manager, who might have taken the joke a little too seriously.

While some might clutch their pearls at the thought, most of us saw his antics as a genuinely entertaining bonus to our shifts. Everyone knew exactly what he was up to—even the managers. The punishment, if caught, was dismissal, and no one wanted to be responsible for someone losing their job.

His mischief brought a little levity to the long days spent in the store—moments where laughter rang out more easily than our efforts to push sugary products through the factory's relentless demands. Even if those higher up the food chain fretted over inventory losses, we couldn't help but admire the boldness that Fingers had cultivated in the most unlikely of settings. The lively banter that erupted whenever Brian entered the room transformed the harsh reality of warehouse work into something that felt less like a grind and more like a family affair.

I realised I was part of this wild tapestry of characters at Rowntree's, where each person added a unique thread to the narrative of our daily escapades. Fingers' magic had a way of igniting a sense of playful defiance amid the long hours of labour, reminding us that it didn't have to be all serious business.

Of course, one day, the game was up, and soon everyone knew that Fingers' magic had come to an abrupt halt. Senior management had finally caught on to his antics, much to the dismay of his amused followers, who had thrived on the excitement of it all. Firemen, who also doubled as security, took up positions in the warehouse, waiting for him to strike.

With a smirk and a flurry of mock innocence, Brian somehow managed to evade discipline with his usual wit and charm, leaving us all in disbelief.

In the years that followed, as I looked back on my time at Rowntree's, I couldn't help but fondly remember Brian "Slippery Fingers"—the man who turned our days into performances filled with laughter, mischief, and a little bit of chocolate magic. After all, it was those little escapades that created the sweetest memories in the rollercoaster ride we called life.

Looking back, I think those early encounters made me wiser in later years—better at spotting those who were spinning the BS.

CHAPTER 19
Shaking the foundations of the village

Tragedy struck us hard in our early twenties, shattering the fragile fabric of our lives with the sudden loss of dear friends. The shockwaves rippled through our close-knit village community, leaving everyone struggling to come to terms with life's harsh unpredictability.

It was a typical evening when four of our close friends decided to hop into a car with a boy from the village—someone we all knew but were not particularly close to. Unfortunately, he had been drinking, and the warning signs were obvious. Yet, in their youthful recklessness, they paid little heed; the appeal of a quick and free ride home outweighed the caution that should have prevailed.

As the car sped down Hull Road toward the village, everything changed in an instant—it swerved violently and crashed into the wall next to the Black Bull Pub, coming to a sudden, devastating stop.

In the front seat, Keith—an enormous man with a heart of gold, known for his hearty laughter—died instantly upon impact. Keith had spent a great deal of time with Graham and me. A larger-than-life character, the thought that he could be gone in an instant was unfathomable. Although there wasn't a mark on his body, the stark reality of the accident felt heavy and profound. We were left shattered, grappling with the loss of a friend who had touched our lives in so many ways.

Another of our close friends, "Beddy," was also killed in this tragic accident. His family faced the unimaginable pain of losing another son—made even more devastating by the fact that his twin brother had tragically taken his own life a few years earlier. The weight of such sorrow was unbearable, leaving us all questioning the fragility of existence and the cruel hand of fate.

Cags, with whom I had played golf and cricket since childhood, was also in the car. He miraculously survived, but not without lasting consequences. The accident left him with severe brain damage, fundamentally altering who he was. Watching one of our own suffer like that was heartbreaking—a stark reminder of how precious life is and how quickly it can be snatched away.

Then there was "Pele." He survived without a scratch, despite being drunk and having travelled in the boot of the car.

As if the tragedy couldn't deepen further, two girls who had also been in the car lost their lives—each life extinguished before it had truly begun. The final, grim twist? The driver was the son of our local vicar—a detail that only compounded the unbearable weight of guilt and sorrow, hanging in the air like an unwelcome fog. All who lost their lives were far, far too young to be taken.

The funeral that followed was a sombre affair, heavy with grief and disbelief. Three village lads were laid to rest together, and the contrast between our shared laughter and memories and the finality of death left everyone at a loss for words. It was a time when sorrow took on a tangible presence in our small community; each tear shed spoke of the love we had for these boys and the gaping hole their absence would leave in our lives.

As we stood together, supporting one another amidst the bleakness, I realised that these experiences would forever shape us. They forced us to grow up quickly, to confront the reality of loss, and to cherish every moment we had. Each life lost served as a stark reminder that our time together was finite.

Through the pain, I drew strength from my remaining friends, bound by the shared anguish of our loss. We found solace in stories of laughter and joy, reminiscing about the incredible moments spent with Keith and Beddy. In those harrowing times, we learnt to lean on each other, transforming our grief into an unbreakable bond that would endure for years.

In the aftermath of the tragedy, our small village stood united in remembrance. A plaque was placed in the lounge bar of the Derwent Arms, allowing us to share a drink with them in spirit. Though the shadows of loss lingered, the legacy of our friendships shone brightly, lighting the path ahead and reminding us that love, though interrupted, is never forgotten.

CHAPTER 20
Entering the Digital Age

At this point, Rowntree's had been taken over by Nestlé, following a bidding war with Suchard. In the end, at least for me and my career, the best firm won. Nestlé Group Distribution had now moved into the digital age, with its logistical operations becoming increasingly computerised.

Along with this change, a brand-new, thirty-thousand-pallet automated warehouse had been built in York, and I was transferred there. I quickly realised that the landscape of modern warehousing was evolving at an impressive pace. While I had honed my skills in logistics, there remained a significant gap in my knowledge—one I needed to bridge to ensure our efficiency kept up with changing demands.

This gap lay squarely in the realm of computer programming and load planning, and I had found myself in the right place at the right time.

The warehouse was equipped with a complex system designed to streamline operations, manage inventory, and optimise load planning. However, navigating this technological maze was no easy feat, and it became increasingly clear that I needed to develop my proficiency in these systems to lead effectively.

I threw myself into learning the intricacies of warehouse management software, eagerly devoting my evenings to familiarising myself with programming languages and data analytics.

During this learning period, I was given a fascinating—albeit daunting—assignment involving a time-and-motion analysis. The company had brought in an expert to scrutinise the efficiency of our operations, particularly my own. The aim was to gather data on how we could enhance productivity by identifying inefficiencies in our workflows.

I vividly remember the day the time-and-motion analyst shadowed me in the computer room. The expert arrived, clipboard in hand, ready to dutifully record my every move—only to be immediately swept up in the whirlwind of my daily routine.

I was zigzagging across the room, tackling a barrage of tasks that would make anyone's head spin. "Wait! Where did you go?" became the refrain I heard as I darted to and fro, managing the team's various duties while simultaneously orchestrating the seamless delivery of pallets from the warehouse and planning loads.

Needless to say, they gave up after thirty minutes, barely able to keep up with my pace and the chaos unfolding around us. Despite their best efforts, they ultimately looked more like a deer in the headlights—frozen, overwhelmed by the symphony of activity. I could see the bewilderment in their eyes—the stark contrast between the high-speed operations and their painstakingly slow recording process.

But what truly ignited my enthusiasm was the exhilaration of joyriding the cranes—navigating the lofty heights of the warehouse while ensuring loads reached the waiting teams. Riding the crane with the electricians became an unexpected perk of my position, allowing me to oversee our meticulous operations while immersing myself in the magic of the machinery that powered our loading and storage processes.

Perched high above the ground, I felt the vast potential of our operation. The crane wasn't just a tool for allocating space efficiently—it became a vantage point from which I could observe, strategise, and motivate my teammates below.

Learning the intricacies of programming and load planning transformed my approach to workforce management. I embraced the digital age, collaborating closely with IT to tailor our systems to our specific needs. Through my programming courses, I honed my ability to manipulate data, enabling me to develop more effective load plans and forecasts.

As I became more comfortable with these systems, I took on the responsibility of training my team. Instilling confidence in my colleagues became a priority; I wanted everyone to feel capable of accessing and utilising the technology essential to our evolving environment. I challenged myself to bridge the gap between seasoned warehouse veterans and the new wave of technology, ensuring that everyone could harness its potential.

The days of relying on manual processes for planning were rapidly fading, and I thrived on helping my team adapt to these innovations. I implemented strategies that capitalised on our data—analysing past performance, measuring output patterns, and forecasting demand based on historical trends. This newfound insight created a dynamic planning system that enhanced our entire workflow, allowing us to manage our time and resources more effectively.

Embracing the world of computerised logistics opened doors to greater efficiency and team empowerment. Together, we optimised our load plans, streamlined our processes, and strengthened the essence of teamwork—an orchestra of interconnected roles working in harmony within the bustling warehouse.

As I embraced this dual life of physical and digital management, I recognised the importance of continual evolution—you can no longer stand still; you must adapt. The journey of learning programming and mastering load planning became a cornerstone of my leadership style, fostering a modern and efficient workplace while motivating my team to face the future head-on. The synergy between technology and human insight was invigorating, and I looked forward to the continued growth that awaited me within the realm of logistics.

CHAPTER 21

The Misadventures of Trevor the "Slopa"

In every workplace, there tends to be a character who adds a unique flavour to the daily grind, and in our warehouse team, that character was undoubtedly Trevor. Now, it's worth mentioning right off the bat that while "Slopa" (as we affectionately dubbed him) wasn't the sharpest tool in the shed, he brought an unexpected brightness to the otherwise serious atmosphere of the warehouse with his unintentional humour—amplified by the fact that the poor chap had a stutter.

Slopa had a knack for making everything seem slightly more entertaining—albeit unintentionally. Lazy didn't even begin to cover it, hence the nickname "Slopa"—he had an incredible talent for vanishing just when the workload was heaviest. It felt as if he possessed a superpower dedicated to self-preservation. Just as we'd be gearing up for a busy shift, he would slip out of sight, leaving behind a trail of expletives from the others.

Unfortunately, his "magic" somehow propelled him to the role of trade union shop steward for logistics—a position that conveniently afforded him ample Fridays off to get through his paperwork. A term that, I assure you, should be taken lightly.

While his absence was often noted with a mix of frustration and disbelief, it was his astonishing inability to handle the role of shop steward—consistently capitulating to everything management put to him—that truly pushed the staff over the edge.

One infamous day, in a moment of exasperation, a group of colleagues decided to put a forklift to creative use. They playfully rigged it up with the intention of "hanging" him—metaphorically, of course! It was a light-hearted joke meant to address the growing tension. The scene was absurdly funny; he remained blissfully unaware of the resentment brewing around him, while we burst into laughter as they hatched their plans. In the end, this act achieved exactly what most people had hoped for—he resigned as shop steward the very next day.

Outside of work, he was quite the character on the golf course. He played with a group of us weekly, bringing his signature mix of talentless ability and comedy to the fairways. I vividly recall one day when he was struggling to carry his clubs around the course, moaning about how heavy they felt after just five holes. In an attempt to lighten his bag, he unzipped the side pocket, only to discover that his kids had taken it upon themselves to become amateur comedians—sneaking in two hefty building bricks. The look on his face was a mix of disbelief and exasperation as he exclaimed, "No wonder this feels so heavy!" The entire group erupted into laughter.

He never failed to deliver comedy, and just a week later, he did it again. Striding proudly up to the first tee, he brandished four shiny, expensive golf balls—each painstakingly bought for £1, a pretty steep price for a ball back then.

With a confident swing, he teed off, sending the ball soaring straight into the cornfield to the left of the fairway.

"W-W-W, where did it go?" he asked.

I couldn't help but laugh as I replied, "Put it this way, you're a pound down, mate."

He huffed and grumbled about his misfortune, his frustration brewing into comedic rants for the rest of the round. By the end, all four balls had disappeared into the wilderness, never to be seen again.

As with most things "Slopa," I saved the best golf story for last. He was the guy who simply kept on giving.

We were playing golf at Pike Hills Golf Club, just on the outskirts of York—a place we frequently visited. That week, we were on the afternoon shift, so an early morning start was required. It was July, a beautiful summer's day, with the sun shining and birds chirping.

Towards the end of the round, we approached the 17th tee. This was an elevated tee box with steps made from railway sleepers. There stood Slopa, ready to take his tee shot up the hill towards the green.

Unbeknownst to him, one of the sleepers was protruding slightly above the grass—no more than a couple of inches.

Bang! He struck the ball, and as we all looked up the fairway, there was no sign of it anywhere.

He had somehow managed what should have been impossible. He'd clipped the very top of the sleeper, sending the ball skyward. Then, in what must have been a ten-million-to-one chance, it came hurtling straight back down—smacking Slopa on the head and knocking him out cold.

I have never laughed as much as I did that day. Pure comedy gold, yet again, from the one and only Slopa.

Beyond golf, he had a creative spark—dabbling in homebrewing beer and, before joining us in the warehouse, working as a carpenter. He took great pride in building a sturdy shelf to showcase his collection of home-brewed bottles in his garage. Convinced he had crafted the ultimate male sanctuary; he saw it as a place to boast about his brewing prowess.

However, the universe had other plans.

About three hours later, he returned to the garage only to find that his self-made shelf had succumbed to gravity's call. In a comedic twist of fate, the bottles had tumbled down, shattering on the floor and creating a glistening puddle of his once-prized beer.

And there, sprawled out amidst the wreckage, lay his dog—clearly inebriated, having indulged in the very essence of his homebrew endeavour. Out cold and blissfully unaware of the chaos it had caused.

These misadventures became the stuff of legend, bringing the team closer together through ridiculous stories and shared experiences. He embodied the spirit of our group—his antics were never malicious, and somehow, he became our lovable mascot of sorts.

In a world that often needed a bit of light-heartedness, he reminded us how humour and friendship could blend seamlessly into the day-to-day grind, whether in the warehouse or on the golf course.

Through every escapade—whether it was bricks in bags or drunken dogs—we found ways to connect and create lasting memories across those long work shifts. As the years passed, I lost touch with him, but hopefully, he's still out there, creating laughter—unintentionally, of course.

CHAPTER 22
Rising Through the Ranks

A few years later, as Nestlé evolved, so too did my role within the company. Gone were the days of loading trucks from a dimly lit back landing or working with computer programming. With the arrival of a sprawling, state-of-the-art automated warehouse—teeming with innovation and efficiency—came new opportunities. It was a whirlwind of activity, the air thick with the hum of machinery and the excitement of what lay ahead.

Two figures had a significant impact on my transition into leadership: Ron Fisher and Eddie Reynolds. With their guidance, I stepped into new territory, taking on the role of charge hand. Managing groups of burly warehouse men was a daunting task, filled with challenges I hadn't quite prepared for.

The old team I had once known had largely disappeared, replaced by new shifts and unfamiliar faces. It was a brave new world, where each individual brought their own experiences, strengths, and challenges. This transformation required me to not only adapt but also master the intricacies of leadership and management.

Managing teams with diverse personalities—many of whom were accustomed to doing minimal work—was an education in itself. Early on, I realized that conflict often stemmed from misunderstandings, differing work styles, and the pressures of a high-intensity environment. Learning to handle these conflicts effectively became paramount. This was my first experience managing people, and I still bear the scars to prove it. Yet, surprisingly, my previous life experiences had equipped me well for the challenge.

The militant presence of the trade union in our warehouse required a careful and strategic approach. Striking a balance between management decisions and staff welfare was essential. I quickly learned to respect the union's role while fostering a relationship built on mutual understanding.

At the centre of it all was Tony, the main shop steward at the time—a pipe-smoking character who referred to all his colleagues as "brothers," regardless of gender. A fiercely militant figure, he made the legendary Arthur Scargill look like a corporate executive. Tony and I clashed often during my time in management at Nestlé Group Distribution, but despite our battles, we developed a mutual understanding of where we each stood.

As I settled into my new role and navigated its challenges, I experienced unexpected growth. I came to understand that management was not just a title but a responsibility—an opportunity to foster a thriving work environment. Under the guidance of Ron and Eddie, I began to recognize my potential and develop skills that would serve me well throughout my career.

In this rapidly evolving warehouse landscape, I became more than just a charge hand; I became a leader—one who could inspire, resolve conflicts, and drive productivity. This period of transformation deepened my understanding of what it truly meant to contribute—not only to the company but also to the people I worked alongside.

As new challenges arose, I embraced them wholeheartedly, ready to face whatever lay ahead with resilience and determination.

Cutting my teeth as a chargehand was not for the faint-hearted. It was a baptism by fire, filled with challenges that tested my resolve and pushed my limits. Each difficult day brought experiences that left their mark—often quite literally. I earned a few battle scars along the way, learning how to manage and motivate a team of strong personalities, many of whom had been at Rowntree's far longer than I had.

At times, the warehouse floor felt like a battleground. The gruff nature of some veteran warehousemen often led to clashes, with tempers flaring and disagreements erupting over logistics or shift arrangements. But through these encounters, I learned invaluable lessons in conflict resolution and how to assert myself as a leader who could earn my team's respect. I quickly realised that being a manager meant juggling compassion for my colleagues while also maintaining the discipline needed to keep everything running smoothly.

As Ron Fisher's retirement drew near, I felt a shift in the winds of my career. He had been a mentor, guiding and encouraging my growth, and now, with his impending departure, I was offered the opportunity to step into a new role as Shift Operations Manager. It was a dream come true, but also a daunting challenge. With new responsibilities came a heightened awareness of the broader challenges facing the business.

Working in the confectionery industry often felt like riding a rollercoaster, defined by its peaks and troughs. Seasonal demands meant high-pressure periods that swung into overtime, leading to significant costs. As I stepped into my new role, I quickly grasped the impact this had on our operations. The highs were sweet—busy shifts filled with productivity—while the lows brought frustration. I realised that changes were needed to optimise efficiency and manage costs.

One of the key initiatives I introduced was a system known as annualised hours, and I had the opportunity to work alongside a consultant who specialised in this field. This innovative approach provided greater flexibility in scheduling, helping us tackle the challenges posed by the erratic nature of production demands. With this system in place, we could roster staff on and off with precision, seamlessly balancing hours worked against business needs. My contribution was to develop an additional banking system of hours, making the process even more efficient. This allowed us to track working hours and determine who was next up for shifts based on both availability and demand.

Negotiating with the union was undoubtedly one of the more delicate aspects of introducing this system. I drew on the relationships I had built over my time at Rowntree's, emphasising the benefits for workers while ensuring management needs were met—all while avoiding the picket lines and burning oil drums. Armed with data and a solid understanding of employee concerns, I framed the proposal in a way that demonstrated it was not only advantageous for the business but also for the workers themselves. Navigating the discussions smoothly, I successfully implemented the system during my first year as Shift Operations Manager.

As we integrated the annualised hours, I witnessed a noticeable improvement in both morale and productivity. Workers were less stressed by conflicting shifts; instead, they could manage their time better, balancing busy work weeks with time off more seamlessly. The newfound flexibility invigorated the warehouse atmosphere, creating a tangible energy that powered us through even the busiest days.

With the success of this initiative, I finally felt like my career was truly taking off in the world of logistics. Each hurdle I had overcome prepared me for this moment of recognition and validation. I was no longer just a manager navigating interpersonal dynamics—I was now influencing change and driving improvement across the entire operation of our busy warehouse.

As my responsibilities grew, I embraced the challenges this role brought, tackling everything with the same resilience that had served me well until now. The landscape of Nestlé continued to evolve, and within it, I found my footing—an emerging leader in the world of logistics, ready to face the next adventure awaiting me around the corner.

It was also during this time that I met Carol—not to be mistaken for my sister, Carole with an e. She was a Glaswegian who had joined Nestlé on their graduate training programme. She had a brain the size of a planet and looks strikingly similar to the singer Belinda Carlisle, who I'd always thought was hot. She brought a balance of both personal and professional fulfilment that I hadn't realised I needed.

It was at this stage that Tony and I would have our final battle. I had been pushing them to improve their workload, as the data reflected that their output was falling behind others. Tony felt it was time to show me the true might of the Trade Union. He marched into my office and announced, "We're on a work-to-rule."

I simply replied that it was their right—just as it was my right to implement regulated breaks. As Tony left the office, I thought, This will go one way or the other.

Being a data junkie, I pulled out the output report at the end of the shift, and to my delight, they had done more work that night than on any shift in the previous two weeks of daily reports. As they all waited on the shop floor to go home, I walked out and asked if I could have a moment.

"Would it be possible," I said, "for you to continue working to rule for the rest of the month? The output tonight was the best we've had."

I walked back into my office, and the noises from outside told me everything—they were not happy, and Tony was feeling their anger.

The following evening, they worked as normal. The loads kept coming out, and I reinstated their extended breaks. Not long after, Tony resigned as shop steward.

That evening was one of the many lessons I learned throughout my career. This one taught me to stand tall—there is more than one way to deal with a problem. Confronting it head-on doesn't always give you the result you're looking for.

Perhaps that's why I've always told people to look at the data to build their story. The facts are your partner when tackling challenges.

CHAPTER 23
A Defining Moment

In the wake of my success in implementing annualised hours, a significant opportunity knocked on my door. The Nestlé York HR Director approached me, expressing an interest in my skill set and asking if I would consider moving into the Human Resources department. It was a moment that would prove transformative—a spark igniting a career path that would take me around the world, working with some of the leading organisations in their field. They commended my ability to negotiate with the trade unions, acknowledging how I had navigated our complex workplace dynamics with a deftness that caught their attention. Although I had built a strong career in logistics, I now felt the need for something fresh, and human resources offered just that.

Embarking on this new journey felt thrilling yet daunting, as I knew it would take me into uncharted territory within the organisation. It also meant going to university, studying Human Resources, passing exams, and working at the same time. Shortly after making my decision, I transitioned to the

Smarties production plant—a hive of activity where the sweet little candies we all loved rolled off the line in vibrant colours. My aim was simple: to introduce new ways of working, improve output, and contribute to the success of the plant while enhancing the experience for all employees.

However, the journey began with a hiccup. Just three months into my new role, the Managing Director who had hired me unexpectedly departed. In his place came a new leader—a stark contrast to his predecessor. The new MD, notorious for his ruthless style and often referred to as "the Ass," quickly gained a reputation for his strict and, at times, questionable management approach—one that sent shivers down the spines of many employees.

It was during this period that I learned one of the most critical lessons of my career: the art of managing people and the vital importance of trust in the workplace. The MD's tactics relied heavily on authority and fear, a style that stifled creativity and motivation across teams. Meetings became tense, loaded with frustration, as employees focused more on avoiding reprimands than striving toward shared goals.

Watching this unfold was both sobering and enlightening. I unintentionally became a keen observer of how not to manage effectively. People followed directives because they had to, not because they wanted to. The difference was palpable—output was dropping, and no one was willing to go the extra mile for a manager who commanded no respect. Toxic managers, whose leadership forces employees into compliance, only ever get the bare minimum in return—nothing more!

From my past experiences, I knew that fostering a culture of trust, respect, and mutual collaboration was the key to improvement. Drawing on my time managing warehouse teams, I began to put these principles into practice. The lesson became crystal clear: without trust, teams would operate in a state of compliance rather than engagement, and the only outcome would be a ceiling on performance.

Determined to make a difference, I threw myself into creating a positive work environment while standing my ground with the MD. At the Smarties plant, I prioritized open communication, empowerment, and teamwork. Instead of waiting for input, I actively sought my colleagues' ideas on improving processes, encouraging them to voice their suggestions. I worked to sustain a supportive environment where individuals felt valued and recognized for their contributions.

Gradually, I began to witness a subtle but positive shift. People became more engaged in their work; a spirit of innovation emerged in discussions, and the overall energy transformed. With each new suggestion implemented, I could sense trust being rebuilt—at least in certain areas. People were no longer just working to avoid consequences; they were contributing because they believed in the vision we were cultivating together.

As I navigated the complexities of this new role, I realised that trust was the cornerstone of effective leadership. My time at the Smarties production plant became a defining chapter in my professional journey, shaped by the lessons learned amid the harsh realities presented by the MD.

With every challenge faced, I grew more determined to champion management practices built on trust, engagement, and collaboration. Though the path was far from easy, I recognised that each step was a building block toward a future filled with promise—a career fuelled by my passion for people and productivity. This new chapter was not just an opportunity; it was a calling—one that would shape me into a leader ready for whatever came next.

In the end, although I had made some progress, the MD's management style continued to affect operations, leading several senior leaders to leave for other parts of the business where their skills would be better utilised. As luck would have it, an opportunity came my way—a route back to logistics, this time as Head of HR.

I still recall the moment I stepped into the MD's office and said, "I've decided to take another opportunity within the business and will be leaving this role." He snapped back instantly, fixing me with a stare that resembled that of an unhinged madman. "You will never come back here to work if it goes wrong," he sneered.

I replied swiftly, "That's the plan, old chap. That's the bloody plan."

It was a moment of pure joy as I swivelled around and walked out, chuckling to myself, but also breathing a massive sigh of relief—I was finally out of that toxic environment. Others outside had caught wind of what had taken place, and as I walked down the corridor, several of them high-fived me.

Sometimes, you just have to have that moment.

Reflecting on this chapter of my career, I recognised the vital importance of effective communication, credibility, respect, and, most of all, trust—both in leadership roles and personal relationships. This experience not only solidified my approach to HR and operations but also reinforced the idea that understanding and collaboration are key to navigating challenges in any organisation.

I am eternally grateful to Nestlé for sponsoring my university education, which enabled me to gain my qualifications in Human Resources. This opportunity has allowed me to explore various facets of my profession. However, I firmly believe that experience is irreplaceable, and sometimes those who have attended the "university of life" earn far higher grades than those who have simply followed a traditional academic path.

CHAPTER 24

Getting Maui'd and the Mysteriously Sober Stag Night

After what felt like a thousand years of dating, filled with the ups and downs of life's escalator, Carol and I decided it was finally time to tie the knot. The prospect of a traditional church wedding—complete with a big white dress, a towering cake, and a guest list packed with relatives we might see once a decade—was about as appealing as a root canal. We wanted something different—something memorable that wouldn't require a second mortgage. Enter our plan for a destination wedding on the paradise island of Maui, Hawaii.

Why Maui, you ask? Well, it's a breathtaking island paradise, and my sister lived in California, meaning she could zip across the Pacific without risking her luggage ending up in another country. We discovered a company called Happily Maui'd to arrange our ocean-side matrimonial adventure. The name alone promised a level of cheesy charm we simply couldn't resist, and their portfolio assured us they wouldn't just plonk us down in front of any old volcano.

But before the Hawaiian extravaganza, there was a crucial rite of passage: the stag night, brilliantly orchestrated by my brother-in-law, Russ, who had clearly missed his calling as an events planner. He rounded up a lively crowd of my friends in California, all too eager for another adventure in San Jose.

Our night out was a living homage to brotherhood and chaos as we hopped from one quirky bar to another. Laughter echoed through the streets until we eventually stumbled upon the infamous Kit Kat Club. This venue bore no relation to the chocolate bar, though one could argue it offered a different kind of sweet experience.

Upon entry, it was immediately clear that I was as prepared for the "entertainment" as a fish attending a bicycle convention. The dancers approached with professional charm, and when one asked if I wanted to dance, my nerves kicked in. "Sorry, my dear, I'm dreadful at dancing," I replied earnestly. Russ erupted with laughter, clapping me on the back. "She'll dance for you!" he chortled, his face turning every shade of red I had. Feeling my bachelorhood hanging precariously, I sought refuge at the bar.

The only catch? The strip clubs weren't licensed to serve alcohol. Non-alcoholic beer was the order of the day—specifically, Coors Cutter, a brand so committed to temperance it might as well come with a halo. Yet, our friend Greg appeared to grow increasingly inebriated, despite the nature of his drinks. He swore he could feel the buzz of Bacchus himself, perhaps from the mere suggestion of drunkenness wafting through the air or the charged ambiance.

Our curiosity about Greg's state evolved into comedic hypotheses about how he was pioneering a new level of placebo intoxication. Meanwhile, I analysed his antics, wondering whether he was simply enchanted by the club's mood lighting or had indulged in some magic white powder we knew nothing about.

Amidst the laughter, mock debates about turning H_2O into wine, and Greg's possibly vodka-less vodka shots, I did, in fact, accept that dance. That girl had the flexibility of an octopus—truly professional!

As the night wore on, tales grew taller, and jokes sharper. The evening was an unabashed success, proving that even a non-alcoholic stag night could spark legendary stories.

With sides aching from laughter and a treasure trove of Greg's imaginary tipsiness firmly etched in our minds, this stag night was the absurdly perfect prelude to our wedding adventure in Maui. It turns out that a little taste of chaos is often the best preparation for love's grand leap.

The day of the wedding dawned, and the air was thick with a mix of excitement and the faint odour of wedding jitters. The ceremony was scheduled for late afternoon, leaving me with the morning to kill. Naturally, this called for a legendary outing with Russ—a trip to Denny's was a must to nurse our slightly throbbing heads from the night before. Nothing says, "I'm about to get married" like tucking into a Grand Slam breakfast while eyeing the clock in mild panic.

At the hotel, Carol was getting ready with my sister and mother, along with her own family—a delightful crew filled with love, supportive wishes, and the occasional eye roll directed at Dottie.

Now, Dottie is a character. Although she had settled down with Ken—who was about as laid-back as they come—she still had a habit of flipping the switch and doing what the family called "a Dottie" whenever the spotlight threatened to shine elsewhere.

Today, Dottie decided it was all about "Keira needing fries." Now, to the untrained ear, this might sound like a cry of parental concern. But to those of us who knew better, it translated to, "I'm starving and need to be the centre of attention." Ah, the nuances of family communication!

As the clock ticked closer to wedding time, Russ and I wrapped up our Denny's adventure, got suited and booted, and made our way to Kapalua Beach—the idyllic venue that "Happily Maui'd" had assured us was perfect. We weren't interested in one of those conveyor belt affairs in a hotel—we wanted a beach. And let me tell you, this beach was rated among the top ten most gorgeous beaches in the world. Sand, surf, and serenity awaited us. Best of all, we were fashionably late, which meant the beach was nearly empty—music to our ears. The perfect backdrop for our wedding.

Now, what happened next could only be described as something straight out of a film. Out of nowhere, a vicar roared down a sandy pathway on a Harley-Davidson—a sight that felt tailor-made for a quirky indie movie. He dismounted, radiating cool confidence. Draped in flowing robes, with a long ponytail trailing behind him and aviator sunglasses perched on his nose, he took a moment to survey the scene, as if about to deliver the performance of a lifetime.

In that instant, I half-expected him to whip out a guitar and serenade us with a rendition of Love Me Tender.

As we gathered, the atmosphere crackled with anticipation. The contrast between this laid-back, biker-vicar and our heartfelt vows was utterly surreal. The sun shimmered on the water, a gentle breeze tousled my hair, and, quite frankly, I couldn't have written a more perfect script if I tried.

The guests—Carol's family, my sister and hers, Dottie and Ken—were all smiles, which only heightened the joy of the day. My heart raced as I glanced at Carol, radiant in her dress, then over at Russ, who had the rings yet pretended—just for a moment—that he had lost them. Today was all about love, laughter, and the mystery of whether Dottie would manage to secure her fries before the vows were exchanged.

And just like that, with the sun dipping lower in the sky, the most breathtaking sunset I had ever seen appeared. Perfect, I thought. After the service, and a few bottles of champagne on the beach, we headed to Lailani's Beachside Restaurant for a wedding supper. What a perfect end to the day!

After the wedding, with the ink barely dry on our marriage certificate, we spent a few days in Maui and decided to try our hand at surfing, envisioning ourselves as laid-back beach bums, riding the waves like pros. As I paddled out, I was filled with delusions of grandeur. I caught a wave, stood up… and immediately wiped out spectacularly. I was never going to be good at this sport.

Carol and I then set off on our epic five-week honeymoon across America. It was a journey so grand it could easily fill a VHS tape—and luckily, we had our camcorder to document every ridiculous moment!

Our first stop? Las Vegas, where the infamous tagline "What happens in Vegas stays in Vegas" echoed in our ears as we rolled into town. We had been to Vegas a number of times before, but never as a married couple!

As we entered Sin City, the streets were alive with neon lights flashing like a hyperactive disco ball. Our first mission was to explore the Strip, and I proudly held the camcorder, ready to capture every over-the-top spectacle. We wandered past the extravagant hotels, each more outrageous than the last, when we stumbled upon the iconic "Welcome to Fabulous Las Vegas" sign. With a grin that could have rivalled its sparkle, I rushed to get Carol in frame.

"Say 'Viva Las Vegas,'" I instructed, just in time for her to roll her eyes while laughing.

The allure of the slot machines called to us like sirens, so we decided to test our luck.

"Watch and learn," I declared, confidently approaching the nearest machine. Moments later, I was dropping quarters as if I were handing out party favours.

"What's that? Another dollar down the drain?" Carol was already laughing, pointing out that I was a casino's dream client.

After surrendering our hard-earned dollars to the slot machines, we decided to indulge in one of the famed Vegas buffets. Here, we discovered a gastronomic wonderland! Plates piled high with everything from shrimp cocktails to decadent chocolate fountains made for a feast fit for royalty.

When Carol declared, "This is one impressive food pyramid!" I knew it was a moment for the camcorder.

"Let's capture the epitome of '90s indulgence!" I said with glee, waving my plate as if it were a trophy of success.

Next stop was the Hoover Dam, a colossal marvel of engineering that left us in awe. Joining a guided tour led by a man who spoke with the enthusiasm of a game show host, we learned about the dam's breathtaking scale

"This dam can hold back more water than a kiddie pool could ever dream of!" he quipped.

I leaned over to Carol and whispered, "Let's get out of here—there's a cocktail with my name on it waiting somewhere!"

Then it was off to the Grand Canyon, a destination that promised to be beyond breathtaking. As we approached, I felt our excitement swell, and I couldn't help but crank up the camcorder.

Standing on the edge of the canyon, I finally understood why people stood in awe of nature. It really does look like a painting.

The thing with such an awe-inspiring place is that after 20 minutes, you've seen it and think it's time to go—well, I did, anyway.

Determined to explore, we set out on a trek, buoyed by excitement and the promise of adventure. Surrounded by majestic views and snapping pictures left and right, we truly embraced the experience.

As the sun began to dip lower, I turned to Carol and playfully lamented, "We should have taken that helicopter ride—we would've been back in time for dinner!"

After our desert adventures, we returned to San Jose to stay with my sister for a week. It was a good opportunity to regroup and recharge.

Finally, we headed to Los Angeles and Disneyland, where childhood dreams were about to come true—at prices so high, you'd almost have to sell a kidney to pay for the pleasure.

With the camcorder ready to roll, I approached the park with the enthusiasm of a child unwrapping gifts on Christmas morning. The rides had us screaming with a mix of thrill and terror—especially on Space Mountain and The Haunted Mansion.

My adventure on Splash Mountain was one for the books, too. I underestimated the power of a perfectly timed wave, and before I knew it, I was drenched—clutching the camcorder as if it were a lifeline. Carol caught the entire ordeal, from my stunned expression to my valiant attempt to maintain dignity as I posed for photos—soaked but determined to document the fun.

Finally, we made our way to San Diego, where sun-kissed beaches awaited us. Eager to embrace the surf and sand, we quickly changed into our swim gear—me sporting classic

90s-style swim trunks and Carol confidently donning a floral bikini.

We spent the day basking in the sun, indulging in fish tacos from a nearby stand, and marvelling at how every adventure—no matter how chaotic—was another feather in our cap as a newly married couple. With the camcorder rolling, we pulled silly faces, laughed over the day's misadventures, and relished every new experience.

This honeymoon was shaping up to be a delightful tapestry of unforgettable moments—one we'd look back on and cherish for years to come, filled with love, laughter, and a whole lot of fries.

CHAPTER 25
The HR Transition and the Lion City

Returning to distribution as Head of HR felt like stepping back into familiar territory—yet this time, I was armed with a wealth of experience that provided a fresh perspective. My role focused on people-related matters within the newly established automated warehouse in Leicester, which, at the time, held the distinction of being the largest in the UK. The thrill of working alongside some of the old management to implement changes in this high-tech environment was invigorating, and I threw myself into the role wholeheartedly.

Having previously navigated both human resources and the business side of operations granted me invaluable insight. My earlier encounters with the trade unions proved beneficial, positioning me favourably when negotiating necessary changes. I had built a rapport and credibility with a large percentage of the management and workforce—not just from my years on the warehouse floor. To most, I was no longer just "the HR guy" but a leader with a genuine understanding of the complexities of logistics operations.

One meeting stands out vividly—sitting before a table full of managers, I presented a strategy for restructuring along with a timeline for implementation. The room was divided; some knew of my distribution background, while others—who had come from locations I had never interacted with—saw me solely as the HR representative.

Just as I elaborated on the plan I had crafted, one manager, oblivious to my past, stood up and bellowed, "You HR people come in and spout your stuff without knowing our business!" A chuckle rippled through the room, and without missing a beat, I replied, "As I said in my introduction, I've sat in your chair and done this before; hence, this is the strategy that will work."

The shift in the room was noticeable. My history with the distribution team granted me immediate credibility, quelling any lingering doubts. This deep understanding of both HR and business became my calling card. The teamwork and plans we had forged during late-night hotel stay as a crew only strengthened our bond. Those nights often dissolved into laughter and drinks—sometimes very messy—turning challenges into shared experiences.

Though I was primarily stationed in Leicester, my home base remained in York, where the main office for distribution HR was located. I shared a PA with one of the Directors of HR, whose name I'll keep out of this—for reasons that are about to become evident.

One day, as I was heading to Leicester from my office in York, the unexpected happened. My shared PA jumped in front of my car, tears streaming down her face. "I need to talk!" she cried out. Before I could respond, my phone rang. It was the Director—yes, the same one I shared a PA with. You guessed it: the PA and the Director had been engaged in a secretive affair during business trips, and now the wheels were coming off the cart.

Time seemed to slow as I absorbed the explosive situation unfolding around me. This secret, which had the potential to shake the very foundation of our HR department, was about to blow up—and I was in the wrong place at the wrong time. Yet, amid the chaos, I was determined to focus on the task at hand and push through my responsibilities.

In the end, I simply looked at her, chuckled to myself, and said, "It happens. I'm sure it will be fine," before driving off.

As my one-year assignment in Leicester came to an end, I was invited back to the York factory for a corporate HR role. I had one final presentation planned for the logistics board, outlining the strategy I'd prepared for the next two years.

Little did anyone know that, at the same time, Carol had just secured a job in Singapore. She had left Nestlé a few years earlier to become a chemistry teacher and had now landed a role at one of the world's leading schools—the United World College of Southeast Asia.

Despite the York corporate head assuming I was negotiating for more money, I decided to be upfront. During our discussions, I told the Director of HR, "I'm actually leaving."

The revelations continued to unfold; each moment layered with its own complexities. I'll never forget my mother's words when I told her I was moving to Singapore and leaving Nestlé: "What about your bloody pension?" Well, as someone in my early thirties, pensions weren't on my mind—adventure was.

Then came the day of the big strategy presentation. The Director in charge of logistics, about as popular as a dose of the clap, wielded an iron fist and was anything but approachable. In a moment of mischief, perhaps emboldened by my impending departure, I decided to make my last slide an image of the Singapore flag.

As I reached that part of my presentation, the Director leapt to his feet, glaring down at me with wide eyes. "What the hell is that?" he bellowed in a broad Scottish accent.

With a smirk, I replied, "Oh, that's the Singapore flag, and I'm moving there—so you'll have to find another muppet to implement all this."

The room erupted in laughter, and the moment became a defining story that would echo for years across the UK logistics network. My light-hearted farewell turned into legend—not just as my grand exit but as a sign of a shifting workplace culture, where humour and camaraderie could thrive even in the midst of serious business matters. Of course, had the Director not been such a thoroughly dislikeable character, I would have been far more professional.

As I closed that chapter of my career, I felt an overwhelming sense of liberation and excitement for the adventures that lay ahead in Singapore. Life had a funny way of unfolding, and this moment was just the beginning.

As we packed our bags for this exciting new chapter in Singapore, I felt a surge of enthusiasm tinged with apprehension. Leaving behind everything familiar was daunting, yet the promise of adventure lay ahead. Singapore was about to become our home, and the anticipation of what awaited us was exhilarating.

It didn't take long for Singapore to capture my heart. Without a doubt, it's one of the best places I have ever lived—a vibrant melting pot of cultures, seamlessly woven together in a clean and safe environment. The blend of modernity and tradition was striking; sleek skyscrapers stood alongside lush greenery, making every street feel alive. Beyond its stunning cityscape, Singapore offered every convenience imaginable, making the transition smooth and settling in an absolute pleasure.

As Carole settled into her new job, I took on the task of exploring our new home. With her busy schedule, I had plenty of time to wander the city, map in hand, eager to get my bearings. I roamed bustling markets, discovered serene parks, and took in the mesmerizing skyline. The air was thick with the enticing aromas of curry, sambal, and chilli, leaving me perpetually hungry. Determined to uncover the best spots for food, fun, and affordability, I embraced the adventure wholeheartedly.

Some Sundays, we would escape to the veranda of the world-famous Raffles Hotel, sipping Singapore Slings as we watched dramatic tropical storms roll in—a ritual that quickly became one of our favourite pastimes.

At the time, finding familiar British comforts felt like a treasure hunt. The everyday home foods we take for granted now were far less accessible then. So, when I stumbled upon something as unexpected as Branston Pickle in a local shop, it felt like striking gold.

Branston Pickle—a staple in any British household—was the last thing I expected to find in Singapore. So when I spotted it on a shop shelf, my heart raced with excitement. I knew I couldn't risk running out, so I didn't just buy one or two—I grabbed five jars on the spot. Stocking up felt like securing a piece of home, a small but significant comfort in this new chapter of life. After all, who knew when—or if—I'd ever see it again? A strange darkness clouded my mind as I imagined a future without my beloved pickle and cheese.

Each day in Singapore felt like a new adventure—immersing myself in local Flavors, meeting people from all walks of life, and revelling in the vibrant exchange of cultures.

Hawker centres became my playground, overflowing with tantalizing dishes from across Asia. The smells, the colours, the sizzling of woks—it was a feast for the senses. I quickly learned how to navigate the bustling markets, where lively chatter filled the air, and every visit became a crash course in culinary delights. From flavours I had never encountered to dishes I couldn't yet name, every meal was an exploration, and I embraced it wholeheartedly.

While immersing myself in exploration, I began to unravel the joys of living in such a connected and welcoming society. Everywhere I went, I was met with warm smiles and kindness—the locals eager to share their stories and recommendations. It was a refreshing contrast to the often-stoic interactions back home, and Singapore quickly taught me the value of a lifestyle built on community spirit.

As weeks turned into months, the city became a canvas on which I painted my adventures. I couldn't have asked for a better place to be—world-class facilities, a thriving nightlife, and an environment that felt both safe and endlessly enriching. And, of course, an abundance of golf courses to enjoy. We often took the ferry to one of the nearby Indonesian islands, indulging in weekends of relaxation and golf, a perfect escape from the city's energy.

That first year was one of discovery, growth, and adventure. The Branston Pickle jars stood proudly on our kitchen shelf—a small but comforting reminder of home amidst the thrill of new beginnings. Singapore was about to redefine our lives, and I was ready to embrace every moment—challenges and all.

As we settled into our new life in Singapore, excitement and change came in waves—and it seemed everyone wanted to be part of our adventure. My mother, Dottie, and Ken were among the first to visit, though the airline tickets we sent them may have played a role in that decision. Wanting to keep our family close, I often arranged for them to visit, thrilled at the chance to reconnect and create new memories together.

Dottie and Ken quickly embraced a globetrotting lifestyle, splitting their time between Asia and America. They visited us in Singapore and explored the wonders of California with my sister, their travels a stark contrast to the chaos of our childhood. Each trip brought new stories of adventure, laughter, and the joy of strengthening family bonds across continents.

It was fascinating to witness the transformation in my mother after marrying Ken. The shift in her demeanour was striking—almost as if she had undergone a complete personality change. Once caught in a whirlwind of emotional volatility, Dottie now radiated a calmer, more nurturing energy. Ken's steady influence seemed to have tempered the chaos that once surrounded her, allowing her to flourish into a more loving and grounded presence.

Their dynamic was heartwarming, filled with moments where Dottie would light up with laughter at Ken's gentle teasing or the way they shared stories over dinner with a tenderness that felt both new and familiar. Ken had a remarkable ability to let Dottie know when she had overstepped without causing conflict—an impressive skill in itself. Their relationship, built on mutual respect and understanding, was evident in even the smallest interactions.

When they visited us in Singapore, our home buzzed with stories of their travels and adventures. Ken's infectious excitement as he recounted his experiences added a vibrant energy to our family gatherings. He relished every opportunity to indulge in chilli crab—one of Singapore's most popular dishes and a personal favourite of his.

Ken had endured his own share of childhood trauma, including the painful separation from two of his sisters, who had been sent to Australia. I encouraged him to visit them, hoping he would take that final step toward reconnection. Sadly, he never made the journey, though he remained dedicated to calling them weekly, keeping their bond alive in the only way he could.

During their time with us, we embraced the richness of Singapore's culture together. From savouring the delights of famous hawker centres to wandering through lush parks, we immersed ourselves in the beauty of our surroundings, creating memories to cherish. We travelled beyond Singapore as well, venturing to Bintan, Batam, Malaysia, and even Kuching in Borneo. Watching my family connect in ways I had never imagined, I felt a deep sense of gratitude—marvelling at how far we had all come.

I recall one trip to Kuching when we needed a taxi to take us back to the hotel. We reached the front of the line and found ourselves faced with a rather battered-looking cab. Behind the wheel sat a very old man, his presence radiating patience. Though I wasn't particularly eager to get in, I reasoned that he had waited his turn, and it was only fair to give him the fare.

Once we were all settled inside, he set off—at a pace so slow that calling it "walking speed" would have been generous. He turned the corner, and BANG! He crashed straight into the car ahead. That was our cue to exit. We climbed out and caught the next taxi in line, but I couldn't help feeling sorry for him. Before we left, I slipped him the equivalent of twenty British pounds in Ringgit.

Carol's parents also visited us frequently, and during one of their trips, we had planned to attend the launch of the Malaysian F1 Grand Prix. While I've always loved speed, I've never quite seen the appeal of sitting in a stand watching cars zoom around a circuit. Nonetheless, we set off from Kuala Lumpur, taking a taxi to the track—a fair distance outside the city. Naively, I told the driver, "I'll meet you back here at the end of the race." In hindsight, I would soon learn that finding a specific taxi at an F1 event was wishful thinking.

Once inside the track, we settled into our seats, waiting for the race to begin. I noticed people inserting earplugs and some even wearing full industrial earmuffs. Having never been to an F1 race before, I found it puzzling—until the first car roared past. I had never heard anything so deafening in my life. It took mere seconds for me to sprint to the concession stand, where I paid an outrageous amount for four sets of earplugs—the most expensive earplugs in the world, but worth every penny when you're a captive audience!

I also revelled in the understanding that our experiences in Singapore—filled with adventure and laughter—stood in stark contrast to the struggles of our past. It was a poignant reminder of how far we had come, not just in geographical terms but in emotional well-being too. Life's transitions often set the stage for growth and renewal, and seeing my mother thrive in her relationship with Ken reinforced this notion.

As Carol and I navigated our time together, I felt an overwhelming sense of gratitude for how life had unfolded. The refreshing shift in family dynamics had granted us new perspectives, bridging gaps that had once seemed insurmountable. It felt as though Dottie and Ken's journeys mirrored our own, each a testament to the strength found in love, support, and resilience.

While the memories of our past lingered, they became more of a foundation upon which we could build anew. Our time in Singapore served as a reminder that, no matter where life takes us, fostering connection and nurturing the relationships we hold dear can transform even the darkest moments into a tapestry of joy, love, and understanding. It was a beautiful new chapter we were writing together, one filled with promise and hope—a testament to my family's ever-evolving story.

CHAPTER 26
The Idiosyncrasies of Global Media Organisation

After three months of exploring Singapore and lounging by the pool with the "expat wives," it was time to re-enter the workforce. I was offered a role at a financial media company—the home of a world-renowned Wall Street newspaper. Looking back, it turned out to be the best job I ever had—great people and an incredible experience.

Joining them in Singapore felt like stepping into a whirlwind of excitement and challenge. After three months there, I returned from a well-earned holiday in Bali, feeling refreshed and recharged. At the time, Bali had yet to become the world's go-to destination—it was far less developed, with an airport that was little more than a small building by the runway. The sunshine, surf, and sand provided a welcome escape from corporate life, but I had no idea that darker clouds were gathering on the horizon.

That morning, as I sipped my coffee at my desk, relishing the peaceful stillness of the office, I was abruptly interrupted.

The Managing Editor burst in, slightly sweaty, panic flashing in his eyes.

"He's been looking at porn again!" he exclaimed, his urgency sharpening the air and instantly catching my attention.

"Morning, Bob," I said casually, offering a polite smile. "My holiday was great, thanks for asking." The contrast between my calm demeanour and his frantic state was almost comical.

"So, who's been looking at porn—again?" I asked, raising an eyebrow, intrigued yet puzzled as to why I was only now hearing about this outrageous situation.

With a stutter in his voice, Bob launched into an account of the high-profile reporter on our team—a familiar face on CNBC—who had been printing out explicit images and leaving them on the communal printer.

"This has now upset the office lesbians—they're up in arms," he added, using words I could hardly believe had just left his mouth. I chuckled inwardly at his exaggerated phrasing.

"OK, let's bring the reporter in here and get to the bottom of it," I suggested, figuring a straightforward conversation might help unravel the chaos.

Bob nodded, and I made my way to the COO's office, where I relayed what had transpired. The COO grimaced, mentioning that they had spoken with the reporter just the week prior and had received a promise that such antics would cease.

"Well, that seems to have had the desired outcome, doesn't it?" I quipped, barely concealing my smirk as the absurdity of the situation sank in.

Gathering my resolve, we brought the reporter into the office. He strolled in, exuding confidence, and offered a flimsy explanation for his actions, seemingly oblivious to the gravity of the situation. I made it clear that this wasn't his first strike and, as such, we had to suspend him pending investigation.

He looked momentarily deflated and a little panicked, yet the bravado remained.

I escorted him to his desk to collect his belongings. "Don't touch your computer, just gather your things," I added, ready to usher him out of the building.

As we moved, my curiosity grew. What else had the chap been up to, and how deep did it go?

The COO and I then made our way back to the reporter's desk, determined to uncover the evidence behind the chaos. What we found was astonishing—an open program titled Adult Finder, a site where people could connect for various sexual activities. It was a blatant manifestation of his personal life, making any notion of professionalism seem laughably distant.

While going through his desk, we uncovered piles of paperwork and twelve boxes of diskettes—no USB drives back then—each one holding the promise of questionable content. I silently pondered the irony; if the reporter had put as much effort into his job as he had into organising his adult materials, he might have secured a Pulitzer Prize by now.

Among the chaotic stash were categorised subjects like "Big Dicks," "Fivesomes," and "Water Sports." It was a bizarre and hilarious collection, and the sheer absurdity of it all caught me off guard.

Just as we were beginning to process this unusual find, our unsuspecting head of IT happened to walk by. "Hey, can you take a look through these disks and report back as soon as possible?" I called out, fully aware of the mischief brewing in my request, knowing all too well what awaited him in those files.

The COO took the mountain of documents to review, and when we reconvened the following day, he couldn't contain his disbelief. "I've never seen anything like it," he remarked, shaking his head. "Clearly, the reporter has some serious issues."

In a surprising twist, we also discovered that the reporter was having an affair with a woman from the office—a deeply religious woman whose faith stood in stark contrast to the chaotic life she had been leading. There was a tinge of irony as we exchanged incredulous looks, barely suppressing our laughter at the absurdity of such a union.

When our head of IT returned, he looked as if he had just stepped out of a horror film—his bloodshot eyes wide with shock. "They're bloody disgusting," he muttered in his thick Irish accent, his voice laced with disbelief.

The COO and I exchanged a glance before bursting into laughter, the sheer implausibility of the situation overwhelming us. With a chuckle, I quipped, "No wonder your eyes are red, you perv," before strolling back towards my office.

We had all the evidence we needed, so we called the reporter back into the office to deliver the news that he was being let go. It was a necessary step, but not without its own comedic absurdity. The entire situation felt surreal—a bizarre blend of professional boundaries being crossed and personal chaos spilling into the workplace.

As we sat him down, I couldn't help but feel a mix of sympathy and frustration. I understood the complexities life could bring, but I also knew the importance of maintaining professional standards

"Listen," I began, keeping my tone measured despite the sheer absurdity of the circumstances. "We can't overlook the seriousness of what's happened. This isn't the first time we've had to discuss your behaviour, and unfortunately, we need to act."

He looked at me, a flicker of defiance in his eyes.

"You can't be serious," he retorted, attempting to regain control. I could see he was struggling to accept the reality of his situation, but the evidence was irrefutable. The laughter and levity that may have accompanied this absurdity would not save him from the consequences of his choices.

"What am I going to tell my wife?" he asked.

"I'm sure you'll figure something out. We won't be announcing the reasons for your departure, so don't panic about that," I replied, trying to offer some comfort.

The decision was final, and as I escorted him out of the building, I felt a strange sense of closure. It was time to move forward, to clean up the mess and restore the workplace's rightful focus. As the door closed behind him, I quietly vowed to myself that I would continue to foster an environment of trust and respect—the very values I had worked to build within the HR team.

The combination of the reporter's antics and the events surrounding them became legendary within the office, even though senior management never uttered a word about it—a story that would be recounted at gatherings and lunches for years to come. These things have a way of circulating.

However, it was not quite the end of the saga. A few months later, his wife called and asked me why he had been fired. I told her I couldn't divulge any information and that she should ask him why he was no longer working here. It turned out he had disappeared, and she had no idea where he was.

Things took an even weirder turn when, some months later, his mother called from Europe asking to speak to him. I explained that he no longer worked here and suggested she speak to his wife to find out what had happened. At that moment, I felt total dread, and I will never forget her response.

His mother burst into tears and said, "He's married? I didn't know he was married! Who to?"

I did bump into him a few months later and gave him both barrels about how he had treated his poor mother. Although we never really know the stories of others and why they do certain things, I wasn't judging him—after all, I had no idea about his childhood.

As my career continued to flourish in HR, I reflected on the series of events that had shaped my understanding of people and relationships in the workplace. In that peculiar world of corporate life, the need for empathy often clashed with the realities of maintaining structure. I learned that it was vital to treat each person with dignity, regardless of their choices, but that the bottom line also needed safeguarding.

Through all this, the friendship among my colleagues remained strong. We supported each other through the ups and downs, navigating the complexities of corporate life together. Whether it was sharing a laugh over the latest absurdities or gathering to discuss new goals and strategies, we remained a cohesive unit, pushing each other towards success.

In the end, the story of the "porno king" of Central Plaza became a comedic footnote in the greater narrative of my career journey. As I moved forward, I remained committed to fostering a workplace where productivity thrived on trust, camaraderie, and a strong sense of purpose—values that would carry me through the intricate dance of professional life for years to come.

Life within the media provided me with an abundance of madcap and hilarious stories, so let's continue the ride for now.

CHAPTER 27

Did Someone Mention Fraud?

Just as I thought things were settling down in my new role, a storm was brewing. Beneath the polished exterior of our operations in Asia, an alarming situation began to unfold—one involving a reporter who had been paid through one of our partners rather than directly by the company. This red flag set off alarm bells, and it became clear to me that there was an opportunity here he couldn't resist—one that potentially involved less-than-honest dealings.

Our COO, ever astute, had been suspicious for quite some time. A slew of questionable expenses had been crossing his desk, cloaked in vague justifications but lacking sufficient clarity. It was time for a closer inspection—no more sweeping things under the rug. We decided it was crucial to meet with our partner and audit the expenses over the past 24 months.

As we gathered the documentation for review, we quickly discovered that the reporter had ostensibly been entertaining not just sources but an entire entourage in Singapore. The scale of the expenses was staggering—lavish dinners at high-end restaurants, extravagant gifts, and, surprisingly enough, even mundane items from his weekly grocery shopping. Our suspicions confirmed the need for urgent action, and it was time to bring him into the office and confront him with the evidence.

When the day of our meeting arrived, the atmosphere was charged with tension. As the reporter walked into the office, I could immediately tell that he knew he'd been caught red-handed. His demeanour was a mix of bravado and apprehension, yet I was determined to get to the heart of the matter.

I started with a straightforward question: "You have a receipt here for $500 for meat and groceries from Carrefour. Can you explain that?"

His voice trembled as he replied, "I was entertaining the President of Singapore."

Of all the answers he could have given, this was by far the least plausible one I had ever heard. "Really?" I challenged, raising an eyebrow. "So, if I call their office now, they'll confirm that, will they?"

Silence filled the room. I could almost see the gears turning in his mind as he scrambled to come up with a response, but nothing came. The weight of his misdeeds hung heavily in the air, and I knew then that there was no escaping the reality of the situation.

With a deliberate tone, I said, "We are suspending you pending further investigation. Do not contact anyone in the office or at our partner during this time." It was a decision rarely taken lightly, but the misconduct was clear. After escorting him to collect his belongings, I couldn't shake the feeling that this was just the beginning of an unexpectedly intricate saga.

It soon became apparent that there were deeper issues at play. As we pieced together the mounting evidence, it culminated in an audit that exposed the reporter's activities, which amounted to a few hundred thousand dollars in fraudulent claims. The magnitude of the situation began to sink in, and my thoughts shifted to the next steps. This man was clearly living beyond his means.

Determined to confront the issue head-on, the reporter appointed a lawyer, and we arranged a meeting to discuss the matter. As we gathered in the meeting room, the atmosphere was thick with tension. The journalist, flanked by his lawyer, appeared nervous yet still attempted to play it cool. His lawyer reminded me of someone—then it struck me. Yes, he was the spitting image of Tattoo from Fantasy Island, although this was no fantasy!

At the meeting, the reporter immediately launched into a weak explanation of his actions, clearly aware of the precariousness of his situation. "This is just a misunderstanding," he insisted. But as the discussion continued, my patience wore thin. His lawyer then stated that they wished to resolve the matter swiftly and, therefore, had an offer to make to rectify this "administrative error." "We are offering $50,000 in full and final settlement."

"You have to understand," I began, "there are numerous claims here that do not look correct. Let's not forget your utterly ridiculous answer about entertaining the President of Singapore in your own backyard." I told them we would not be accepting the offer and that they should come back with a more realistic proposal for us to consider. The meeting ended, and we all went our separate ways.

Upon returning to my desk, I turned my focus to the files we had gathered from the reporter's office. The depth of his fraudulent activity was staggering. I had already shared my initial findings with the COO, and as we dissected the files further, it became clear that the situation was even more serious than we had anticipated.

When the journalist's lawyer called later that afternoon, they requested a further meeting with us to negotiate terms. Before agreeing, I asked, "What is the revised offer?" "$75,000," came the reply. I told them I would take it away for discussion, though I strongly suspected it would be rejected. I didn't hesitate to share my thoughts with the Managing Editor, who was now on vacation. Anxiety crept in about how to proceed. I phoned him, relaying my stance that we should hold out for more. "We have the upper hand in this situation," I said confidently. "I suspect there's more money to come."

Not known for his courage in tough situations and always worried about how he would appear to his superiors, he hesitated and expressed his concern about walking away with nothing.

"I think we should accept this; I have to report back to New York," he explained, clearly feeling the pressure of external expectations. "Let's hold out," I urged. "We're in a strong position here. If you're worried about the repercussions, I understand, but I believe we can negotiate for better." He paused for a moment before coming back to me. "Okay, go back and reject it, but if this all falls through, it's on your head." The call ended, and the COO, who had been on the line with me, chimed in at that moment. "What a wimp he is," he muttered, and we both chuckled, finding a brief moment of levity amid the growing tension.

The following day, I received a call from the reporter's lawyer requesting another meeting. We entered the room once again, and the reporter, now visibly shaken, returned with yet another offer. This time, it was a meagre increase of $5,000, bringing the total to $80,000. I looked the reporter straight in the eye and calmly said, "Do you really want to be someone's bitch in Changi Prison? Because that's where you'll end up without a serious offer by 5 p.m. tomorrow."

The meeting adjourned, and I returned to my desk, uncertain but hopeful that my firm stance would yield results. The next day, as the clock ticked towards 4:50 p.m., a creeping sense of doubt began to settle in—I started to wonder if they had called my bluff.

But just before 5 o'clock, my phone rang. It was his lawyer on the line. "We will offer you $150,000," he stated, his words carrying an unmistakable urgency.

"Deal," I replied without hesitation, but added, "I want the money by close of business Monday, and not in a personal cheque—a banker's cheque." This needed to be a clean exit from the mess. "I also want you to send me an email now outlining your offer, so I have a record." With that, I ended the call.

Afterwards, I shared the news with the Managing Editor, who responded enthusiastically, "That's great!" When I told him the figures, I couldn't help but grin from ear to ear. A few days later, I received a congratulatory call from a very senior figure in New York. "Well done, Simon! Getting that money back was a fabulous result. Everyone here is delighted."

However, during the conversation, it became clear that the Managing Editor had tried to claim the glory for the situation. But New York reassured me, saying, "We know who did the work and made this happen. Well done again, Simon."

This experience taught me a valuable lesson about recognition: managers should always ensure that those who do the work receive credit for their efforts. People should be able to celebrate their achievements and receive the acknowledgment they deserve. This principle became a guiding tenet in my leadership philosophy, reinforcing my belief that success is always a collaborative effort.

In reflecting on the chaotic yet enlightening journey that led to this moment, I felt a profound sense of accomplishment. Managing the intricacies of corporate life and navigating the constant unpredictability of human behaviour had sharpened my skills exponentially. I understood that while the corporate world often feels burdened by pressures and expectations, moments of levity—like chuckling at the Managing Editor's hesitance or the absurdity of the reporter's antics—were essential for maintaining perspective.

When the cheque finally arrived, it symbolised more than just a financial victory; it epitomised resilience, negotiation, and the strength of upholding values in the face of challenges.

The journey ahead promised further growth, new opportunities, and the chance to help shape workplace culture—fostering trust, respect, and collaboration. I carried with me the lessons learned from each of my roles, determined to advocate for a company culture rich with potential, driven by people empowered to bring their best selves to the job.

CHAPTER 28
The Day the World Changed

The world changed forever on 11 September 2001, and for those of us in the human resources field within the organisation, that day remains etched in our memories with a profound sense of loss and disbelief. Every year, we would convene as an HR team to discuss strategy, set new initiatives, and foster connections among colleagues. At that time, we had planned an eventful week in New York, filled with meetings, networking, dinners, and a breakfast gathering scheduled to take place on that fateful day in the iconic World Trade Centre. I had been to Windows on the World a few times before, mainly for evening drinks. A fabulous location, it offered breathtaking views across Manhattan and the Hudson River. It also had a glass floor along the windows—meant only for those with a strong stomach.

By a miraculous stroke of fortune, the HR meeting had been pushed back to the following week at the last minute. As I sat in Singapore, absorbed in the day-to-day rhythm of my life, my good friend Tony was visiting from Australia. Tony, the Editor in our Sydney Bureau, was in town for a few days. I walked into my lounge, where the television flickered, and casually asked Tony, "Which film are you watching?" The sound of the TV was swallowed by the growing horror in Tony's eyes. "It's really happening," he whispered, his voice barely audible above the static. "It's an attack on the World Trade Centre." The words hung in the air, heavy with disbelief. My stomach plummeted. We were supposed to be there.

In that moment, my heart pounded as the realisation gripped me like a vice. I said it aloud, as if speaking the words would make the shock more tangible: "We were supposed to be there." Had we gone ahead with our plans, I could have easily been trapped in that building, with no way out of the nightmare unfolding before my very eyes.

As details emerged throughout the day, the sheer scale of the tragedy became painfully clear. From across the ocean, I listened and watched in disbelief as reports of the attacks continued to roll in—America was truly under attack. The events of that day impacted countless lives, including many friends and colleagues who were directly affected. Our office was situated just across the road from the Twin Towers, and many of my colleagues bore witness to the unthinkable—people falling from the buildings, scenes of chaos, confusion, and terror unfolding right before their eyes.

We all had BlackBerrys back then—no iPhones. But the network was down, so I couldn't even check if my colleagues were safe.

I felt a deep sense of sorrow as I learned about the individuals who wouldn't return home that day. Others would be forever impacted by what they had witnessed. I struggled to fathom the sheer terror experienced by those inside the towers, desperately trying to escape the flames and destruction. There are no words to capture the fear and helplessness felt in those urgent moments.

As I processed the harrowing events, a strange sensation washed over me—an unsettling mixture of horror at the devastation and gratitude for the fortunate turn of fate that had kept me out of harm's way. It felt as if someone had truly been watching over me, protecting me from a disaster that could have cost me everything.

In the days that followed, as the world mourned, I joined my colleagues in honouring the lives lost and the heroes who emerged in the face of adversity. The tragedy united many in a profound way; we reached out to one another, recognising our shared humanity amidst the horror. Our team discussions became deeper—not only focusing on business strategies but also on how we could support each other, emphasising the importance of mental health and solidarity in the wake of such a distressing event.

The aftermath of September 11th fundamentally shifted our conversations within the organisation. We found ourselves questioning the future of our world and how we could approach our work and lives with greater care. We also reinforced the need for resilience within our team, creating initiatives aimed at supporting not just our operations but the well-being of everyone involved.

The office was now uninhabitable; it was closed. We had several offices around the city where people relocated, as well as our campus in Princeton. New York-based employees were offered cash incentives to relocate to Princeton on a permanent basis. Eventually, the New York office would reopen, but it would never be the same as it once was.

As I look back on that heart-wrenching day, it serves as a powerful reminder of the fragility of life and the importance of connection. In a world where chaos can erupt unexpectedly, I hold dear the lessons learned—about compassion, vigilance, and the strength found in solidarity. September 11th remains a touchstone in my journey, shaping my awareness of the human experience and solidifying my belief that through every shadow, whether personal or collective, we can emerge with a deeper understanding of ourselves and each other.

My tenure as HR Director for Asia Pacific spanned from 1999 to 2006—a period that was as challenging as it was transformative. The region I oversaw was vast and varied, encompassing everything from India, Pakistan, and Sri Lanka to New Zealand, reaching all the way up to China and Japan. Each part of this diverse tapestry brought unique challenges and rewards, but my time in Asia would be marked by dark episodes that underscored the dangers journalists often face in the line of duty.

During my tenure, we faced a tragic incident that left an indelible mark on our organisation—the kidnapping of Daniel Pearl, a reporter based in our Pakistan bureau. Daniel was a talented journalist, widely respected for his work in international reporting. He was kidnapped in January 2002 by members of a militant group linked to al-Qaeda, an organisation that was rapidly gaining notoriety for its violent tactics and radical ideology.

I remember vividly the day I received the call from our bureau in Pakistan, reporting that Danny had gone missing. The voice on the other end was shaky, but the urgency was apparent. "I'm calling to let you know Danny has not returned from a meeting," they said. My heart sank as I quickly ran through questions in my mind. "When did this happen, and is New York aware?" The responder confirmed that they were and were dealing with it, yet I could already sense the rising tension among the staff in our region.

It became imperative for me to act quickly and decisively. I immediately contacted our head of security in New York, Joey, a former FBI agent who always carried a gun while working in the U.S. office. I asked if there was anything I could do to assist. He said he would keep me abreast of events and let me know. Joey had a knack for presenting himself like a covert operative, complete with a serious demeanour that could intimidate even the most hardened criminals—and now it was time to leverage his expertise. As I maintained contact with Joey, we found ourselves locked in an almost daily rhythm.

During this tumultuous period, the Washington Editor was a steady presence in the office in Pakistan. Known for his unwavering commitment to journalism and his deep compassion for his team, he played a crucial role in navigating the unfolding events. He was a man of great integrity, often taking the time to communicate openly with the staff about the emotional impact of the crisis. I would have much more interaction with Lee in a few years' time when he moved out to Hong Kong.

Time passed agonisingly slowly as we waited for any news. Then came a glimmer of hope—proof of life. We received a photo of Danny holding a newspaper, the date clearly visible—a stark reminder that he was still alive, but the circumstances were dire. At the time, Danny's wife was pregnant, expecting their first child, which added to the emotional weight of the situation as we wrestled with feelings of helplessness.

Despite those small signs of life, the mood remained tense. Unfortunately, the nightmare reached its horrific conclusion when a video of Danny's execution was released. The impact of this news on the organization was nothing short of devastating. It sent shockwaves through our offices, shattering the sense of security that many had taken for granted. Danny had been a well-respected member of the company, a talented storyteller whose passion for reporting was evident to all; losing him felt like losing a part of ourselves.

In the wake of this tragedy, the company rallied around Danny's family, offering full support to his wife, Marianne. To honour Danny's legacy, a college fund was established for his son, and his colleagues created a memorial at the main office. As you entered our headquarters, his desk—complete with a telephone and writing pad—stood just outside the elevator, greeting visitors. It served as a poignant reminder of his contributions and the dangers faced by those in journalism.

Additionally, his name was added to the Wall of Remembrance in Princeton, commemorating him alongside other colleagues who had lost their lives while carrying out their work. Each name inscribed was a silent testament to the risks reporters face and their unwavering commitment to uncovering the truth, even at great personal peril.

While this tragic episode was a harsh lesson in the realities of our profession, it also served to galvanise our organisation, fostering a deeper sense of community and dedication among our team. Danny's story reminded us all of the fragility of life and the extraordinary courage of those who devote themselves to the pursuit of journalism.

CHAPTER 29

A Dark Time in Singapore

One of the darkest times of my life occurred in Singapore—the passing of my father. By then, our relationship had rekindled in meaningful ways. As I reached my mid-twenties, I grew much closer to him in ways I had longed for throughout my childhood. We frequently spoke on the phone; he had even come to see me play with Three Billion Things in the early '90s. We played snooker, and life between us was great. Even when I was in Singapore, we spoke every week, and I would share stories of my adventures with him.

My dad was overjoyed to hear that Carol was pregnant with my son, Rory, who was due to be born in March of the following year. He was so excited about the impending arrival of another grandchild that he shared the news with all our relatives, eagerly awaiting the newest addition to the family.

However, my father had been ill for some time, and during one of our calls, I asked if he had seen a doctor. With his characteristic humour, he quipped, "Yes, in about 1956." That was my dad—always able to lighten the mood with a touch of wit, even when discussing something serious.

In November, while chatting with my sister, who still lived in San Jose, California, we received disturbing news: Dad had been admitted to hospital. This made us reassess the situation more seriously. We both agreed that we needed to fly home to see how he was, as the prognosis wasn't looking good. Given my sister's background in emergency services, she had a clearer understanding of his condition than I did, and her immediate concern only heightened the gravity of the situation.

I arrived at the hospital in York first, and my heart sank upon seeing my dad in the high dependency unit. He lay flat on his back, making that dreadful rattling sound no one ever wants to hear from a loved one. It felt surreal to see him like this—a man once so full of life and strength.

My sister arrived what felt like mere minutes later—no small feat considering we had travelled from opposite sides of the globe. As she stepped into the room, a wave of relief washed over me; we were finally together, side by side, as we faced this difficult moment. At the sight of Dad's frail form, Carole immediately sprang into action, propping him up in bed.

Miraculously, he seemed to come around, looking surprised to see us.

"What are you doing here?" he asked, his voice raspy yet warm. I responded with sincerity, "We came to see you and check what's happening." He smiled faintly, clearly pleased to have us by his side. After getting him a drink of water, we agreed it was time to speak with the doctors, whose news was nothing short of bleak. My stepmother and my younger siblings, Nick and Lisa, were there too. They hadn't fully grasped the situation or its seriousness. To be fair, unless you have medical knowledge, doctors rarely explain the details in depth. Thankfully, Carole could speak with them in their terms of reference, so we finally knew exactly what was happening.

The doctors informed us that Dad was in critical condition and, at best, had about a week to live. At that moment, the logical decision seemed clear: we needed to bring him home. The hospital staff explained that there was nothing more they could do, so we arranged for a nurse to visit daily to provide support with oxygen and morphine when needed.

That night, as preparations were made to take Dad back to Stamford Bridge, my brother Nick, my sister, and I decided to stay with him at the hospital.

I remembered how Dad had confided in me months before, expressing a desire to visit Singapore to escape some tensions with Margaret. We had made plans that summer—each conversation filled with the anticipation of exploring new places. My dad's brother had been taken prisoner during the second world war in Singapore and sent to Changi Prison, before being sent to the notorious Burma Railway. I had visited the memorial site at Changi and wanted to take my dad to see it too. My biggest regret now was that those plans would never come to fruition.

As the night wore on, we settled into a side room. We exchanged memories, laughter, and even a few tears, cherishing the time together. I stepped outside for a moment, taking a breath to collect my thoughts and emotions—and to grab a cup of tea. When I returned to the room, Nick was talking to Dad, a solemn look on his face. "Simon," he said quietly, "this is for you. He thinks I'm you."

At that moment, my heart felt heavy. I looked at my dad, who was clearly struggling but seemed to draw some comfort from our presence and connection. I could see his eyes searching for familiarity amidst the haze of illness, and it struck me just how momentous this was for all of us.

In that shared silence, I felt the weight of our family history and the bittersweet nature of the night pressing down on us. It reminded me of everything we had faced together—the struggles, the love, the laughter, and the hardships that had strengthened our bond over the years.

As I sat down next to Dad, I knew we were navigating these waters together for whatever time we had left. It was during this precious time with him that I began to process the depth of emotion that would come with saying goodbye. I was grateful for the memories, the laughter, and the life lessons my father had imparted—even in the most challenging moments. Each experience we had shared shaped the person I had become, influencing not only my career but also my understanding of family, connection, and love.

As the hours passed in that hospital room, we continued to share stories, reminiscing about our adventures and the little moments that had woven our lives together. With each laugh, each tear, and each heartfelt moment, I felt the heaviness in my chest gradually lift. There was beauty to be found even amid the shadows of impending loss—it lay in the love we shared and the memories we created.

When dawn broke, I left the room for a brief moment, stepping outside to breathe in the fresh morning air. It was a new day, yet everything felt suspended in time, as if the world around us was aware of the profound moment we were living through. My heart ached, but I also felt a surge of gratitude for having had a father who, despite his flaws, had always tried his best for me and my sister—even if things didn't always work out as he had hoped.

Returning inside, the quietness of the room welcomed me back, and I saw my father resting, looking a little more at peace. I took his hand and squeezed it gently, feeling the warmth of his spirit even in that frail body. "We love you, Dad," I whispered softly, hoping he could hear me. He could. He responded, "I love you too."

The next day, Dad was placed in an ambulance and transferred back to Stamford Bridge. A bed had been prepared in the front room downstairs, ready for his arrival. We embraced the precious moments we had left, surrounding him with familiar sounds and smells, sharing our hopes and conversations, and keeping the warmth of our family bonds alive. I had brought a scan of my baby son to show Dad, knowing he would never meet him in person, but it was still a joyous moment. Dad's face lit up with excitement as he held the image, a huge smile spreading across his face. That little scan of a new human was something magical.

At that moment, it felt as though life had replayed itself. My own grandfather had been killed a few months before I was born, and now here we were—my father about to pass, and my son due to be born in a few months. Is there a curse on our family? I wondered for a moment.

I spent around 20 hours of each day with Dad. We spoke about everything that had happened, made peace with the past, and left nothing unsaid. I recall one night as I sat next to him, watching him wired up to the oxygen. I must have drifted off for a moment, but in the distance, I heard a faint clicking sound—like a lighter being flicked. I opened my eyes in horror. Dad had placed a cigarette in his mouth and was trying to light it. Moving faster than a gazelle, I flicked the cigarette out of his mouth and sent it flying across the room. "What are you doing?" he asked, his voice filled with massive disappointment. "Dad, you're wired up to oxygen, and fire and oxygen are a deadly combination. If I hadn't flicked that out of your mouth, you would have blown the whole house up. Now, you might be ready to meet God, but for me, it's a little too soon. So, let's take the oxygen off first." We both laughed like there was no tomorrow. Even near death, Dad was still funny as hell!

As the week progressed at home with my father, the crisp November air carried a sense of both anticipation and nostalgia, particularly with Bonfire Night looming on the 5th. This annual celebration, commemorating Guy Fawkes and his infamous attempt to blow up the Houses of Parliament, was always a time for gathering with friends and loved ones. It was a cherished tradition, filled with the excitement of fireworks illuminating the night sky.

We decided it was time to put on our own firework display for Dad in the front garden, and I can still hear his laughter as he delighted in the festivities. Nick and I took charge of lighting the fireworks, setting off as many as we could get our hands on. Dad had always loved Bonfire Night, revelling in the bright displays and the magic of fireworks bursting overhead. I can still picture him as a child, running up and down the garden with a Roman candle in his hands— probably not the safest thing to do, to be honest. This year, however, as we prepared for the celebration, the joy of the occasion felt muted, shadowed by the reality of his condition. Nevertheless, we did our best to honour the spirit of the night, staying close to his bedside and making sure he could still be part of it in some way.

On 7 November, the evening unfolded with the quiet intensity that had become all too familiar. Carole, Nick, my sister's boyfriend Dennis, and I had gathered to keep vigil by Dad's side. We knew this was likely to be his last night with us, so we all stayed close. By this point, he was heavily under the influence of morphine, drifting in and out of consciousness—his body frail, yet still holding on.

That evening, something happened with a strange synchronicity—one of those moments that feel almost beyond explanation. In a surreal twist of fate, we all fell asleep at the same time, gathered in the living room we had transformed into an oasis of comfort for him. It was peaceful until Dennis gently tapped my shoulder and spoke the words that hit me like a freight train: "I'm sorry, your dad has passed."

I jolted upright, disbelief and sorrow intertwining as I looked across at my dear father. It was almost as if he had waited until we were all asleep before he left. There he lay, stubbled and silent. My heart ached—this was the finality of a journey that had spanned so many years, a bittersweet goodbye that left me feeling hollow.

As I took in the moment, my gaze lingered on Dad's stubbled face, and a surge of resolve washed over me. The funeral director was on their way, and my poor sister—due to her medical background—had essentially called the doctor, who certified his death over the phone. I couldn't bear the thought of him looking unkempt as he left the house for the final time.

Taking out his battery razor, I began to shave him, determined to present him with dignity when the time came. In that intimate moment, I focused on each stroke, my emotions pouring out with every pass of the razor. The act felt oddly sacred as I prepared him for the journey ahead. "You wouldn't have liked to be seen like this," I murmured softly, remembering how, as a child, I had always seen Dad in a suit—always looking presentable, a trait I had long admired in him.

Once I finished, I stepped back, taking a moment to appreciate the peaceful face of the man who had shaped my life in countless ways. It was a final act of love—a way of honouring the father I had grown to admire, even with all his flaws.

In the quiet that followed, as my family began to wake and absorb the reality of our loss, I felt a bittersweet mix of grief and gratitude for the time we had shared. The memories of laughter during past Bonfire Nights mingled with the weight of sorrow, and as we gathered together, the bonds of family wrapped around us like a protective embrace during an otherwise heart-wrenching time.

As the funeral director arrived, I stepped outside to gather my thoughts, standing in the crisp November air, which carried the faint scent of smoke from distant bonfires. It felt like a strange juxtaposition of life and death—one being celebrated while another was being let go. I realised just how much Dad had taught me through our time together—lessons of resilience, humour, and the importance of family.

In the days and weeks that followed, those moments spent with my father during his final days became treasures I carried with me. I knew I would encounter periods of reflection in the years to come, weaving together the narrative of our lives—the highs, the lows, and the promises of joy worth cherishing amidst the shadows. Now, it was time for his funeral.

My father's funeral was a challenging day for us all. It was an exceptionally cold day, and the funeral car carrying Dad's coffin arrived at his house in Stamford Bridge, its presence a stark reminder of life's finality. As is tradition with funerals in the UK, a man in a black cape, cane, and top hat walked solemnly ahead of the hearse as we moved towards the end of the street. Our black funeral cars followed closely behind, the atmosphere thick with grief as we made our way to the crematorium in York.

Upon our arrival, the grey, dreary sky mirrored the sombre mood. A light rain began to fall, adding to the melancholy that enveloped us. As my brother, the funeral attendants, and I carried Dad's coffin into the room, a gathering of family and friends filled the space with love and shared sorrow. My father had never been a religious man, so there were few references to God during the service. Instead, my sister and I took turns sharing stories about Dad—each tale a reflection of the positive impact he had on our lives.

Yet, when I reached the part about how my dear old dad would never get to see his new grandchild, the weight of emotion surged within me. I struggled to keep my composure as the reality of that loss hit me like a tidal wave. In that moment, with a deep breath, I handed the speech over to my sister to finish. As always, she was there when I needed her most. Her steady presence provided comfort amidst the grief as she continued to honour Dad's memory with stories of joy.

After the service, we made our way to The Marcia village pub in Bishopthorpe, a customary venue for post-funeral gatherings. The atmosphere felt a little lighter as we reconnected with family I hadn't seen in years, sharing memories and recounting stories about Dad that sparked laughter amidst our tears. It was heartwarming to see the smiles as we reminisced about the good times—a reminder of the love he had fostered within our family.

Yet, as the afternoon drew to a close, the stark reality of our parting hit us all over again. We went our separate ways, each carrying the heavy burden of loss. In the wake of my father's passing, I learned that he had not made a will—not that he had ever been particularly organised. In the weeks that followed, Margaret sorted through his belongings, and the only items handed to me were a broken pair of cufflinks and a well-worn pen—not much to represent a lifetime of love and memories from a dad who had left an indelible mark on my heart.

In those quiet moments of reflection, I felt a pang of bitterness mixed with gratitude. Though the physical items were few, the lessons, love, and experiences Dad had given me were boundless. It became clear that while material possessions may fade, the legacies we carry forward—the love, the laughter, and the memories we forge—remain eternal. My father may not have left behind grand gestures, but he had instilled values and stories that I would carry forward, ensuring his spirit lived on within me and our family.

CHAPTER 30
Our family grows.

Deciding to start a family later in life felt like embarking on a thrilling new adventure—one I had anticipated for many years. Carol and I had spent our early adulthood exploring the world, pursuing our dreams, and embracing countless experiences that enriched our lives. We wanted to ensure that when the time came, we could fully embrace parenthood and create a nurturing environment for our future children.

Living in Singapore provided a unique set of advantages, making the prospect of raising a family feel somewhat easier than in the UK. For starters, most families in our community had the luxury of a maid to assist with cleaning, laundry, and general household chores. Knowing that someone was there to help manage daily tasks meant we could focus on the joy of starting our family without feeling overwhelmed by the logistical challenges typically faced by new parents. Moreover, once children arrived, having an on-site childminder was a tremendous benefit, offering us peace of mind as we navigated the challenges of new parenthood.

When we decided to try for a baby, we were pleasantly surprised by how quickly Carol became pregnant. I always felt for couples who struggled to conceive. Life can present unexpected challenges, and I was grateful that our journey towards parenthood unfolded naturally and swiftly.

As we prepared for this incredible new chapter, we sought a midwife to guide us through the pregnancy. Anne Haggarty came highly recommended by a friend who had experienced a miraculous delivery with her assistance—one that had actually saved his wife's life. Her reputation preceded her, and when we finally met, I felt a wave of relief wash over us. The care she provided was second to none, each interaction brimming with warmth and expertise that put us at ease.

For the first few months, everything seemed to be progressing normally. The excitement grew with each appointment and ultrasound as we marvelled at our growing baby. However, as the pregnancy reached its later stages, an unexpected complication arose—Carol was diagnosed with preeclampsia, a condition that became a significant concern and had the potential to complicate the birth.

When contractions began, we found ourselves navigating a wave of uncertainty. Unlike in the UK, where expectant mothers might be sent home during early labour, the protocols in Singapore were markedly different. We were swiftly admitted to Mount Elizabeth Hospital, a highly respected establishment known for its excellent care, and from there, preparations for the delivery unfolded.

The atmosphere in the hospital was a mix of excitement and apprehension. Nurses and staff moved deftly around us, their professionalism infused with a reassuring warmth. I could feel the weight of anticipation in the air as we braced ourselves for the arrival of our son.

Every moment felt monumental, my senses heightened as we awaited the culmination of our journey. Watching Carol prepare for labour, I admired her strength and determination, knowing we were about to experience the most profound transition of our lives.

As the day progressed in the hospital, Carol began experiencing increasingly frequent contractions. Anne, our midwife, kept us informed with printouts and detailed instructions, guiding us through each step of the process.

There was some discussion about inducing labour, but thankfully, it wasn't necessary. By 5:00 PM that March day,

Rory had decided it was time to enter the world, propelling us into the delivery room with a mix of urgency and excitement. I had already made a personal vow to avoid looking south of the hips during the proceedings—I figured certain sights might haunt me forever. Some images are better left undiscovered, and I was determined not to let them alter the way I saw my wife in those sacred moments.

When Rory finally made his entrance, I saw the extraordinary and surreal in the ordinary—life was being born right before my eyes. Anne asked if I was ready to cut the cord, and in a moment filled with awe, I did so, feeling the weight of the experience wash over me. But as I looked at our newborn son, I couldn't help but notice that his head was shaped like a cone. It was the result of pressure during his passage through the birth canal, and my first remark was, "For the love of God, he'll have to wear a hat for the rest of his life with a head like that!"

Anne chuckled, sensing my nervousness, and reassured me, "Don't worry, it will go back to normal shortly." Relief flooded through me as we began to settle into the reality of parenthood. With Rory safely taken to the nursery for observation, Carol and I were escorted to our private room, allowing us a moment to take in the incredible events of the day.

In the excitement of the occasion, I felt an overwhelming urge to share the news with family. I quickly reached for my phone, the joy bubbling within me. The moment my mother answered, I blurted out in delight, "It's a boy! Rory has arrived!"

However, her response took me aback. "Is he Chinese?" she asked.

That was, of course, typical of my mum's penchant for asking silly questions when it came to family matters. "Don't be ridiculous, of course not!" I replied, half-laughing, half-shocked. I joked that if he had been, there would have been far more pressing questions I'd have needed to ask. She was, of course, referring to his nationality, given that he was born in Singapore—which, incidentally, is geographically a long way from China!

Carol remained in hospital for a few days following Rory's delivery, giving us the opportunity to bond with our newborn. I even managed to spend a few nights in the hospital room, as they provided proper beds for husbands—a pleasant surprise that made our stay more comfortable.

As I settled into the rhythm of hospital life, I quickly learned that infants in Asia are wrapped tightly in blankets, cocooned against the bustling world outside. It felt like a practice steeped in warmth and tradition, and I couldn't help but smile as I watched the nurses care for new-born Rory with tender precision.

Though the hospital food was not particularly Western in nature—often comprising dishes I wasn't quite accustomed to for comfort, like fish ball noodles, char kway teow, and carrot cake (not the Western version, but a savoury dish)—I was grateful for our saviours, Ian and Sheila, who came to our rescue now and then. They brought along ham sandwiches that provided the familiar comfort I craved. I would occasionally nip out to the nearby shops to grab snacks that reminded me of home, each outing a small but welcome escape.

Those early days with Rory solidified the bond of our new family unit. They were filled with love, anxiety, and joy, even amidst the unfamiliarity of new parenting. Every glance at my son served as a reminder of our journey—one filled with promise, hope, and remarkable experiences that would only deepen our connection. Yet, I couldn't help but feel the sadness that my father would never get to meet his grandson. However, I was ready to embrace the rhythms of fatherhood, navigating the challenges and joys that lay ahead, forever grateful for the wonderful surprise that had entered our lives.

Rory's first trip overseas was an exciting adventure to Perth, Australia, when he was just three months old. Joining us on this trip were his maternal grandparents, Kerr and Agnes, who had arrived from the UK. It felt like a joyous family reunion and the perfect opportunity to introduce our little bundle of joy to the wonders of the world beyond Singapore. The excitement in the air was palpable as we boarded the plane, ready to embark on a journey that would set the stage for many more family adventures in the years to come.

Perth was enchanting, with its vibrant beaches, warm weather, and a spirit that celebrated life. It felt as though we were wrapped in sunshine and joy, exploring the sights and sounds of a city that was new to us all. The trip was nothing short of spectacular, with each day bringing new experiences filled with laughter and adventure as we navigated this beautiful, sun-soaked landscape together. A visit to Fremantle for fish and chips at Cicerello's was a highlight—my first real fish and chips since I was last in the UK. The smell of vinegar on hot chips made my mouth water. Signs were posted everywhere warning, Do not feed the seagulls or they will SOY! I'm sure you can guess what those letters stood for.

But the adventure didn't stop there. A few months later, when Rory was six months old, we headed to Disneyland in California. The excitement of being back together in a place filled with magic heightened the experience for all of us—especially now that we had our son with us.

I watched as children bustled around, their faces alight with wonder and laughter, each seemingly happier than the last. And, true to his nature, my little Rory chose this momentous occasion to achieve a significant milestone: he learned to crawl!

The only catch? He decided to go backwards rather than forwards. There we were, in the happiest place on Earth, yet Rory was determined to roll away from the attractions instead of towards them. It was both adorable and comical, as we found ourselves chasing him around the hotel room, laughing at his stubborn spirit.

Every time he crawled, he pushed harder, propelling himself backwards with gusto as he carved out his own little path of exploration. Watching him figure out how to navigate the world filled my heart with joy and pride. It was a perfect introduction to the unpredictability of parenting—reminding me that, even in the most magical of places, children march to the beat of their own drum.

Thankfully, he quickly realised that moving forwards was far more effective than going backwards.

Those early trips, whether to Perth or Disneyland, laid the groundwork for future family adventures. They became the foundation of shared experiences, bonding us through laughter and love. As we navigated the journey of parenthood, I cherished these moments that defined Rory's early days, knowing that each destination wasn't just a place on a map, but a stepping stone to building memories that would last a lifetime.

Reflecting on those times, I realised it wasn't just the places we explored that mattered, but the precious connections we nurtured along the way. Each trip was filled with joy, discovery, and the growing understanding that we were crafting a unique story as a family—one woven with love, laughter, and the beautiful unpredictability of life itself.

Rory had always been a remarkably well-behaved child. Our routine was peaceful; his last feed at 11:00 PM ushered in a blissful night's sleep that lasted until 7:00 AM. With the help of our live-in maid, Nur, we navigated the early days of parenting with a surprising sense of ease. This calm and order lulled us into a comfortable routine, making the idea of raising another child seem just as manageable.

After several months of this blissful existence, we decided it was time to expand our family once more. It wasn't long before Carol announced she was pregnant again. From the start, this pregnancy felt smooth—there were no signs of the complications we had faced previously, such as the preeclampsia that had overshadowed Rory's birth. With that concern lifted, we allowed ourselves to relax and truly enjoy the experience.

We chose not to find out the baby's sex in advance, preferring to embrace the suspense of the delivery room. As the months passed and the due date approached, excitement grew within us. Each passing day carried the promise of new beginnings and the joy of welcoming another child into our lives.

September arrived, and one morning, I woke with an unsettling feeling. The air felt charged with unspoken anticipation, and I sensed that something wasn't quite right. Knowing we were close to the due date, I decided not to go into work that day. Instead, I chose to stay with Carol, determined to be there for her and observe how things unfolded.

As the hours passed, I noticed Carol's contractions becoming more frequent. My concern grew, and I urged her repeatedly, "Let's go! We need to get to the hospital." After much persuasion, she finally agreed around 10:30 AM. We jumped into the car, adrenaline surging through my veins.

Typically, Singapore traffic was a nightmare on the route to the hospital, plagued by endless traffic lights and heavy congestion. However, on this particular morning, fortune smiled upon us. I swear, every single light turned green. It was as if the universe had conspired to clear the way for our new arrival, and we sped towards the hospital, buoyed by the miracle of effortless navigation.

I dropped Carol off at the hospital entrance, watching as she made her determined waddle towards the main reception—a sight to behold. She moved swiftly, and excitement surged through me as I hurried to park the car, eager to join her in the maternity ward.

Racing up to the ward, I was driven by an overwhelming sense of urgency. But as I arrived, a wave of panic crashed over me—Carol had already been whisked away to the delivery room. Heart pounding, I followed closely behind, propelled by a mix of adrenaline and anxiety.

Inside, the atmosphere was tense, with medical staff moving swiftly in response to an urgent situation. I quickly learned that our baby had the umbilical cord wrapped around her neck. My breath caught as I watched the doctor spring into action, her years of experience evident amidst the organised chaos. Though it felt as if time had stood still, within mere seconds, we welcomed our daughter into the world.

Anne, our doctor, looked at me and asked if I was ready to cut the cord. Overwhelmed with emotion—delight surging through me as I realised, we had a daughter—I found myself frozen, tears rolling down my face. It was a moment of pure joy as I saw her for the first time. In the aftermath of the chaos, Ailsa had arrived—our precious girl had finally graced us with her presence.

The moments that followed were a blur as the nurses worked swiftly, ensuring Ailsa was safe, using pumps to clear any fluid she had swallowed due to the cord. Then, as I held her in my arms, the weight of love and responsibility settled deep within me. Ailsa was the embodiment of hope, filled with endless potential, ready to carve her own path in this world. As we embraced this new chapter of parenthood, I was acutely aware that our family had grown—not just in number, but in love and joy.

Looking back, the journey to that moment felt surreal. The chaos of labour had swiftly transformed into serene joy, shaping the foundation of our lives as a family. Just like her brother, Rory, Ailsa would become an essential part of our story—a narrative woven with warmth, laughter, adventure, and the sweet complexities of life. I could not help but look up to the sky, grateful for her safe arrival. I'm not a spiritual man, as I've mentioned, but I did wonder if someone had been watching over Ailsa that day. Thanks, Dad, I thought, a big smile spreading across my face.

As our family grew, so did the challenges we faced—one of the most difficult being Ailsa's frequent health issues. From a young age, she seemed plagued by ailments that had us in and out of hospitals, particularly during our travels. I vividly remember two pivotal incidents that profoundly affected me: one during our time in Australia and another while visiting family in York.

The trip to Australia should have been filled with sunshine, excitement, and the joys of new adventures, but it turned into a harrowing experience when Ailsa fell ill. The love and warmth of our surroundings faded in the face of watching my little girl suffer. Each cough and fever brought a whirlwind of anxiety, leaving us feeling helpless amid the picturesque scenery.

However, it was our visit to York that left an indelible mark on my memory. During that trip, Ailsa's condition worsened significantly, making a hospital visit unavoidable. I remember walking into York Hospital, the crispness of the air mingling with the antiseptic scent that lingers in places dedicated to healing. A knot of anxiety tightened in my stomach as we were escorted to the children's ward—a place designed for comfort yet filled with the sounds of little ones in distress.

With Carol staying at my mother's house to care for Rory, it fell to me to spend the night with Ailsa. As I settled into the small room, pushing the uncomfortable chair closer to her bed, my heart sank. There was nothing worse than watching your child suffer through illness and pain—lying there in discomfort while I felt woefully inadequate to help her.

Adding to the heartbreak was the fact that she could not yet speak, leaving her unable to tell us what she was feeling. I wished I could trade places with her, take away her pain, but I was left powerless, utterly dependent on the doctors and nurses tasked with pulling her through this ordeal.

Despite my heartache, I held her hand, hoping my presence would bring her comfort. I read her stories and whispered reassurances, trying to stitch together threads of normalcy in a hospital room filled with machines and medical jargon. The gentle beeps of heart monitors and the rustling of nurses performing checks became part of the late-night symphony that tucked us into a restless sleep.

Ailsa's condition improved over a couple of days—something that felt like a miracle under the circumstances. When we received the announcement that she could finally go home, a wave of relief washed over me. We had endured sleepless nights filled with worry, and the thought of returning to the comfort of home, to familiar surroundings and routine, felt like an oasis after the emotional toll we had faced.

Driving home, I was overcome with a mix of emotions—relief, gratitude, and an overwhelming appreciation for the healthcare providers who had cared for Ailsa with such tenderness. While this experience had been deeply difficult, it had also strengthened the bonds within our family.

I was reminded that parenting often comes with difficult choices, and watching your child endure illness brings a depth of empathy and perspective that lasts a lifetime. Ailsa's struggles became part of her growing story, shaping her resilience in ways that would serve her well as she journeyed through life.

Those trials offered pivotal lessons; they taught me that every smile shared and every challenge faced as a family was a testament to our connection. No longer would I take for granted the ordinary moments of joy without recognising the shadows that sometimes lurked behind them. In the end, witnessing Ailsa's recovery filled me with even greater love and devotion, strengthening my resolve to support her through life's challenges—both the mundane and the extraordinary—as a united family.

After the birth of my children, the onset of what many affectionately call a midlife crisis felt both imminent and inevitable. The weight of parenthood pressed heavily on my mind, and I soon realised that it was time to reclaim a sense of individuality and adventure. I had long fantasised about owning a Harley-Davidson motorbike. The allure of the open road, the wind rushing past, and the freedom it promised called to me like a siren's song.

In true Singaporean fashion, there was a designated area known for selling an assortment of motorbikes, and among those dealerships, a few specialised exclusively in used

Harley-Davidsons. Among them, I discovered Sun Hog Motors, a reputable dealer known for its expertise and impressive inventory. After considering various models, I set my sights on a limited edition—the 1996 Harley-Davidson Softail Nostalgia.

This motorcycle was nothing short of a masterpiece—a stunning racing green beauty, blending classic style with modern performance in a way that utterly captivated my senses. The Softail's smooth, flowing lines and retro styling evoked the true spirit of the open road. Its deep green colour glistened in the sunlight, catching the eye with every gleam and curve.

The chrome details were striking—from the gleaming custom exhaust to the elegantly crafted beach bars, designed for a comfortable grip. The seat—plush yet firm—ensured hours of riding pleasure, cradling me in comfort as I took to the roads of Singapore.

The bike's powerful 1340cc V-twin engine roared to life with a distinct growl—an exhilarating sound that echoed through the air and turned heads. The Softail's remarkable handling made it a joy to ride, allowing me to navigate the winding roads and the last remnants of long country lanes on the city's edges. But the bike's nostalgia ran deeper than its aesthetics—it embodied a sense of freedom and adventure that stirred my soul.

Taking to the roads of Singapore, I felt an adrenaline rush with every ride. The early 2000s presented a unique blend of city life interwoven with remnants of jungle and greenery—pockets of nature that had yet to be fully consumed by urban development. As I cruised along long stretches of open road, I embraced the serenity of the ride, my spirit lifted by the wind and the rhythmic sounds of the world around me.

I would often weave through towering palms and dense foliage, occasionally pausing at scenic viewpoints to take in the breathtaking vistas. Each ride felt like a brief escape, a chance to step away from the responsibilities of family life and immerse myself in the sheer joy of the open road.

Joining the Singapore Hogs introduced me to a brotherhood of like-minded riders, adding yet another layer of fulfilment. Weekends often saw us gathering in groups, weaving through the island's winding roads before heading to the legendary Colbar for a traditional British fry-up—a relic of Singapore's colonial past. The café, once frequented by British soldiers during their time on the island, stood as one of the last remaining glimpses of that bygone era.

Yet, amid the thrill of motorbiking, I was reminded that stepping into this new phase of life came with its own set of reflections and realizations. The call of adventure intertwined with the responsibilities I now carried as a father, fuelling my desire to set an example for my children—not only through my role as a parent but also by showing them the importance of pursuing one's passions, no matter the stage of life.

Owning that Harley-Davidson Softail became a symbol of rediscovering a part of myself—an embodiment of freedom intertwined with the lessons I had learned along the way. It was more than just a motorcycle; it represented a commitment to balance—choosing to embrace adventure while staying grounded in love and family.

As I rode through the streets of Singapore, I felt invincible, yet I also understood that family was my anchor. Navigating midlife changes required a certain bravery, but I was ready to embrace it all, knowing that the road ahead would be rich with experience, joy, and opportunities to share with my loved ones.

When my brother Nick and his wife Sarah decided to visit us in Singapore, the excitement was palpable. Having family around always brought a refreshing energy into our lives, and I was eager to show them everything this vibrant city had to offer. From the moment they arrived, we plunged into a whirlwind of activities, starting with a round of golf that set the tone for the rest of their visit.

The warm sun and lush greens of the golf course provided the perfect backdrop for laughter and friendly competition. Nick and I had always relished pushing each other to our limits on the course, and this trip was no exception. The sibling rivalry was evident as we battled for the best scores, each swing accompanied by playful banter and a competitive edge.

As evening fell after a day on the course, we made it a point to explore Singapore's bustling nightlife. Every night became an adventure—a chance to experience some of the city's most exciting spots. On one particularly memorable evening, after I finished work, I whisked them away to lively local joints brimming with culture and energy.

That night, we found ourselves in a lively bar where the atmosphere buzzed with music and revelry. Our spirits were high, and before long, we were belting out classics during a spirited karaoke session. With laughter erupting from our group, we sang Dancing Queen, our voices harmonising in joyous disarray. It was a moment that transcended any concerns about hitting the wrong notes—we were there to have fun, and we certainly succeeded.

As the clock struck 2:30 in the morning, we wandered into Denny's at Holland Village, a late-night diner that had become a staple for night owls. Over plates of hearty breakfast fare, we recounted the highlights of our evening, thoroughly enjoying the beer-infused madness. The laughter and stories flowed as effortlessly as the coffee, making it clear that we'd had an exhilarating night.

The next morning, I rose early for work, my energy slightly drained from the late-night festivities. However, as I returned home that evening, the sight of Sarah still in bed signalled a successful night of fun—if she was still catching up on sleep, I knew they had thoroughly enjoyed themselves, even if she did look a little green.

While Nick was a zealot on the golf course, he was equally competitive when it came to tennis. Our evenings transformed into intense matches on the courts of our condominium, both of us sweating under the tropical sun, our shouts of triumph and faux indignation echoing as we smashed the ball back and forth. It was a classic display of brotherly competition—no surrender, always striving to outdo each other, yet the stakes were never quite as serious as our laughter made them seem.

Amidst it all, those moments with Nick and Sarah reminded me of the importance of family. They enriched our lives with joy and connection, grounding us in the ever-changing flow of life that sometimes felt turbulent or chaotic. Their visit became a treasured encapsulation of fun and happiness.

In the end, as I reflected on their time in Singapore, I was reminded that moments of familial connection bring the deepest sense of fulfilment. Through these shared experiences—golf outings, karaoke nights, and spirited tennis matches—we strengthened the bonds that anchored us, preserving our connection as we navigated life's adventures together.

CHAPTER 31
The Challenge of SARS

The arrival of Lee to lead the editorial team of Asia's foremost financial newspaper marked a significant turning point in the region. With Lee at the helm, we witnessed an unwavering commitment to the highest standards of journalism and a renewed drive for excellence. His reputation as a world-class journalist was well deserved, and I felt honoured to work alongside him. However, as with any leadership change, it came with some peculiar managerial decisions that occasionally left us scratching our heads.

As the dust settled on this new chapter, an unexpected challenge emerged: the outbreak of SARS (Severe Acute Respiratory Syndrome). This highly contagious respiratory disease, caused by a coronavirus, began making headlines in late 2002 and reached its peak in 2003. Compared to the world-altering events of COVID-19 in recent years, SARS was relatively contained but posed its own serious challenges.

As news of the outbreak spread, so too did the anxiety surrounding it. Hong Kong, bearing the brunt of the crisis, became ground zero, with a significant number of cases reported in a short span of time. It was clear this posed a threat to everyone in the region, and I knew swift action was essential to protect our staff and ensure the continuity of operations.

Working closely with Lee and the management team, we implemented strict measures to safeguard our employees. We swiftly introduced work-from-home protocols, advising those with relatives in healthcare facilities or anyone displaying symptoms to stay at home. At a time when being proactive rather than reactive felt imperative, reports of SARS cases continued to rise daily.

With the urgency of the situation, we enforced guidelines to limit physical interactions within our office space. The necessity of social distancing became clear, and we aimed to create as much isolation as possible, recognising the risks posed by close quarters in a bustling office environment.

At the time, the world of communications was still evolving; video conferencing was in its infancy, and we relied heavily on traditional conference calls to stay connected. As we gathered on those calls, I could feel the tension—everyone trying to navigate their roles while simultaneously grappling with the uncertainty of the outbreak. It was a frightening time, especially with the awareness of how rapidly illnesses could spread.

I also felt the weight of the situation pressing down on my personal life. My son, Rory, had been born just a few months earlier, in March 2003, at the very peak of the SARS outbreak. As a father, I was keenly aware of the need to protect him from the outside world and its potential dangers. The thought of bringing a new life into such uncertainty added an extra layer of anxiety, but it also strengthened my resolve to ensure that everyone around me, including my family, felt safe during these tumultuous times. It was about finding the balance between protection and carrying on with life as normally as possible.

Then one day, as the SARS crisis escalated across the region, he called me in a frantic tone. "We have to get everyone out of China," he urged, worry evident in his voice. The virus was certainly spreading like wildfire within the country.

I paused, taking a moment to assess the impracticality of the situation. "That's impossible," I replied. "No country on the planet will take them, and we have about 150 Chinese nationals. Where would they go?"

The enormity of what was being asked sank in. Even if we could do that, the logistics alone would be difficult. "We simply can't achieve that. We need to think about what can be done within the country to protect our people," I said.

The travel restrictions were far-reaching, and fear had spread through nations like wildfire. I knew that we couldn't just magically extract people from a place where borders were tightening and safety protocols were stringent.

We spent the next 30 minutes chewing over ideas to create a sensible, workable plan—one we could actually achieve. Communication was critical at this point to ensure everyone knew what to do. The moments spent coordinating our response to the crisis demanded my full attention, and I watched the situation unfold with a mixture of dread and anticipation. We needed to remain calm and united in our efforts, prioritising the well-being of our colleagues and their families. That was our goal.

In those early days of uncertainty, I grappled with the boundaries of leadership and protection. My thoughts always circled back to Rory, my newborn son, whose small hand had wrapped around my finger just days after his birth—a tender reminder that the world was filled with love and hope, even amid chaos. I was determined to shield him from panic and fear, wanting his early days to be filled with warmth and security.

As we worked diligently through this tumultuous period, I held tight to the hope that, together, we could navigate the challenges ahead. My ultimate goal was to lead us through this crisis, ensuring our workforce felt secure and supported during a time of uncertainty. I wanted to create a safe environment not only for my colleagues but also for my family, ensuring that Rory would grow up in a world where he could thrive—free from the shadows of fear that so quickly emerged in the adult world.

After the tumult of SARS had passed, life in Singapore gradually settled back into a rhythm of normality. The world was moving forward, and with it came the anticipation of returning to our regular business trips, particularly the annual Society for Human Resource Management (SHRM) conference held in America. The event rotated locations between the East Coast, West Coast, and Central regions over three years, and this year, we were bound for the glitz and glamour of Los Angeles.

Dolly, a great leader and a bright beacon of kindness who managed our global HR team, was the mastermind behind organising our trip. On the first day, we were having drinks on the balcony of our hotel when she turned to me, eyes sparkling with excitement—or perhaps the wine.

"Does your sister still live in San Jose?" she asked, a smile playing on her lips.

I nodded. "Yes, she does!"

"Good! Let's get her down here to have some fun!" Dolly exclaimed, already formulating a plan in her mind. And just like that, we arranged for my sister to join us for a few days, making the trip even more special.

When my sister arrived, the atmosphere was electric. Dolly had gone all out, hiring a luxurious limo to whisk us around the vibrant streets of LA. A sense of adventure filled the air, and I felt a buoyant thrill as we prepared to hit the town.

In addition to the glamorous ride, Dolly had brought along a special treat for us all—bottles of Rubicon wine from Francis Ford Coppola's vineyard. It was an incredibly generous gesture, especially given the prestige and price of such a fine wine. We raised our glasses and toasted to friendship, the anticipation of the conference, and the opportunity to enjoy life's luxuries together.

The next few days unfolded in a whirlwind of laughter, exploration, and unforgettable memories. We visited iconic locations, dined in delightful restaurants, and revelled in the communal joy of shared experiences. The backdrop of Los Angeles, with its palm trees and sprawling landscapes, felt like the perfect escape from our busy lives back in Singapore.

Dolly had also arranged a trip for Mark and me to the famous Riviera Golf Club. A PWC representative took us and said, "I have an account—get something you'd like." I chose a waterproof jacket, which I still have to this day.

As our fabulous time in LA drew to a close, anticipation for the following year's conference began to build. The next SHRM conference was set to take place in the vibrant city of Las Vegas. Once again, Dolly was at the helm, securing us all luxurious jacuzzi suites at Caesars Palace—an extravagant arrangement that promised another unforgettable adventure.

As luck would have it, my sister was also in Vegas for a concurrent medical conference. The chance to reunite in such a lively setting felt serendipitous, and our group expanded once more as we welcomed her back into the fold.

In Vegas, the energy was infectious. The city's lights pulsed with excitement, mirroring the atmosphere among our group. Each day was filled with seminars and networking opportunities, while our evenings overflowed with laughter, fun, and a touch of indulgence.

From exploring the iconic Strip and its lavish hotels to sharing stories over drinks, those moments became treasured memories woven into the fabric of our lives. Dolly was eager for us all to have dinner at the famous Toby Keith restaurant, named after the country and western singer. The sense of connection was palpable; we had forged bonds that transcended our professional lives, becoming friends intertwined in shared experiences.

One afternoon, I was sitting at the bar with Dolly, enjoying cocktails. I mentioned that I was heading off to call my family back in Singapore and would return in about thirty minutes. When I came back, Dolly looked distressed and wasn't making much sense.

"Dolly, what's wrong?" I asked, taking a seat next to her. At first, I thought she had simply overindulged in the two-for-one cocktail offer.

Then she revealed that she had decided to play blackjack while I was away and had lost a decent wedge of money—she swore she was never playing that game again. We both laughed, and I said, "Never mind, you might make it back on the slots!"

That evening, we focused on making the most of our remaining time in Vegas, hopping between various bars. We revelled in the memorable moments we had shared earlier in the week—delicious dinners, wonderful company, and the joy of exploring the city together.

In the wake of that trip, I was reminded of the importance of supporting friends and being there through life's ups and downs. Life is short—don't dwell too much on what's happened; focus on what's to come!

CHAPTER 32
The Z Chronicles and the panty stealer

Working in a large organisation, you encounter a number of issues that, while serious, can sometimes add a touch of humour to the situation. The New Zealand office of the wires presented its fair share of challenges, but it was also home to a truly remarkable individual—Fred.

A genius in financial markets, he was not only well-respected within the media community but also a genuinely kind and personable figure. He possessed an astute mind, capable of dissecting complex economic issues and translating them into digestible insights for our clients. His ability to analyse and report on market trends made him the go-to expert for up-to-the-minute information, earning him a level of credibility that few others could match.

His journey into journalism was a blend of natural talent and years of dedication. With a background steeped in economics, he had studied at a prestigious university before breaking into reporting. His intellect and work ethic quickly established him as one of the leading figures across our Asian bureaux, particularly within the newswires team. However, as brilliant as he was, he faced significant challenges due to his ongoing battle with diabetes. The condition frequently impacted his health, leading to a series of medical complications that gradually took a toll on his performance.

Despite these struggles, he was still able to file directly to the financial wire—an unusual privilege, as most journalists had to go through an editor at the news desk in Sydney or the main desk in Singapore. This direct access was a testament to the level of trust management placed in him, reflecting his expertise and ability to deliver high-quality work, even in challenging times.

One particularly hectic afternoon would go on to become legendary in our office lore. As he sat at his desk, surrounded by papers and immersed in data, he was preparing to write a critical piece. The exhaustion of managing both his condition and the relentless demands of the newsroom had begun to take its toll. Somewhere in the depths of his struggle to gather his thoughts, fatigue overtook him, and he succumbed to sleep—leading to an unforgettable incident.

As fate would have it, his nose landed squarely on the "Z" key of his computer keyboard, causing multiple "Zzzzzzzzzzzz" entries to shoot out live to financial institutions across the globe. Of all the keys to hit with his nose, it had to be the "Z" key. The unintended comedic timing was absurdly perfect—here was a financial genius, poised to report serious market news, inadvertently sending out a stream of snores instead.

When the news spread through the office grapevine, laughter erupted everywhere. As management, I knew we had to address the incident, but I also believed in using humour to diffuse the situation. So, when he returned to work, I called him for a light-hearted chat. "So, I see your article on the market took an unexpected nap."

Despite the stress of the incident, he took it in stride, chuckling along with the rest of us and quickly regaining his focus. Perhaps some of those financial institutions needed a reminder that life can't always be serious!

A few years after that episode, I found myself making plans with Brian, the editor, to fly down to Wellington and work through an exit strategy for Fred. Sadly, his health had continued to decline, and it had become apparent that we could no longer rely on him in the same capacity. It was a difficult conversation, as Fred was not just a valued colleague but a wonderful human being whose presence had enriched the workplace.

The journey was a long one—two stops from Singapore and over 11 hours on the plane to Wellington. I remember that after our meeting, as we boarded the plane the next day, one of the crew members looked at me and said, "Didn't you just get off this plane?" I looked at her and sighed, "Yep, we certainly did."

When we arrived in Wellington, we approached the situation delicately. But this was business, and the outcome needed to serve both the company's interests and Fred's well-being.

Reflecting on Fred's journey reminds me that every individual leaves behind a legacy of talent, humour, and friendship. The light-hearted memories—like the Z Chronicles—serve as a powerful reminder of his significance, bringing laughter into our days even amid the challenges we faced.

Amidst this whirlwind period of my career, I encountered numerous characters and challenges. One such story revolved around a colleague who managed a geographical area for circulation operations. For the sake of discretion, let's refer to him as the Head.

The task of increasing readership numbers was never straightforward. To facilitate sales, we enlisted agents who would receive a percentage for every subscription they sold.

As time went on, we began to grow suspicious of some of the circulation numbers. They simply didn't add up—it was concerning enough that we decided to dig a little deeper. Our investigation uncovered something startling: the Head had set up a shell company, appointing his secretary and her mother as directors alongside himself. It was a scheme woven through layers of deceit, one that posed a serious threat to our integrity.

Realising the gravity of the situation, I knew we had to act decisively. Following the old adage "divide and conquer," I planned our approach while the Head was away travelling. We brought his secretary into the office for questioning, understanding that her position made her more vulnerable to scrutiny. Bless her—she wasn't the sharpest tool in the shed and would likely spill the beans without much prodding.

Sitting across from her in the office, we crafted our inquiry with care. "Given the magnitude of this situation, we may have to involve the police," I told her, watching as fear flickered across her face. It didn't take long for the floodgates to open; she revealed everything in a rush of panic, eventually even bringing her mother in to corroborate the details. It became increasingly clear that neither of them fully grasped the legal ramifications of their actions. They believed they were operating within the confines of legality, oblivious to the gravity of what they had become ensnared in.

Armed with this newfound evidence, we prepared to confront the true mastermind behind the scheme—the Head himself. The moment he walked into the room was unforgettable, a curious blend of Del Boy Trotter and Mr Bling. Clad in a flashy suit that practically shouted, "Look at me!" he filled the space with an air of misplaced confidence. What stood out most, however, were the furry tufts sprouting from his ears—an odd sight that was somewhat off-putting as we engaged him in conversation. "What's up, fellas?" he said in a deep voice.

We informed him that he had been summoned to discuss the situation, as our teams had crunched the numbers related to the fraudulent circulation that had funnelled through his shell company. Those figures amounted to a few tens of thousands of dollars—a reasonable sum, but hardly worth the effort and the risk of losing his job.

At our first meeting, he exuded bravado, seemingly unfazed by the inquiries we threw his way. That was until we laid out the evidence—the statements from his secretary, the company documentation, and the damning numbers.

The shift in his demeanour was immediate. His bravado evaporated like a puff of smoke as we laid out the full extent of his actions, exposing how he had been quietly creaming off the top of the circulation figures he was meant to oversee. The façade of confidence cracked, revealing the trepidation beneath.

In a surprising display that underscored his desperation, on his second appearance, the Head walked in with a small card peeking out from the top pocket of his jacket. The card bore an image of Jesus alongside the words, "GOD WILL FORGIVE YOU." It seemed as if he was attempting to claim the moral high ground amid a tide of deceit.

As the meeting wore on, he continued to project a hardened exterior, but one could sense the anxiety mounting beneath the surface. Eventually, I leaned forward, fixing him with a steady gaze.

"You may hold a card that says God will forgive, but we won't," I stated firmly. "If we don't see our money returned by the end of the week, we will seriously consider moving forward with criminal proceedings for theft."

As the implications of my words settled in the room, a charged silence followed. With newfound urgency, he grasped the gravity of his situation.

By the end of the week, he returned with a cheque covering most of the money he had swindled, handing it over without a trace of the bravado he once exhibited. Following this ordeal, he was dismissed, along with his PA—the unfortunate accomplice in his scheme.

Looking back on that episode, I recognised it as a testament to the importance of diligence and integrity in the workplace. While challenges are inevitable, managing them with transparency and accountability is crucial to preserving the values we hold dear—especially within such a respected organisation.

This experience also reinforced my belief in the necessity of ethical leadership. Holding people accountable for their actions ensures that we uphold the standards guiding our work and maintain trust among our colleagues. At the end of the day, I took pride in ensuring our workplace remained a space where integrity flourished, strengthened by the lessons learned from these misadventures.

When people work in large groups, you will always encounter moments that leave you questioning why certain things happen. One particular incident, involving a senior colleague who shall remain nameless in this narrative, stands out as a prime example of how unexpected situations can arise in the corporate world—and how often people fail to think through their choices.

We were in the midst of discussing a potential move to our Singapore office for this colleague—an exciting opportunity that required navigating the intricacies of immigration criteria. Singapore is known for its strict regulations regarding who is permitted to live and work in the country, with a checklist that includes education, medical, and even criminal background checks. It should have been straightforward, but as I soon discovered, it would be anything but.

During our preliminary discussions about the relocation, I casually asked if there were any criminal issues, we should be aware of that might impact his application. I assumed I was merely probing into minor matters, such as a speeding ticket or some youthful indiscretion. Expecting a light-hearted chuckle in response, I certainly didn't anticipate what would come next.

A few days later, he sent over a set of documents outlining various charges against him—a shocking revelation that left me speechless. To my complete disbelief, I discovered that he had been caught stealing his neighbour's underwear from the washing line—not once, but multiple times! The sheer absurdity of the situation was hard to digest, as I pictured our colleague sneaking around with an armful of laundry, trying to evade the watchful eyes of his unsuspecting neighbours. And why do these people always steal clean clothes? I often wonder.

However, that wasn't all. The document contained a list of other, more serious offences, the details of which I will spare you for the sake of discretion. Suffice it to say, my jaw practically hit the floor as I read through each line. Here was a senior individual, applying for a prominent role, with an unexpectedly colourful legal history that I never could have imagined.

Now, faced with this new reality, I knew I had to have a difficult conversation with him. I called him on the phone, striving to maintain a professional demeanour despite my lingering disbelief.

"Look, given these details, we will not be able to submit your application to the authorities in Singapore," I stated plainly, carefully gauging his reaction.

Instead of the shock or concern I had anticipated, he seemed oddly indifferent, brushing off the gravity of the situation. My mind raced with the thought: if I were in his position, I would have handled this very differently. It felt like an opportunity had slipped through his fingers, his future in Singapore now overshadowed by the absurd but troubling antics of his past.

I couldn't help but think that a more judicious approach might have been to say something like, "My wife is having second thoughts about the move, and we may have to reconsider." Perhaps then, he could have bought himself some time to reflect on the implications of sharing such vivid details about his criminal history.

"Just leave it with me for a few days while I discuss it further," I would have suggested if I were in his position. Instead, he had opted to send over the rather incriminating evidence straight away, turning what could have been an exciting opportunity into an administrative debacle.

As I relayed the unfortunate news to my superiors, my colleagues found endless amusement in the whole scenario.

It became a running joke—a reminder of the unpredictable twists' life could throw our way. "What's next?" we'd laugh in disbelief.

Despite the light-hearted banter, a valuable lesson echoed through that experience: the importance of transparency and the understanding that every action has consequences. In a world governed by rules and regulations, honesty truly is the best policy. While the comedy of errors would forever amuse us, it also reinforced a deeper understanding of ethics within professional spaces—one that I would carry forward throughout my career.

In the end, as we collectively chuckled over the tale of the Laundry Thief, I couldn't help but appreciate how incidents like this added colour to our professional lives, strengthening the bonds among colleagues while imparting lessons we would never forget.

CHAPTER 33
Thailand and the Ladyboy

For around 40 years, I have nurtured a deep love for Thailand—a country that has never ceased to amaze me with its breathtaking landscapes, warm-hearted people, and tantalising cuisine. I recall as a 16-year-old, receiving a post card from my friend who had travelled to Bangkok. He simply wrote – "never has a place been so aptly named" During my time in Singapore, my mates and I would frequently travel to Phuket, indulging in rounds of golf, scuba diving, and enjoying cold beers while basking in the sun. In fairness, the guys I travelled with were interested in the local nightlife but had no real interest in the girls. Instead, we were always on the lookout for good fun, plenty of beer, and a McDonald's stop on the way home.

During those late nights amidst the vibrant atmosphere of Bangla Road, I had a front-row seat to the eclectic nightlife that defined Patong. The road pulsed with energy, its bars alive with laughter, music, and the promise of adventure. People danced, revelling in the carefree nature of the evenings, and the night became a Patchwork of colourful lights and smiles.

In those days, girls danced naked in the bars—to the point that, for a frequent visitor, you hardly even noticed. It was a sensory overload—exotic drinks, music that seemed to vibrate through your very soul, and an endless array of characters adding to the vivid scenery.

I recall one particular night when I nearly started a war. As the girls danced naked on the bar in front of me, I casually tapped one on the hip. She leaned down to speak, clearly hoping for some business. Without missing a beat, I said, "Would you mind moving slightly to your right? I'm trying to watch the football on the screen behind you."

If looks could kill, I wouldn't be writing this book.

One memorable trip, I had the pleasure of introducing a friend who was visiting from the UK to all the wonders that Thailand had to offer. Fresh from a divorce, he approached his new adventures with a sense of curiosity and liberation, eager to explore the depths of life post-marriage. We hit the nightlife scene together, and one night while walking back to the hotel, we stopped at a street vendor to grab some delicious BBQ chicken—an aromatic treat that left our taste buds begging for more.

As we savoured our snacks, two girls on a motorbike pulled up beside us, and I could immediately see my friend's interest piqued. With the carefree spirit of the night guiding me, I decided to help facilitate the budding connection. Negotiating a price was effortless; I figured since it was near my friend's birthday, I'd treat him—£20 wouldn't break the bank for a night to remember, after all. My friend headed off to the beach with this girl and I decided to hang back with the other girl while my friend went off with his newfound companion.

As I chatted with her, as we sat on two plastic chairs by the roadside, she miraculously produced two cold beers from somewhere, and we enjoyed the relaxed atmosphere while waiting for my friend to return. He emerged after some time, a gleam in his eyes. "We used one of the beach beds for our… activities," he said with a mischievous grin, clearly revelling in hiding the details beneath layers of bravado.

He then mentioned what had happened while he was on the beach – a moment that would become widely recounted with hilarity within our group of friends. As my friend recounted his escapade, he mentioned that while they were in full flight in their beach activities, he felt a sudden tap on his shoulder.

Spinning around, he found a man – clearly from Africa- smiling widely and asking "would you like to buy a melon"

The exchange was comedic in its absurdity. The man, with his grand designs of selling fruits, stood comically coupled against my friend's euphoric state post-encounter. The spectacle of it all propelled the humour to the forefront, and laughter bubbled forth between us.

Fast forward a few years, and my friend found himself back in Phuket, having developed a taste for the escapades we had once shared. He was still naive in many ways when it came to how things worked. This time, he arrived a few days before me, and we agreed to meet at the hotel bar once I arrived. He was practically buzzing with excitement, eager to tell me about a "wonderful girl" he had met the night before—one who had apparently given him the most unforgettable experience (and you can probably guess what I mean).

As we exited the hotel and made our way to Bangla Road, he couldn't stop gushing about her, recounting the many charms that had completely enchanted him. As we walked down the bustling street, I casually asked, "Which bar did you meet this girl in?"

A puzzled smile spread across his face as he pointed toward a side road. Back in those days, that particular street was well known for its ladyboy bars.

"So, this is the road?" I asked, raising an eyebrow in curiosity as we stepped in. Sure enough, we stopped at one of the bars, and he eagerly beckoned a petite, attractive girl over. She glided toward us effortlessly, and my friend, beaming with pride, introduced me to his newfound love. We exchanged polite chatter, wrapped in warm laughter, as I took in the unfolding irony of the moment.

However, after about ten minutes, curiosity got the better of me. I casually leaned in and asked, "So, when did you have the operation?"

She looked at me and, without skipping a beat, graciously replied with a smile, "Two years ago. Would you like to see some pictures?"

I glanced sideways at my friend, who was rapidly losing colour in his cheeks as her words sank in and the realization hit him.

"Come on, let's get out of here!" he gasped, hurriedly making his exit.

I turned to his new love and said, "Forgive us, my dear. I think my friend has suddenly taken ill, and we must go."

As we walked away, he turned to me with earnest eyes and said, "Don't tell anyone about this, will you?"

I couldn't help but burst into laughter, revelling in the absurdity of the situation. "Well, it's safe to say I've shared this story with anyone who would listen."

Although, in fairness, I never revealed exactly who it was. He certainly wasn't the first Farang to fall for that, and he definitely wouldn't be the last.

Those escapades in Phuket became a lasting part of my life story. That was the beauty of it—those strange moments turned into stories we'd share with nostalgia over a drink or two, our faces lighting up as we recounted the events with exaggerated gestures and laughter.

In many ways, my time in Thailand—filled with golfing, late-night escapades, and amusing encounters with characters like my friend—was a vital part of my journey. It helped shape the person I was becoming—someone who could embrace laughter amid chaos, find connection in friendship, and carry forward the lessons learned in the most unexpected circumstances.

The vibrant nightlife of Thailand, with its cultures and characters, continued to play a significant role in my life, leaving me with a treasure trove of memories and stories worth sharing for years to come. Although now, I visit more for family reasons, as well as for golfing and beer.

Through it all, I learned that no matter where life took me, the bonds formed through humour, friendship, and shared experiences would remain steadfast—enduring the test of time and the journey ahead.

CHAPTER 34
The Move Back to the UK

As the years passed, my children thrived in the vibrant surroundings of Singapore. Life felt enjoyable—a harmonious blend of work and family. We relished our weekends, filled with adventures to the zoo, the Night Safari, and the Bird Park, exploring the wonders of wildlife and nature right at our doorstep. The memories of those days—filled with laughter and the thrill of seeing animals up close—remain vivid. Ailsa's favourite was the polar bear as he swam in his pool; she would always give him a little wave.

My love for golf flourished as well, thanks to my membership at the stunning Bintan Lagoon Golf and Country Club, with its luxurious hotel. Just a short ferry ride away, it was a frequent weekend delight where I could indulge my passion for the sport while the family enjoyed the hotel's many pleasures. I would get out early on Saturday and Sunday mornings, savouring the quietness of the course before the day's heat set in, relishing the competition with fellow golfers and immersing myself in the lush greens of paradise—where monkeys and monitor lizards roamed freely around the course.

Yet, amid these joys, the winds of change were quietly gathering strength back in the UK. My father-in-law had fallen ill with prostate cancer. Although this type of cancer is generally slow-moving and not typically fatal, the anxiety it brought into our lives weighed heavily on Carol's mind. She became increasingly restless, yearning for the comfort of family during this challenging time, which led us to consider moving closer to our loved ones.

As if fate had aligned, an opportunity within the organisation presented itself during this turbulent period. A restructuring was underway, and I was approached about taking on the new role of VP of International HR, EMEA/APAC. It was an exciting proposition—a chance to advance my career while ensuring my family had the support they needed during this uncertain time.

After deep discussions with my wife, we realised this could be a positive step forward. Still, the prospect of leaving our idyllic life in Singapore felt daunting. We had also secured residency in Australia, and our original plan had been to migrate there; however, the growing need for family closeness during my father-in-law's illness weighed heavily on our decision.

With a mixture of hesitation and hope, we agreed to move back to the UK. Plans began to take shape swiftly as we prepared for the transition. We looked towards that familiar homeland, memories of childhood and past adventures intertwining with our reasons to return. Yet, in the back of our minds, we couldn't help but wonder how we would adjust to the colder climate and shifting lifestyle after so many years of tropical bliss.

The decision felt like standing at a crossroads—a leap into the unknown yet onto familiar ground, carrying both apprehension and the promise of new beginnings. As I prepared to embrace my new role in early 2006, I also knew that our journey as a family would lead to even more growth and adventure, with the resilience we had built during our time in Singapore guiding us through the inevitable changes ahead.

While it was bittersweet to leave behind our cherished life and connections in Singapore, we understood that family and community were the true treasures worth seeking. As we prepared for the move, I held onto the belief that every ending opens the door to fresh beginnings, and I looked forward to what awaited us in this new chapter of our lives.

As the day of our move finally arrived, the movers descended upon our apartment like a whirlwind, carefully packing away the memories of our years in Singapore. Each box filled marked the end of one chapter and the beginning of another, sending my mind racing through a mix of nostalgia and anticipation.

To help ease our transition back into Western life, we decided to bring Nur, our maid, along with us. After so many years together, she had become an integral part of our family, adding her own warmth and care to our home.

Nur was bubbling with excitement about the move, though I couldn't help but wonder how an Indonesian woman would adapt to a British winter. To prepare her, we kitted her out in full winter attire—thick coats, sturdy gloves, and scarves to help her battle the chill. Watching her don those layers, I felt a wave of amusement; she had always been the sunbeam in our home, and now she was about to face her first winter in a climate so drastically different from the tropical warmth she had known.

Before our departure, I took the time to say goodbye to my friends at the fencing club in Singapore. They had gathered to wish me well, presenting me with a shirt signed by all the members. Their camaraderie and support meant the world to me—a fitting farewell gesture that became a symbol of the strong bonds we had built during my time in the club.

I cherished the moments spent with our coach, a remarkable Singaporean who had once competed in the Olympics. His unwavering encouragement had invigorated my practice, and it was bittersweet to part ways, knowing I was leaving behind connections I had come to value deeply.

Finally, we boarded the plane bound for the UK, carrying hopes and dreams in our hearts as we prepared for a fresh start. The flight became an opportunity to reflect on the whirlwind of emotions that had accompanied our journey. As we soared above the clouds, I looked forward to the possibilities that awaited us, even as I acknowledged the anxious uncertainties surrounding our return.

Upon arrival, the global mobility team had facilitated our relocation, ensuring the transition went as smoothly as possible. We were settled into temporary accommodation—a charming house on a farm just outside the village of Tring, providing a picturesque backdrop for our new adventure. It felt idyllic, a stark contrast to the urban sprawl of Singapore, with open fields and wide skies offering the promise of exploration for our children, though the drastic change in weather made things more challenging than we had hoped. Still, it was the perfect setting to let their imaginations run wild.

In our family's efforts to make the move more comforting, we also brought along our two beloved cats from Singapore. Katya and Moshi, both Russian Blues, had become treasured companions to the children. Their silky grey fur and playful personalities made them an integral part of our family, and I knew the kids would find comfort in having familiar faces with them during this transition.

Special pet transfers were arranged to ensure their safe arrival, and just a few days later, they joined us at the farm. Watching the cats acclimate to their new environment was a spectacle in itself. They tentatively explored their new home, wide-eyed and curious, as if trying to make sense of the vast open spaces around them.

The first few days were filled with adjustment, laughter, and new discoveries—the kids were thrilled with their newfound freedom to roam, while Katya and Moshi pounced on every shadow, eagerly claiming their territory. As we navigated our way through this transition back to the UK, I couldn't help but feel a wave of optimism wash over us—though, ironically, I was the one struggling to adjust the most.

Some things took a little longer to get used to than others. For example, supermarkets closing at 4:00 pm on Sundays was completely alien to us, as we had been accustomed to stores being open seven days a week—often 24 hours a day. Twice, I made the mistake of arriving at 3:55 pm for my shopping. Not once, but twice—can you believe it? To be honest, even to this day, I still can't get used to British opening hours.

Every change, every new adventure we embarked upon, embedded itself into our story. As laughter echoed through our temporary home, I found comfort in the realisation that, together, we would face whatever came next, embracing the unpredictability of life with resilience honed through our shared experiences. Our journey back to the UK was not just a return or a fresh start but a beautiful continuation of our story.

After a month of searching, we finally found a house to rent in the charming town of Berkhamsted. The moment we stepped into the three-bedroom home, I knew it would serve our family well in the short term while we figured out exactly where we wanted to settle. One bedroom was allotted to the children, another to Nur, and the third to Carol and me. The house overlooked the picturesque canal system that wove its way through Berkhamsted, providing a stunning backdrop and making for pleasant morning strolls to the train station.

The canal added an enchanting dimension to our daily routines. I simply loved walking along its winding paths, past brightly painted barges and serene waters. The peaceful surroundings were a welcome contrast to the hustle and bustle we had experienced in Singapore. I particularly appreciated the tranquillity of these walks as I prepared for the long commute to my London office. Though the journey was a hefty 90 minutes each way, I found solace in those quiet moments along the canal as I strolled towards the station.

On occasion, I would stop for a quick pint at one of the charming pubs dotted along the waterway on my way home. It felt good to unwind after a long day of work, and I enjoyed the warm atmosphere of the local pubs, often engaging in friendly conversations with the regulars. It was a delightful way to transition from the rigours of professional life back to the comforts of home.

Then came the day our furniture arrived, bringing back a sense of normalcy to our living situation. As the movers unpacked and set everything up for us, I felt that familiar rush of excitement as our belongings took their rightful places. However, once they left, a strange smell began to permeate the room. Carol, ever the eternal worrier, voiced her concern.

"Something must have contaminated the furniture," she said, her tone hovering between disbelief and anxiety.

After a few moments of sniffing around, feeling slightly frantic ourselves, we decided it would be best to err on the side of caution. Off we went to the local hospital to have ourselves checked out, just in case some hidden ailment was lurking beneath the surface. Thankfully, back then, we didn't have to contend with the chaos that now plagues the NHS. We could quite literally walk straight into A&E without an agonising wait—a convenience that felt almost foreign now, given that today, you could wait up to five hours to see a doctor, if you were lucky.

Arriving at the hospital, I was pleasantly surprised by how organised the system was at the time. The staff were efficient yet warm, ushering us in and swiftly preparing us for a check-up. We explained our odd situation—the strange smell and our fears about possible contamination. There was a peculiar comfort in the surroundings; a place dedicated to health and safety that offered reassurance during moments of uncertainty.

We were taken to the front desk, where a doctor emerged. He asked a few questions, then, in a sudden state of panic, urgently told us to step back. Can you imagine the state of my wife at this point, with two small children in tow? We were then instructed to walk outside the building, retracing the exact route we had taken in. Once outside, they spoke to us from a distance to assess the situation. Only after they were confident that we weren't about to infect the entire hospital did they allow us back inside.

After running a few tests and thoroughly examining us, the medical staff concluded that we were perfectly fine, alleviating our fears about any contamination. The source of the smell, it turned out, was nothing more than a collection of packing materials that had absorbed an odour during transit. Relieved but slightly embarrassed, we thanked the staff for their assistance and headed home, chuckling at our overreaction.

The experience reinforced the realization that adapting to a new environment often came with its own challenges. Settling into our new home and becoming part of the Berkhamsted community felt like a fresh start—a reboot of our lives. The laughter of my children and Nur created an uplifting atmosphere as we began weaving memories in our new surroundings, gradually transforming the house into a home. Each hiccup along the way, from the moving day chaos to our hospital adventure, became threads in the fabric of our family story—reminders of resilience, wrapped in love and gentle humour, guiding us forward.

By this time, we had purchased a Honda SUV to get around, and Nur had started driving lessons. Nur was vertically challenged—standing at just 4 foot 6 inches tall. Seeing the car moving down the street without a visible driver was quite an unnerving experience for the observer.

The Hertfordshire countryside was a breath-taking canvas of rolling hills, verdant fields, and charming villages—most with an excellent pub for a relaxing drink—a perfect playground for our family adventures. Most weekends, we'd pile into the car, exploring different corners of the surrounding counties, often finding ourselves drawn to our favourite spot: Waddesdon Manor. The sheer scale of the manor was impressive, and we loved spending hours wandering its grand rooms, imagining the lives that had unfolded within its walls.

For Rory, however, the true magic lay outdoors. He was captivated by the aviary, where a multitude of birds—from brightly coloured parrots to majestic peacocks—filled the air with their vibrant calls. The manor's extensive grounds provided endless opportunities for adventure. He could often be found exploring the winding pathways, discovering hidden nooks and crannies, or simply revelling in the vast open spaces. These family outings to Waddesdon Manor created a treasure trove of cherished memories, which we still fondly recall to this day.

CHAPTER 35
A New Home in Aldbury

After months of searching for a suitable house to buy, we finally found a charming 500-year-old Tudor home in the picturesque village of Aldbury. Given its size, we faced the daunting task of selling much of our furniture. The contrast in living arrangements was stark; our apartment in Singapore had been significantly larger than any house we could find in the UK.

Aldbury was straight out of a storybook—a village where the iconic TV series Midsomer Murders had been filmed, along with the beloved Shillingbury Tales. Finding a house over 500 years old felt like stepping back in time. We marvelled at the Tudor-style beams that adorned the ceilings, each piece of wood holding stories of its own. One wooden beam in the kitchen caught my eye—an old mast from a warship that had met a sorry end. It was a captivating reminder of history, blending seamlessly with our daily lives.

Small wouldn't quite describe the house. It had originally been three cottages knocked into one home, though you wouldn't necessarily realise it at first glance.

The village of Aldbury was quintessentially English—charming and full of character. The two pubs, one at each end of the village, were likely the envy of many, offering a warm atmosphere and the chance to connect with locals over pints of ale. At the heart of the village, a serene pond reflected the sky, while nearby stood the old stocks—a relic of a bygone era where unfortunate souls had once been placed for public ridicule, enduring rotten vegetables thrown in their direction.

Our new home was surrounded by lush forests, inviting nature walks and adventures just beyond our doorstep. The tranquillity of the setting put us instantly at ease, providing the contrast we had yearned for after the hustle of urban life in Singapore.

Not to be overlooked, the village had its own primary school just a short walk from our house. The thought of being part of such a close-knit community, where the school felt like an extension of our home, resonated deeply with us. It was the perfect setting for Rory and Ailsa to grow up—surrounded by nature and a supportive environment.

Settling into life in Aldbury felt rejuvenating. We carved out new routines and created memories within the walls of our historic home. Family picnics by the pond, Sunday roasts at the local pubs, and school events at the primary school quickly became the foundation of our life in this enchanting village.

The warmth of the community, the history of our house, and the beauty of our surroundings blended seamlessly, reminding us that life's journey often follows an unpredictable path, leading to unexpected joys and adventures. In this picturesque village, we found a renewed sense of belonging, love, and shared experiences that would serve as the backdrop for the next chapters of our lives.

Sadly, Nur had decided that life in the UK was not for her; she simply could not adjust to it. So, she headed back to Indonesia. Although she kept in touch for a number of years—mainly to ask about Rory and Ailsa—a chapter in our lives had ended, and it felt as though we had lost a family member.

Rory had started attending the local primary school, and with my flexible work-from-home schedule a few days a week, picking him up became a delightful part of my day. It gave me the chance to connect with him in the heart of our new community, witnessing firsthand the joys and challenges of his early education.

When Nur was part of our household, we encouraged her to speak to Rory and Ailsa in Bahasa, her native language. It was a wonderful way for the children to become bilingual, enriching their lives with an additional skill and a deeper cultural connection. Inspired by this, I, too, dabbled in learning the language, as well as Mandarin. Although I had once been able to converse in a few languages, I unfortunately lost that fluency over time, as life and routines shifted and opportunities to practise diminished. Although I still maintain the ability to speak Thai, not fluently, but enough to get by when visiting.

One day, as I arrived to pick Rory up from school, his teacher pulled me aside with a concerned expression. She was a sweet old lady who had spent most of her life teaching generations of children in the village, and her devotion to her students was evident.

"Rory kept pointing at me and shouting something," she said, looking both puzzled and concerned.

I gave her a puzzled look in return and asked, "What did he say?"

"Wait there a second; I've written it down," she responded, rifling through her papers.

You have to understand, this was before smartphones became ubiquitous, and certainly before Google was widely used. In our remote village school, information was often shared through handwritten notes and word of mouth.

She returned with a serious expression and said, "It sounded like this: 'Kamu Gala Harry inat.'"

It was then that I realised there had been a misunderstanding.

"Oh, I'm sure Rory was just making up his usual nonsense," I reassured her, not wanting her to worry. "I'll have a talk with him later."

As we walked home, the phrase the teacher had shared echoed in my mind. Given my limited knowledge of Bahasa, I tried to decipher the words and soon realised that what Rory had actually said was, "Kamu Gila Hari Ini," which translates to, "You are crazy today!"

When we got home, my curiosity was piqued, and I spoke to Rory. "So, what did you say to your teacher today?" His honesty had always been one of his defining characteristics, and I knew he wouldn't hesitate to tell me the truth.

"I told her she was crazy," Rory replied matter-of-factly, as if it were the most obvious statement in the world.

I felt a mix of amusement and concern as I said, "Rory, that's not a nice thing to say to someone, especially when they don't understand the language."

He looked up at me with a puzzled expression, his brow furrowing in confusion. "But Dad, she is!" he insisted, his innocence shining through.

Once again, I explained, "That may be the case, but it's still not nice to say it out loud. You have to be kind, especially to someone who might not understand the joke."

Rory nodded, his expression shifting as he absorbed my words. "Okay, Dad. I won't do it again," he promised, and I could see he genuinely wanted to make things right.

In that moment, I realised that parenting often involves balancing lessons of kindness with the harsh realities of the world. Rory's innocent observation was a glimpse into the complexities of social interactions. Each of these moments—humorous or serious—became teaching opportunities, shaping his empathy and understanding of others as he grew.

As we carried on with our day, both of us smiling, I knew that settling into our new life in Aldbury would come with its own challenges. But the lessons of kindness, compassion, and communication would remain steadfast pillars guiding us forward. By embracing every little lesson, we would nurture a home filled with understanding and laughter, reflecting the beautiful cultures we had experienced as a family.

Our first Christmas in Aldbury was fast approaching, but before the festivities began, I had our annual HR team Christmas night out. After a festive dinner and a few too many drinks in London, I boarded the train—slightly worse for wear—back to Tring. By now, the taxi fares from various stations between Tring and Wolverhampton were second nature to me; I had often fallen asleep on the train during that journey home on Fridays after work drinks. This year, however, the festive cheer kept me awake until I arrived in Tring.

It was a few miles down a country lane from the station to our house, and in my drunken wisdom, I decided to take a shortcut across the fields. The ground was muddy, and there wasn't much light—even with the faint glow of a mostly full moon—but I set off with a confident stride, completely oblivious to the dangers ahead.

As it turned out, the farmer had recently dug a massive hole in the middle of the field, creating a large, muddy pit at the bottom. I was enjoying my countryside walk, strolling merrily along, when I suddenly lost my footing. Within seconds, I was sliding down into the pit with a resounding splash. After a rather undignified tumble—now covered in mud and with my freshly dry-cleaned suit ruined—I finally managed to crawl out.

I walked into the house, and Carol took one look at me before collapsing into laughter. The very next day, she took my suit and coat to the dry cleaners.

When the dry cleaner opened the bag and saw the muddy clothes, Carol immediately launched into the story, trying to explain the situation. The dry cleaner simply looked back at her and said, "We get a lot of that sort of thing around this time of year."

Christmas in Aldbury was a magical time, when the village came alive with festive cheer, transforming into a winter wonderland. Everywhere you looked, decorations twinkled, Christmas lights wrapped around trees, and villagers gathered to celebrate the holiday spirit. The air around the pubs was filled with the enticing aroma of roasting chestnuts and mulled wine, accompanied by the sound of laughter, and a roaring log fire —creating an atmosphere that felt warm and inviting, a stark contrast to the cold winter nights outside.

This year, Dottie and Ken had come to stay for Christmas, adding extra joy to our family celebrations. Their presence brought even more excitement to the festivities, and we were overjoyed to share the season with them. Along with our children, we took part in various village traditions, embracing the shared warmth of our community during this special time.

The highlight of Christmas in Aldbury was the annual festive panto, organised by the church—a beloved tradition that showcased the talents of local residents. Everyone gathered in the village hall, where anticipation and merriment filled the air—no doubt helped along by an earlier trip to the pub. As the curtain rose, we were treated to an evening of singing, humour, and heartwarming performances—everything one would expect from a proper pantomime.

Halfway through, an unexpected moment brought the house down. The vicar entered, donning a policeman's costume, his helmet shimmering under the stage lights. He wore a serene expression, preparing to deliver his lines. However, just as he opened his mouth to speak, a loud voice rang out from the front of the hall where the children sat.

"Look, everyone! It's God!" Rory exclaimed, his innocent observation cutting through the silence like a bolt.

The entire room erupted into laughter, a cascade of giggles and chuckles filling the space as all eyes turned towards Rory. Even the vicar couldn't help but crack a smile, momentarily breaking character amidst the wave of collective mirth that swept through the village hall. It was a moment of pure joy—a reminder of the innocent perspective that children hold, often bringing fresh light to our lives.

The laughter swirled around the hall, and as Rory turned to look at me, I gave him a big thumbs-up. While the panto carried on, Rory's off-the-cuff remark lingered in the air—a reminder of how the joy of childhood has the power to uplift and unite everyone around it. We still chuckle about it to this day.

Boxing Day in Aldbury was a much-anticipated event that brought the village together in a flurry of excitement and community spirit—well, certainly a lot of spirits, if you get my drift! The day kicked off with the legendary barrel race, where two pub teams competed against each other, pushing a barrel of beer from one pub to another, circling the village pond, and racing back again. The thrill of the competition ignited cheers from the crowd, their voices merging into a raucous symphony of support for their favourite pub.

I, of course, remained neutral, as I generally liked most pubs!

As the competitors barrelled down the street, the energy was electric, laughter ringing out against the backdrop of brisk winter air. The spirit amongst the villagers was infectious as everyone gathered for the event, creating a sense of unity and fun, reminding me of village life as a child. I remembered the scent of winter—a mix of frost and the faint aroma of wood smoke—and felt grateful to be part of such a vibrant tradition.

We had a large log fireplace in the house, a cosy spot where you could sit and keep warm—something I was looking forward to once the races were over. Well in advance, I had relocated the car a few streets away, ensuring it would be safe from damage.

The excitement didn't stop there. Once the adrenaline of the barrel race subsided, the annual tug-of-war unfolded—an event that took the festivities to new heights and added a fair bit of hilarity. I, of course, was never a participant; spectating was more my comfort zone, beer in hand, cheering them on.

With one team positioned on each side, we stretched a hefty rope across the pond, and the stakes were raised. The dramatic challenge promised that the losers would be unceremoniously yanked into the frigid water—an outcome any sensible soul would want to avoid on a cold winter's day.

As the two teams gripped the rope, tension filled the air, and the enthusiasm from the crowd surged. The cheering grew louder, blending with the friendly banter shouted between teams. It all felt wonderfully chaotic—a festive atmosphere that lingered in the bones of the spectators.

Just as the whistle blew, the teams pulled with all their might, the outcome hanging in the balance. The sight of competitors straining as they dug their heels into the ground always painted a picture of sheer determination and competition.

Then, the inevitable happened—the victorious team yanked their opponents into the icy water, eliciting roars of laughter and cheers from the delighted audience. Those who had fallen into the pond emerged, drenched but roaring with laughter, fully embracing the spirit of the day. It was messy and exhilarating, a joyful moment where dignity was abandoned in favour of pure fun.

The local Morris Men were there, dancing along to their merry tunes—it was like a film set!

Once the day's events concluded, the festive merriment continued at the local pubs. With a satisfying return to warmth, everyone gathered together, buoyed by the day's antics. We huddled around a flickering fire, sharing stories and laughter while enjoying copious amounts of beer—far removed from the challenges of everyday life. As the flames crackled and the warmth enveloped us, we felt a sense of connection that made all the winter chill worthwhile.

Boxing Day became a cherished tradition in our household—a highlight that signified not just a day of games and merriment but also the very essence of community spirit. These were the moments I treasured, where laughter and joy flowed as freely as the drinks, bonding us together as we celebrated our shared existence in the idyllic village of Aldbury.

CHAPTER 36
The Relocation of a Major European Publication

As life continued to flourish in Aldbury, a new and exciting chapter awaited me as I embraced the responsibilities of leadership in Europe. I had become acquainted with a global media mogul, the owner of the publication, following the family's sale of the publishing company to him. Our paths crossed several times, allowing me to gain insight into his vision for the future of our organisation. Before long, I found myself entrusted with the significant task of overseeing people-related matters for the relocation of the European headquarters from Belgium to London.

Relocating was no small feat; it came with its own set of challenges, particularly due to Belgium's labour laws, which heavily favoured employees. Navigating this daunting landscape required not only meticulous planning but also a keen understanding of the cultural nuances involved. From the outset, I knew this endeavour would test my negotiating skills to their limits.

This move would once again bring together the old leadership from Singapore. Bob had come over to lead the paper, and I was back working closely with him. He could be frustrating to work with at times, but I always enjoyed it. I also had my sidekick, "Little Steve," as he would forever be known—despite not actually being short.

The day before the announcement, we hopped onto the Eurostar and made our way to Brussels. From the station, we headed straight to the hotel, ensuring we could start early the next day. As I arrived at the office, I could feel the weight of anticipation in the air—the murmurs circulating among the employees hinted that the rumours had been out for quite some time. When we finally addressed the staff and delivered the news of our plans, the atmosphere in the room was mixed. Some seemed relieved that the uncertainty would soon be behind them, while others felt the weight of inevitable change settling on their shoulders.

In preparation for the negotiations ahead, I emphasised the importance of electing a representative group from among the employees to take part in discussions with me and management. This was crucial not only from a legal standpoint but also to ensure that their voices were heard and that the transition would be as smooth as possible.

The announcement had its intended effect, giving employees the agency to participate in the process, though I sensed some trepidation about the impending changes. However, this was merely the first step in transferring the business.

To complicate matters further, the employee representative group announced that they would be bringing along two trade unions, with whom I had no prior experience. This development made me acutely aware of the challenges ahead; navigating the complexities of union negotiations required finesse and strategy, not to mention a willingness to engage in honest dialogue. The atmosphere was often strained as redundancies were discussed. Yet, amidst the uncertainty, a small café near our office became a welcome haven. Their exquisite croque monsieur, served with perfectly crisp pommes frites and accompanied by Belgian beers, offered a bittersweet respite from the difficult realities of the situation.

We established a timeline to complete the relocation within just six months—a task I believed was achievable despite its challenges. The countdown began, and as plans unfolded, I immersed myself in understanding the new legal landscape and union dynamics that would soon come into play.

Weeks turned into intense discussions, with every meeting becoming a test of patience, understanding, and negotiation. I was committed to fostering a cooperative atmosphere, one where trust could grow amidst the uncertainty. I quickly realised that open communication would be the cornerstone of our progress. Each time we convened with employees and union representatives, I took great care to listen to their concerns and suggestions, ensuring everyone felt valued and respected throughout the process. I would then counter their requests and outline my reasons why. And, in fairness to Bob, he stepped up as a leader in this moment, demonstrating his skills in handling the situation.

As we delved deeper into this transition, I began to appreciate the cultural differences that emerged in negotiations. Each exchange was not just about policies and figures; it was also about people and their livelihoods—the dreams and aspirations tied to their work and the future they envisioned within the organisation.

With every meeting, the unions grew bolder, yet there was a clear calculation to be followed, and I would not be easily swayed. Working alongside our external legal partners, we ensured all written communication was legally compliant—

in French and Dutch, as well as in English. We also engaged our in-house legal department in New York.

In the end, as we navigated these challenges together, I grew not just as an HR professional but as a leader who understood the importance of balancing ambition with empathy. The road was bumpy and fraught with obstacles, but with every hurdle overcome, I knew we were shaping a brighter future for the Publication and strengthening the bonds between management and employees.

Through this experience, I realised that while my role was pivotal in overseeing the logistical relocation, it was equally important to prioritise the emotional well-being of the team. The commitment to ensuring we moved forward together would shape not only the success of the transition but also foster a stronger, more resilient workplace in the future.

Just a year after relocating the European headquarters, changes began stirring closer to home. The dynamics of our workplace were shifting, and it became apparent that New York was preparing to implement some changes. Among those affected was a colleague with whom I had shared a professional history over the years. While he was not particularly tough on employees in general, he had a knack for protecting his own interests—especially when it came to negotiating his terms and conditions.

The call from New York felt like a punch to the gut. The decision had been made—they wanted to terminate some executives and appoint a successors. It was a bittersweet moment for me, as one executive had been instrumental in my career. I had a deep appreciation for what this person had done for me; he was not only a work colleague but also a friend whom I admired and respected.

I knew this was going to be delicate. They had always exhibited a volatile streak, especially when their position or ego was threatened. The prospect of their expat life coming to an abrupt end was likely to send them into a defensive spiral, and I was tasked with delivering the news—something that felt both daunting and heavy. Yet, I was equally up to the task. It was business, after all, not personal.

Arranging to meet them for lunch at a hotel, I chose a crowded venue, hoping it would reduce the chances of a scene—a Jerry Maguire moment. The atmosphere buzzed with the murmur of conversations, bursts of laughter, and the clinking of cutlery—a stark contrast to the harsh news I was about to deliver.

As I made my way to the table, the weight of what was about to transpire settled on my shoulders. This was not just a colleague, but also a friend.

"Hey," I began after we exchanged pleasantries, carefully choosing my words. "Thank you for meeting me here."

They leaned back, their eyes searching mine, sensing my seriousness. "What's up?"

Taking a deep breath, I opened with the line no one ever wants to hear.

"This is a without prejudice conversation. I'm afraid I didn't call you here today just to have lunch. I've received word from New York. They've decided to make some changes within the management structure, and unfortunately, those changes are going to affect you. They're terminating your position and will be appointing a successor in due course."

I felt the words hang in the air, thick with gravity, as he processed the information. This was one of the hardest things I had ever had to do in my professional career.

As expected, they reacted first with disbelief, followed by flashes of anger. The noise from the lunch crowd faded into the background as they processed their emotions.

"What the hell? This is total bullshit! I've worked my arse off here for years, and this is what they do to me?" exclaimed, his voice slightly raised, the tension escalating.

I raised a hand slightly, attempting to maintain a sense of control over the situation.

"I understand that this is not welcome news, but the decision is final. Unfortunately, you are not to return to the office after this meeting. I will arrange a suitable time for you to collect your belongings. I suggest you seek legal counsel, and they can contact me for any further discussions. I'm truly sorry that this is happening, and I am here to support you through this difficult period."

Even as I spoke, I couldn't help but think that it all sounded scripted and robotic.

Delivering these words felt like a gut punch—it was one of the most difficult things I had ever had to do, or at least it was up to that point in my career. Here I was, delivering news that could unravel their career and unsettle their life. And despite any previous thoughts, they were a friend, and I felt a deep sense of compassion for them.

As we parted ways, a lingering sadness settled over me as I walked away from the hotel. This person had given me a lot of support over the years, yet the realities of corporate life sometimes demanded making difficult decisions with unforeseen consequences—an unsettling aspect of leadership I was growing all too familiar with.

Reflecting on that day, I recognised that every departure served as a reminder of the volatile nature of workplace relationships, the fragility of careers, and the importance of treating each interaction with integrity and professionalism. My journey continued to evolve, shaping me into a leader who understood both the joys and the responsibilities that came with navigating the complexities of people and their careers.

Just when I thought I had successfully navigated the tumultuous waters of handling one departure, another high-profile executive exit landed on my desk, bringing with it an entirely new set of challenges. Once again, I was tasked with steering the ship through these murky waters. This time, I was dealing with a compensation specialist based in our Princeton office—who, for the sake of discretion, will remain nameless.

Two days before the scheduled date to inform the executive of their termination, I received an email from this individual that sent shockwaves of disbelief through me. The message, written in a tone both casual and careless, simply asked whether the executive was aware they were being let go at the end of the week. However, in a blunder that defied logic, this person had inadvertently copied the very executive in question onto the email thread.

I can still picture the moment I read the executive's swift reply, which landed in my inbox almost instantly: "No, but I do now!" My jaw dropped. I couldn't help myself—laughter erupted from me as I marvelled at how someone could be so comically inept. How on earth could this happen?

With panic rising, I immediately phoned the person in the U.S., unable to contain my incredulity. "Why did you do that, for goodness' sake?" I asked, half-amused and half-annoyed.

The response was almost too absurd to believe: "I was just checking how to spell their name and forgot to remove it from the 'To' address line."

I was momentarily speechless, grappling with the sheer ridiculousness of the situation. All I could muster was, "I'd better go and see them now and sort out your mess."

Putting aside my frustration at the incompetence of the situation, I knew my responsibility lay in addressing the fallout. I walked over to the executive's office, steeling myself for what was bound to be a challenging conversation.

Upon entering, I was met with a mix of confusion and frustration. I immediately apologised for the slip-up, acknowledging that the circumstances surrounding their exit were both unfortunate and mishandled. "I know this has put you in a difficult position, and I genuinely regret the way this information came to you," I said, trying to express my sincerity.

They simply replied, "It's okay. I know you weren't the one who sent this."

From there, I sought to turn the conversation into a productive dialogue about their exit strategy. "Let's just talk about how we can make this process smoother for you," I proposed, hoping to shift the mood. I emphasised the importance of facilitating a respectful and comfortable transition. "Please have your lawyer contact me regarding your exit details, and we will cover a portion of their fees. I want to ensure you're looked after as you navigate this change."

As the meeting progressed, I could see the tension dissipate, replaced by a sense of professionalism that allowed us to navigate the next steps together. In moments like these, my own experiences with transitions and exits reminded me of the importance of clear communication, empathy, and tact—even amid the most chaotic circumstances.

Reflecting on these two notable departures, I recognised that each situation offered invaluable lessons in leadership and the importance of handling sensitive matters with care. Navigating corporate life often felt like managing a predictable ebb and flow, where each wave of change brought opportunities to demonstrate integrity, empathy, and an unwavering commitment to supporting colleagues, even in the most tumultuous of times. Every interaction reinforced the notion that, despite the challenges, the foundation we built would guide us through the complexities of corporate life and the nuanced realities of human relationships within it.

After three years in London, I found myself yearning for something different. The vibrant city had its charms, but the fast-paced corporate world had begun to weigh heavily on me. Dolly had moved on some time ago, and in her absence, I had endured the leadership of two subsequent managers—each more inept than the last. Their lack of direction and understanding made even the best-laid plans feel like navigating a ship without a captain.

Then came "the Makeover Man," as we dubbed him—a figure so enamoured with his own reflection that there seemed to be no room for anyone else in his world. He strutted into meetings with an air of superiority, often blinded by his self-importance. It was as if he believed leadership hinged solely on charisma and not at all on ability, collaboration, and vision. It became increasingly clear that continuing under his management would not be sustainable for my own career satisfaction.

Frustration bubbled within me. I realised this was the push I needed to seek new horizons. With my father-in-law now stable, we no longer had a compelling reason to remain in the UK. I had enjoyed my time there, but the itch for change grew stronger by the day after enduring the recent managerial follies.

As the company became integrated into the parent, new opportunities began to emerge. I was offered several roles in the US but, to be honest, although we were open to relocating, the United States was not among my preferred destinations. The thought of such a significant move felt overwhelming; I wanted to ensure that any transition would be in the best interest of my family.

Amidst this uncertainty, fortune intervened when Dubai World came knocking. The prospect of moving to Dubai was tantalising, offering a unique blend of culture and opportunity that felt deeply enticing. The idea of living in a city characterised by rapid growth, a vibrant expat community, and a stunning contrast between tradition and modernity was hard to resist.

Decision made! Excitement and anticipation filled the air as I shared the news with my family. My mind raced with visions of sunshine, adventure, and new beginnings. We were about to embark on a journey that promised to be both culturally enriching and personally fulfilling. My aspirations were fuelled by the potential for professional growth.

The move to Dubai felt like stepping into a world brimming with possibilities, one that had the power to transform our lives in ways we had yet to imagine. As I prepared for my new role, I focused on what we wanted from this chapter as a family. I sought to create an environment where the children could thrive and explore while I maintained a healthy balance between work and life.

With our bags packed and our hearts full, I knew the journey ahead would bring its own challenges and experiences. But this time, it felt different. I had navigated complicated waters before, learned valuable lessons, and managed the chaos of life. Now, with optimism and determination, I looked forward to immersing myself in the vibrant life of Dubai, embracing the adventures that awaited us as a family.

As we boarded our flight, . the clouds of uncertainty were lifting, and as we prepared to land in our new home, I knew this next chapter would be filled with growth, discovery, and the chance to create lasting memories together. Dubai was calling, and I was ready to answer.

CHAPTER 37
Dubai to Jersey

We arrived in Dubai with two exhausted children, their little faces bearing the strain of the long journey. Thankfully, Dubai World had arranged our accommodation for the first month, securing a two-bedroom apartment in The Greens. It was a practical and comfortable introduction to life in this bustling city.

As we settled into our new home, the rapid expansion surrounding us was impossible to ignore. Dubai in 2009 was transforming at an astonishing pace—construction sites dotted the skyline, and the roads were a chaotic maze of development. The sat nav we had brought along proved almost useless as we tried to navigate the ever-changing landscape. It felt like reading a map of a city still trying to define itself. Everywhere we looked, cranes towered above the horizon, while the iconic silhouette of the Burj Khalifa steadily emerged from the ground, looming over the city like a beacon of progress.

On my first day at work, I was picked up by one of my team members, a friendly fellow named Ahmed. I stepped outside to meet him, and we set off for the office together. Little did I know that our drive would turn into an adventurous trek across the desert. The roads leading to our office were still under construction, forcing us to take a winding, improvised route—an unexpected thrill to my morning commute. The golden sands and vast, empty stretches were a stark contrast to the urban energy of London and Singapore, and I couldn't help but marvel at the surreal beauty of the desert landscape.

When we finally arrived at the office, I was welcomed into a five-storey building that boasted a swimming pool and a restaurant on the top floor. However, much to my disappointment, the pool was strictly off-limits. As this was a government-owned business, regulations were in place to ensure employee safety and compliance. It seemed ironic that such lavish amenities were out of reach—a curious contrast of luxury and bureaucratic restrictions.

Stepping into the main foyer, I was struck by the sheer scale of the projects we were involved in. The office featured a mezzanine floor adorned with models of various developments in progress—intricate representations of staggering projects valued in the billions of US dollars. Each model showcased the ambitious designs that were transforming Dubai and the broader region, igniting a sense of pride in the work we were undertaking—projects that would leave a lasting mark on the world.

As I was shown to my office—which, as expected for a director, was a spacious corner office—I took a moment to take in my surroundings. It was elegantly furnished, but nothing captured my attention quite like the desk in the centre of the room. Allegedly, it had cost an astonishing US$25,000. Madness, I thought to myself. I could only imagine how as a HR leader I could justify having such extravagance—not to mention, all I really needed it for was typing on my computer.

When I inquired about the exorbitant price tag on the desk, I received an unexpected response. "It's a special desk for architects," I was informed. "When we built this office, we designed it around this desk and couldn't remove it once construction was completed." This was my first real encounter with what I would come to think of as Corporate Madness—the absurdities that often accompanied the rapid expansion of this booming city.

As the weeks passed, I settled into my role and adjusted to my new surroundings. The challenges of relocating my family and adapting to a new work culture soon evolved into opportunities for growth and discovery. I immersed myself in my responsibilities while also embracing the distinctive aspects of life in Dubai.

The shifting sands of this vibrant city reflected not only its physical transformation but also the continual evolution of my professional journey. I was ready to embrace the challenges ahead with the resilience and determination I had cultivated over the years, carving out a new life for myself and my family in this remarkable, ever-changing landscape.

In our first week in Dubai, Carol and I embarked on an essential mission: finding a suitable school for our children. It was no easy task, especially partway through the academic year, with limited spaces available in such a competitive educational environment. Each school we visited presented its own challenges, strengths, and complications. Yet, driven by our determination to provide the best environment for Rory and Ailsa, we pressed on. What we found was a resounding "no spaces here" response.

We eventually settled on a school that seemed to fit some, but not all our needs and made our way to meet the headmaster. Carol had a distinguished background as a teacher at Queen Margarets in York, and UWC in

Singapore—one of the leading schools in the world—which added an air of expectation to our search.

That said, as we sat across from the headmaster, I quickly sensed that he was more preoccupied with his own aspirations than with our urgent needs.

In a conversation that felt oddly self-serving, he casually mentioned that he had applied multiple times to work at UWC, only to be rejected on each occasion. I wonder why, I thought to myself, fully grasping the implications behind his struggles. The exchange felt more like an audition for his own relevance rather than a genuine consultation to secure a suitable place for our children.

In an astonishingly brazen move, he remarked, "Why would you want to come to Ryanair when you could afford British Airways First Class with your allowance?" The comment left me momentarily speechless. Here we were, searching for a nurturing environment for our children, and he was comparing schools to budget airlines!

I knew we needed to settle quickly, and ultimately; this was the only option available. While the school was primarily attended by Indian students—which wasn't an issue for us—it wasn't the top-tier institution we had hoped for. We decided it was the best choice for our family's immediate needs. Sadly, Rory struggled to adjust to this new environment, facing challenges that affected his confidence and enthusiasm for learning.

Amidst the school search, I should also highlight another milestone—I bought a car. Being the ever-thrifty Yorkshireman, I wasn't about to follow the trend of buying flashy luxury cars like everyone else. Instead, I opted for a 20-year-old Land Rover Discovery. Sure, it was a bit of a wreck, but it was exactly what I needed for driving around the desert and navigating Dubai's rugged terrain.

I remember rolling into the office for the first time, parking the Discovery in a lot filled with gleaming luxury cars—Aston Martins, Hummers, and BMWs, all glistening in the sun. I entered the building with a chuckle at the sight of my wreck among those pristine vehicles.

Moments later, my second-in-command walked in—a great Indian guy whom I admired for his work ethic. He had a knack for getting things done, although his methods occasionally felt a bit outdated.

He approached me with a serious expression and led me to the window overlooking the parking lot. "Sir," he began, his tone suggesting a lesson was about to be imparted, "a man in your position should not be driving a car like that. Look across the car park and tell me— which car would you prefer to have?"

I couldn't help but smile as I took in the luxurious fleet lined up before me. But instead of succumbing to the temptation, I replied with a grin, "I'd have my car, as it's the only one out there that's paid for."

The chuckle that escaped me felt liberating—a quiet rebellion against the expectations of status and wealth that surrounded us. As he left with a puzzled look on his face, shaking his head slightly, I felt a sense of satisfaction at having navigated the situation with a bit of humour while staying true to my principles.

Yet, these experiences also taught me important lessons about identity and staying grounded amidst new environments and societal expectations. The challenges surrounding our move reminded me of the strength I had built over the years and how important it was to remain authentic to who I was, regardless of where life took me.

These early days in Dubai were filled with challenges and adjustments, both personally and professionally. We had found a lovely villa in The Lakes to rent, on a great street with children from many different countries, which was fabulous for Rory and Ailsa. After school, all the kids would be out in the street playing together, with their maids in tow. It was a wonderful mix of cultures—exactly what my children needed.

We had hired a Sri Lankan helper, who initially started off well. I remember the time it all started to unravel—within just a few weeks. Carol and I were going out for dinner, and the taxi had picked us up. I'd asked our maid to please bath the children and put them to bed, as we had plans for the evening. As we headed off in the taxi, I realised I had forgotten something, so we turned around and headed back.

As I entered the house, I could hear squealing from the back garden. When I went to investigate, I saw Rory and Ailsa in their birthday suits, with our maid firing a hose at them, shampoo in hand. I asked, "What are you doing? I thought I told you to give them a bath." She looked at me and simply replied, "I thought this was a better idea." This, on top of a number of other more serious issues, meant we had to part ways with her—a decision I did not take lightly, as I had given her multiple chances. We needed to find a maid quickly, so we used an agency. Thankfully, we found a wonderful person named Ana, who remains a family friend to this day.

Within the offices, there was a theatre that would put any corporate setting to shame. It was like stepping onto the main deck of the Starship Enterprise, complete with state-of-the-art seating, crafted by Ferrari, and an audiovisual setup that would be the envy of the world. The design was nothing short of spectacular—a testament to the endless resources poured into the building.

The theatre quickly became a cherished space for me. Occasionally, on weekends, I would take Rory and Ailsa to explore its wonders. The kids would dash through the aisles, their excitement overflowing as they discovered the various models on display and explored the intricacies of the theatrical layout. There was something magical about the environment, and I loved watching their eyes light up with joy as they played. It was a playground for imagination and creativity, just as the builders had clearly envisioned.

No expense had been spared in crafting this magnificent building, and it reflected the ambition and forward-thinking nature of the company. Every corner sparkled with possibility, making it the perfect setting for brainstorming sessions, presentations, and the myriad creative endeavours that would unfold within its walls.

After my first few weeks in the new role, I began holding monthly meetings with the CEO, a man whose genius was well recognised. He was eccentric in his approach and had conceived the groundbreaking concept for the Palm—an iconic development that redefined luxury living in Dubai and could even be seen from space. His ideas were big, bold, and often unconventional, and I found our discussions stimulating and invigorating.

One particularly memorable meeting stands out in my mind. The CEO's office was as unique as the man himself, with plush furnishings and a leather floor—yes, a leather floor, folks! And then, there was his parrot—a colourful creature that flitted around the office, perched on desks, and chattered intermittently, adding an unexpected vibrancy to the environment. As I sat there discussing strategic initiatives, I was mesmerised by how the parrot glided through the air, a whimsical distraction amid our serious discussions.

In the blink of an eye, the parrot decided to land on the CEO's shoulder, and what happened next could only be described as both comical and slightly chaotic. Without warning, the parrot relieved itself, leaving a mess down the back of his dishdasha, the traditional attire he wore. I was taken aback, desperately trying to maintain my composure as I processed the absurdity of the scene unfolding before me.

Immediately, like a scene from a comedy, a small Indian man slipped into view from behind the CEO, brandishing a sponge and cloth as if he were a trained magician—a quiet professional whose job was to maintain the pristine appearance of the office and, apparently, the dignity of its occupants. As he sponged the mess from the CEO's back with an efficiency that was almost too surreal to believe, I was forced to suppress a laugh, my thoughts racing at this bizarre yet strangely endearing moment.

Despite the chaos, the conversation continued without missing a beat, demonstrating both the humour and resilience that often accompany corporate life. The contrast between serious business discussions and moments of levity left a lasting impression, reinforcing the idea that even in high-stakes situations, there are opportunities for humour and connection.

These experiences, woven throughout my time in Dubai, were a reminder of the joy and unpredictability of life, where unexpected moments can lead to laughter and insights. As I moved forward in my role, I embraced the unique, often eccentric culture around me, knowing it played a pivotal role in fostering creativity and connection. Life was a tapestry, enriched by its eclectic threads, from the spirits of playful children to the endearing humour of meetings with parroting CEOs.

Living in Dubai opened up a world of exploration and adventure, and my family and I seized every opportunity to discover the breathtaking landscapes and hidden gems scattered across the Emirates. One of our favourite excursions took us to Jebel Hafeet in Al Ain. The drive along the winding road that ascended the mountain was thrilling, with hairpin turns offering stunning views down into the valleys below. Though the scenery was magnificent, the rubber marks on the barriers served as a stark reminder of those who, in their haste, had misjudged the curves and lost control.

At the top of the mountain, we checked into the Mercure Hotel, where the views were nothing short of breathtaking. The sprawling landscapes below, beneath the vast Arabian sky, felt like something out of a fairy tale. The hotel itself was incredibly kid-friendly, with a sparkling pool and a variety of entertainment options that kept Rory and Ailsa enthralled. My children splashed around in the water, their laughter echoing in the warm air, leaving me with a heart brimming with joy.

One of the attractions of the hotel was a roller coaster that extended out to the edge of the mountain. It was always a topic of intrigue among guests and tourists, yet tragically, it was never in use due to safety concerns. The mere thought of speeding along the edge of a mountain on a roller coaster was exhilarating—it was the kind of adrenaline-pumping adventure that left you breathless. However, the reality of safety took precedence, and it remained closed. I often wondered how many other thrill-seekers had been disappointed by its absence, yearning for the rush that seemed destined to remain just out of reach.

Al Ain was also home to a wonderful zoo, another favourite destination for our family. We meandered through the beautifully landscaped grounds, where we encountered animals native to the region, marvelling at the vast array of wildlife on display. Each visit was a chance to engage with nature and learn about the majestic creatures that roamed our planet.

We ventured to the other Emirates, with Fujairah becoming a notable favourite for its stunning beaches and scenic mountains. The laid-back vibe of Fujairah provided a refreshing escape from the hustle and bustle of Dubai, with the peaceful sound of waves lapping against the shore creating the perfect backdrop for family memories.

One of the more adventurous outings included crossing the border into Oman, where we explored the Arabian fjords. This stunning area was a natural wonder, characterised by towering cliffs that rose dramatically out of the water, creating a landscape that felt both enchanting and serene. I recall standing in awe at the breathtaking views, feeling as if I had stepped into another world—an untouched paradise, far removed from the rapid pace of urban life.

There's an old saying in British culture: "They've gone round the bend." This refers to someone who has gone mad or suffered some sort of breakdown. The rumour was that during the British colonial days, there was an island around the corner of the fjord from the main fortress. Individual soldiers would be sent there for long periods, which could occasionally result in them going a little mad with loneliness—hence the saying. I have no idea if this is true, but it is plausible.

As we sailed around the fjords in a dhow, a traditional Arabic sailing boat, each bend in the water revealed new wonders, from shimmering waters to the vibrant green of lush vegetation that flourished in this coastal oasis. We all donned our snorkels and masks and swam amongst the beautiful fish—what a great experience for the children, I thought. Then, it was time to head back to Dubai.

As we navigated the winding roads, I found myself reflecting on the beauty of exploration, not just in a physical sense, but in the connections we forged and the memories we built as a family. The adventures in the Emirates became woven into the fabric of our lives, marking the moments that brought us closer, teaching us about culture, resilience, joy, and the magical wonders that lay hidden around every turn.

Ultimately, our time spent exploring these remarkable places not only brought joy and excitement but also instilled within us a profound appreciation for the richness of life and the adventures that lay ahead. In those moments, discoveries weren't merely about the destinations; they were about the experiences shared, the connections made, and the stories that would follow us home.

As the turbulent waves of the financial crisis slowly hit the operations in Dubai, I found myself at the beginning of a new chapter in my career—one that would lead me to a fresh corporate challenge and a new beginning on the picturesque island of Jersey. As with most of my roles, I had been headhunted—an opportunity that felt like a golden ticket amidst the uncertainty surrounding my recent experiences. The idea of relocating to Jersey was not only exciting but exhilarating, offering the chance to immerse myself in the world of Professional Services, an area that promised growth and discovery.

Before fully diving into my new role, I took the family for a "look-see" visit to Jersey, where we truly felt the weight of its lush, green charm, contrast against the busy world of business I'd left behind. However, calling the weather during my visit "bleak" would be an understatement. It was a stark contrast to the near-perfect warmth and sunshine I had grown accustomed to in December in Dubai. The skies were overcast, casting a muted hue over the landscape as I stepped off the ferry, while drizzle hung in the air like a persistent fog, competing with the gusty winds that swept across the coast.

Jersey, an island in the English Channel, was known for its stunning landscapes, charming villages, and strong sense of community. The transition felt refreshing; I was trading the sprawling expanses of Dubai for a more intimate environment, surrounded by rolling hills and picturesque coastlines. Leaving behind the chaos of my previous role meant I was ready to embrace the opportunities that came with this change.

For the first few weeks after our arrival in Jersey, we found ourselves in another temporary accommodation—an elegant apartment overlooking the beach in St. Helier. Each morning, I awoke to the soft sound of waves lapping at the shore, a tranquil reminder that we were finally settling into this new chapter of our lives. The views were nothing short of breathtaking, with the sun slowly rising over the horizon, painting the sky with hues of pink and gold.

As we explored different rental options around the island, we eventually came across a beautiful farmhouse that captured our hearts. Nestled in a serene setting high above St. Helier, the capital of the island, it offered everything we could have wished for, including its own swimming pool—a feature that sent Rory and Ailsa into a frenzy of excitement. The prospect of having their very own pool felt like an enviable luxury, and the children could barely contain their enthusiasm.

When we moved in, I remember gathering the kids in the hallway, their wide eyes taking in the new surroundings. "Enjoy this, kids," I told them, a proud smile spreading across my face. "This is the best house you will ever live in." I genuinely believed it, even in comparison to the stunning villa we had in Dubai's Lakes. While that home had its own charm, it paled in comparison to the magical ambiance radiating from this farmhouse.

The farmhouse was more than just a place to live; it felt like a sanctuary. Its rustic charm, combined with modern amenities, made it incredibly welcoming. The pool, surrounded by lush gardens and an expansive lawn, became a playground for the kids, where laughter echoed during sunny afternoons spent splashing and playing games.

My fondest memories of those early days involved evenings spent gathered around the dinner table, sharing stories of our adventures or winding down by the pool with the children as they splashed gleefully in the water. The atmosphere was alive with laughter and joy—an intoxicating blend of comfort and excitement that made us all feel at home.

As I looked around at our new surroundings, I felt a sense of peace settling in. The beautiful location, set against the backdrop of St. Helier's beaches, reminded me that we had made the right choice in moving here. The combination of sun, sea, and the warmth of island life provided a rejuvenating atmosphere that invigorated our spirits.

The farmhouse had become a canvas upon which our family's new chapter could be painted, filled with the vibrant colours of happiness, adventure, and connection. With every passing day, our new life began to take shape, and I knew that wherever our journeys led from here, they would be filled with the beauty and love we were cultivating in this idyllic setting.

Settling into the role presented its own set of challenges—but ones that felt invigorating. The first few weeks were a whirlwind of introductions, meetings, and learning about the nuances of the industry. The organisation was divided into Private Equity, private investors, and the C-Suite, and that alone brought another layer of complexity. I quickly realised the depth of talent within the organisation; my colleagues were brilliant, driven, and eager to make waves in the world of professional services.

Jersey's slower pace of life was a welcome change compared to the hustle and bustle I had become accustomed to in Dubai. The crisp sea air, along with the rhythms of island life, enveloped us in a comforting embrace. In my role, I had the opportunity to shape HR strategies in a way that enhanced the working environment, drawing from the lessons learned throughout my multifaceted career.

However, the transition to Jersey was not without its hiccups. Adjusting to a new environment took time, especially when it came to navigating local customs and forging connections in a community that, while warm, could sometimes feel somewhat insular. But as I reached out to my colleagues and built relationships, I began to find my footing. The charm of the island began to unfold before me in delightful ways.

Rory and Ailsa quickly adapted to their new surroundings as well. We had found them a village school just down the road, where they would once again experience the true meaning of village life and friendship. They explored the island's beaches, hiking trails, and family-friendly attractions, thrilled with the new experiences that awaited them. Their laughter echoed through our home, creating a sense of warmth amidst the shifts in our lives.

One particularly vivid memory from our early days in Jersey was the stunning countryside that surrounded us. Long walks became a staple, with the children marvelling at the rolling fields of wildflowers and the olive-green cliffs jutting into the sea—a stark, beautiful contrast to the urban landscapes we had previously inhabited.

In the summer months, Jersey seemed to host a different festival each weekend. Whether it was fish, wine, or boats, we attended and enjoyed them all.

However, within this tranquil setting, I became reacquainted with the complexities of both island and professional life. The nature of my role involved understanding global intellectual property law, a world filled with its own intricate challenges. My experience in negotiations—sharpened through my years in logistics and HR—proved invaluable as I navigated the needs of employees while supporting the broader corporate goals. I implemented new initiatives aimed at fostering engagement and enhancing our workplace culture, determined to create an environment where everyone felt valued. No matter how long you live on an island, if you were not born there, you are never truly seen as an islander—a lesson I learned over time.

Despite the dreary weather, Jersey evoked something within me—a nostalgic sense of familiarity. The island, with its charming villages and rugged coastlines, reminded me of my childhood in the late 60s and 70s—a time when life was distilled to simple joys and the passage of time seemed less dictated by technology and more by nature's rhythms.

Jersey emanated a certain timelessness. Its cobbled streets were lined with quaint shops and charming cafés, with age-old stone buildings standing proudly as testaments to history. The landscape was dotted with stunning cliffs and picturesque beaches, untouched by modernity. Fields of wildflowers and lush greenery flourished alongside the roads, evoking memories of the idyllic countryside back home.

One could almost hear the echoes of children's laughter as families strolled along scenic pathways, exploring the natural beauty that surrounded them. In some respects, it felt like stepping onto a movie set—a place where traditions echoed through past lives, and time had a different rhythm.

The harbour bustled with sailboats and fishing vessels, inviting visitors to discover its hidden coves and immerse themselves in the rich maritime history that defined the island. It was easy to lose track of time as I meandered through the streets, soaking in the vibrant culture and community that Jersey had to offer.

I especially appreciated the locals, who embodied a warm, welcoming nature. The community spirit was evident in the conversations at the market and the smiles exchanged in passing—everyone seemed connected, united by the rhythm of island life. Jersey was also world-famous for its cows, whose milk was unlike anything I'd ever tasted, not to mention the legendary Jersey Royal potatoes.

While I relished the charm of Jersey, I was also acutely aware of the task that lay ahead. The transformation of the global organisation into a company that appealed to potential investors was no small feat. I needed to streamline operations and present the strongest case for growth, all while navigating the complexities of life in a close-knit community.

Travel was always an integral part of my roles throughout my career, flying hundreds of thousands of airmiles, often taking me away from my family for extended periods. While many view business travel as a luxury and envision glamorous adventures in the front of the plane, the reality is far less glamorous, especially once it becomes routine. Yes, there I was, seated in business class, enjoying the comforts it offered, but after watching countless movies and eating enough airline food to fill a small diner, it grew tiresome.

On most flights, I would dive into work—drafting reports, preparing for meetings, and planning strategies. But once the work was done, I faced the question: then what? Long hours confined on a plane, with little to occupy my time beyond the standard inflight entertainment, became increasingly mundane. I found myself yearning for the comforts of home, the laughter of my children, and the familiarity of our daily lives—each of which seemed just a little farther away every time I boarded a flight.

A significant portion of my travels took me to India, where we had two major business units located in Gurgaon and Noida. Navigating Delhi's chaotic traffic could take up to an entire day, and the experience felt like a game of survival—a dramatic ballet of vehicles weaving through seemingly impossible gaps while horns blared incessantly. An Indian friend once shared the essential rules for driving there: "You need three things: a good horn, good brakes, and good luck." I often recalled his words as I made my way through the bustling streets—whether riding in company cars or dodging traffic myself.

As the team held board meetings around the globe, the CEO occasionally preferred to take us on private jet trips. I had to admit that while the flexibility and convenience of private air travel were tempting, it didn't quite match the comfort of commercial business class in terms of the overall experience. Yes, the benefits were clear— bypassing long check-ins and security lines made for a much quicker process. But the indulgence of commercial travel, where you could stretch out and enjoy higher-quality service, was something I missed.

On one such trip to Munich, I decided to voice my thoughts to the CEO about our travel arrangements. Given the leadership team would be flying on one private jet, I suggested we consider splitting our travel into commercial flights for half the team, to distribute the risk. "It's smarter," I explained, hoping he would be open to my suggestion. Yet, as I said this, he replied with a smile on his face, "no, this is cheaper."

I raised an eyebrow as we exited the plane in Germany, wondering how such a scenario would unfold. To my surprise, he quickly dismissed my suggestion, stating, "Leave it with me." I expected we might utilise commercial flights for the return journey, but I certainly hadn't anticipated what came next.

As we arrived at the airport and made our way to the cars, I quickly learned that he had arranged for two separate private jets for our return. "You take half on that one, and I'll take the other half over here. Problem solved!" he said with a confident smile To be fair, he had solved the risk problem!

I couldn't help but chuckle at his approach. It was creatively pragmatic, but it reinforced the reality that our world often operated on the wings of unpredictability and quick fixes. I respected his decisiveness yet felt an overwhelming sense of being caught in the chaos of corporate life—an ever-turning wheel that never truly stopped.

While travel took me far from home. The experiences carved out paths of understanding and growth that would serve me in countless ways as I continued my journey within the realms of business life

By this time, Rory had been diagnosed with autism, a revelation that sent a whirlwind of emotions swirling through our lives. While Carol and I loved our son deeply, we found ourselves holding differing views on how to approach his condition. I firmly believed that Rory could lead a fulfilling, independent life, rich with experiences like any other child. My thoughts were fuelled by the understanding that, with the right support and encouragement, he could find his own path and thrive.

On the other hand, Carol was never quite convinced that Rory would be able to navigate life without challenges. For her, the diagnosis signified an ongoing concern and a need for constant supervision and support, as well as medication. The differences in our perspectives led to countless discussions—some heartfelt, others strained—as we tried to determine the best way forward for our son.

We had irregular visits from a specialist who travelled from the mainland to assess Rory, offering insights and recommendations that sometimes left us feeling more confused than enlightened. Despite those assessments, the variability of professional opinions only added to the emotional weight we carried. I could sense Carol's worry; her protective instincts took over, shaping her perspective on what was best for Rory.

As time wore on and the complexities of parenting a child with autism unfolded, the difficulty of our situation became painfully clear. It was evident that Rory needed additional resources and support—ones we felt would be difficult to access while living on Jersey. After much deliberation whilst on a family Christmas holiday in St Lucia, , we reluctantly decided it was time for us to move back to the UK, where we hoped he would have better access to support as Rory's well-being took precedence over our desires for a lifestyle we had grown accustomed to.

Once the decision was made, we began preparations for our return to the UK. I focused on gathering all the necessary information about educational and medical resources that could help Rory transition smoothly. I wanted to ensure we were equipped with the right tools to support him effectively, no matter what challenges lay ahead.

Remembering the kindness and warmth of our friends and family back in the UK, I held onto the hope that returning home would provide us with both stability and a sense of community. The connections we would forge would not only support Rory but also help Carol and me navigate the complexities of our new reality as parents of a child with autism.

I could feel determination stirring within me. I was resolved to advocate for Rory, ensuring he had every opportunity to thrive. It became imperative that we embraced our journey with love, understanding, and, most importantly, an unwavering commitment to providing Rory with the best life possible—a life rich with potential, no matter how the world outside tried to define him.

This chapter in our story was one of growth and transformation, rooted in the love of family and the courage to face the unknown together. As we navigated this new terrain, I remained dedicated to learning, evolving, and finding joy in the little victories that made our path uniquely ours.

As we made our way back to our house in St Andrews, Scotland, we arranged for some building work to extend it, which meant spending our first month at a campsite with our caravan. Thankfully, it was summer, and the weather was particularly kind to us.

CHAPTER 38
To the Home of Golf

Returning to St Andrews, the home of golf and arguably the most famous golf course in the world, marked a significant shift in our family's journey. St Andrews is a coastal town, and we had purchased the house while living in Singapore, ensuring we had a base. The summer spent relaxing in the caravan was a delightful reprieve. The sound of rolling waves and the gentle breeze created an atmosphere of calm and tranquillity. With soft grass underfoot and picturesque landscapes surrounding us, it was a chance to reconnect with nature and one another.

Knowing my passion for golf, I managed to secure a residency links ticket, which included the famous Old Course—a dream come true. To qualify, you must have a permanent address within the boundary, and when we bought our house, we ensured it met that requirement. I joined The New Club, a prestigious establishment with a rich history in the golf world. I was especially fortunate to have gained entry, as Carol's connection to a former club captain paved the way for my membership. Luck had certainly been on my side, and I couldn't wait to immerse myself in the traditions and passion the club offered.

St Andrews is home to three main golf clubs, each steeped in history and prestige—the Royal and Ancient Golf Club, which organises The Open Championship and oversees the rules of golf in the UK and Europe; The St Andrews Club, traditionally catering to blue-collar workers; and, of course, The New Club, primarily for white-collar members, founded by the legendary Tom Morris in 1902. The New Club was notable not just for its rich legacy but also for having famously welcomed members like Bobby Jones, Arnold Palmer, and Tom Watson.

The atmosphere inside the club was as warm and inviting as the oak-panelled walls of the main bar suggested. I spent many afternoons overlooking the iconic Old Course, lost in the beauty of the landscape while enjoying a drink with fellow members. The grandeur of the club was a sight to behold, and I felt a deep sense of pride in being part of such a storied institution.

As our new home was finally completed, we moved in with eager hearts, settling into a spacious environment that felt both comforting and inviting. With Rory and Ailsa enrolled at the local primary school, their new friends filled the house with laughter, creating a joyful backdrop for family life.

Soon after settling in, I began working on a project involving the merger of two law firms in England. This new challenge was intriguing, if not a tad mundane. Nothing is quite as captivating as sitting down with a group of employment lawyers to discuss the ins and outs of their terms. Each conversation felt intricately woven into the fabric of a corporate world that was both familiar and starkly different at the same time.

My work routine developed a rhythm: I'd fly out of Dundee Airport on Monday morning, arriving at Birmingham Airport before heading to the main HQ for the morning, then travelling to Leicester for the week. I would return to Scotland on Friday afternoons. My temporary residence was a student accommodation flat in a converted warehouse, a stark contrast to the stability of family life. I quickly realised that I was probably the oldest person in the building by several years—a thought both amusing and slightly humbling.

The students in the flat seemed entertained by my presence, perhaps even sympathetic, as I ambled around with my briefcase and business attire amidst their lively, carefree living. They would often knock on my door, inviting me downstairs to join them at the swimming pool for a quick swim and a few beers. Who could turn that down? Though I felt a bit out of place amidst their youthful exuberance, those moments often turned into impromptu gatherings filled with laughter and fun, bridging the generational gap in unexpected ways.

I found myself enjoying the blend of my professional life with youthful chaos, balancing the serious nature of work with the delightful light-heartedness of student accommodation. These experiences added a new dimension to my life in St. Andrews, reinforcing my belief that connection, regardless of age or background, can create vibrant memories and enduring relationships.

As I embraced this new atmosphere, I felt grounded by my family and the community in St. Andrews. The summer days turned into joyful evenings spent with friends, whether from the golf club or my newfound student acquaintances, and these moments became integral to the life we were building together. Ultimately, it was the connection to both my family and the community that enriched this new chapter, creating bonds that would carry us through the years ahead.

As I spent much of my time away from St. Andrews, my circle of acquaintances outside the golf club remained small. My routine revolved around the courses, where I would simply drop in and join others for a round of golf.

It was on one of these occasions— to be precise, May 22, 2012— that I met a man who would soon become one of my closest friends and a trusted companion on many adventures around the world.

Sean was a wee Scottish guy from Alloa who had made St. Andrews his home. When he first spoke, his thick accent made it difficult for me to understand a word he said; honestly, to my untrained ears, it was simply an assortment of sounds! But the spirit of friends on the golf course is universal, and the excitement of the day quickly pushed any language barrier aside.

I distinctly remember the date of our meeting because it marked the beginning of a delightful string of events that would reshape my social life in St. Andrews. We teed off on the New Course, which opened in 1895 and is considered relatively "new" by St. Andrews standards, though its charm and history gripped me right away.

As we made our way around the course, excitement filled the air. At the fifth hole, an unexpected mishap occurred—while preparing for my shot, I somehow managed to slice my finger. I turned to Sean and asked if he had any plasters, but his answer was a simple "Naw." Despite the nagging pain, I resisted the temptation to walk off the course. No, I thought, this is good company. Let's carry on.

We pressed on to the ninth hole, a par 3 running alongside the estuary, with wild bushes lining the right side and a slight dogleg leading to the green. The hole stretched a challenging 235 yards, but I was determined to give it my all. I took out my 3-wood, steadied myself, and prepared for what felt like the most important swing of my golfing life. With a focused mind and a practiced motion, I struck the ball with a confidence I had never felt before.

To my sheer delight, the ball sailed beautifully towards the green. I looked up and noticed a four-ball on the 10th tee, uphill, jumping up and down in excitement. Sean, grinning widely, exclaimed in that unmistakable Scottish accent, "You've made a hole-in-one, big fella!"

I looked at him in disbelief as we walked towards the green. "Don't be daft, Sean... not a chance!" I replied, scepticism clouding my enthusiasm. But as we arrived, my heart racing, there it was—the ball sitting snugly in the hole.

Exhilaration flooded through me, and a burst of laughter erupted as we celebrated the moment together. The disbelief melted into pure joy, and sharing the excitement with Sean made it all the more special. We headed into the clubhouse afterward, beaming with pride. To commemorate my incredible achievement, I received a certificate confirming my hole-in-one, and for a few months, my name adorned the drinks carts—an undeniable badge of honour within the golf community.

So, that's how I came to remember the date I met Sean—an intersection of friendship and the thrill of the game, bonded by laughter in the face of my triumph. That day marked the beginning of a strong friendship, one that would bring adventure and shared experiences beyond the golf course.

Through countless rounds of golf and evenings filled with fun, and a few cold beers Sean became an integral part of my life in St. Andrews, reminding me that friendships can blossom in the most unexpected moments. Our paths crossed through the spirit of the game, and I knew we were destined for more adventures, all fuelled by the shared joy of living life to the fullest.

Although I was enjoying my time in St. Andrews and the legal project, I began to feel restless for overseas work again.

On top of that, my marriage was starting to break down, and time apart might have helped smooth things over. Rory was now settled and thre was no more real concern for him. When a search firm I knew in Dubai called with an opportunity at a leading US insurance organisation, I jumped at the chance. And just like that, it was back to the sandpit for me!

CHAPTER 39
A Solo Return to Dubai

This time, my journey back to Dubai was a solo trip, with the children well-settled in their school back in the UK and Rory soon transitioning to secondary school. With such significant milestones on the horizon for them, it felt both exciting and bittersweet to be heading back to the city that had once felt like home.

Upon arrival, I spent my first month in serviced accommodation—standard procedure for expats adjusting to life in Dubai. The apartment was conveniently located just a short walk from HQ in the Gate Building of the Dubai International Financial Centre (DIFC), an iconic locale that had gained global recognition, particularly after being featured in the Mission: Impossible film series. It was exhilarating to be in such a prestigious setting again, surrounded by the bustling energy of finance and commerce.

The people were incredibly welcoming, and I quickly forged great friendships within the office. After spending time enjoying time with my new work colleagues, we began socialising outside of work, playing golf most weekends under the radiant Dubai sun. As part of my expat package, I was granted membership to The Dubai Creek Country Club, allowing me to once again indulge in my love for the game while deepening my connections with my colleagues.

Settling into my role within financial services felt seamless; I was invigorated and ready to take on new challenges. During my first year back, Carol, Rory, and Ailsa came out to visit for several holidays. By now, Dubai was much more established than it had been on my previous visits. The road systems were nearly complete, and the city felt more connected and accessible than ever before.

I had managed to secure a fabulous apartment in Downtown Dubai—one that felt more like a villa with its gardens and waterfalls, a hidden oasis amidst the city's concrete jungle. Though it was built above a car park, you would never have known. From the pool, I could look up at the Burj Khalifa, the tallest building in the world, and marvel at its magnificence. It was a surreal experience to feel the blend of luxury and excitement as I embraced my new home.

As my role expanded, I was entrusted with managing large human resources and business projects, one of which involved relocating our finance operations and establishing analytics and tech centres in India. This was no small task; it required careful planning and execution to ensure that all processes aligned with our global objectives. The scale of these projects meant spending significant time in India, and I found myself increasingly engaged as a Board Director there.

Bangalore became my hub of operations—a bustling, vibrant city where life thrived amidst the hectic pace. Like much of India, traffic was omnipresent, and the constant symphony of car horns and street vendors created a cacophony that defined the city's character. The culture was rich, the people warm, and each interaction brought new insights into the complexities of doing business in such a dynamic environment.

Seeking some sanctuary from the chaos, I found refuge at The Marriott Hotel, a stark contrast to the hectic streets outside. Its serene atmosphere and luxurious surroundings provided me with a much-needed escape after long days filled with meetings and negotiations.

As time passed, family visits dwindled, and it was primarily Rory and Ailsa who came for holidays. Ailsa sometimes struggled with travel, but thankfully, Rory made it out as often as he could—his presence a welcome boost to my spirits during those solo stretches. My good friend Sean from St. Andrews would often accompany them, bringing laughter and connection, reminding me of the beautiful friendships I had forged over the years.

The hardest part of working away was being apart from my children, and I missed them dearly with all my heart when they weren't with me. I flew back as often as I could. Once, I even flew home just to watch Rory play in his school football team. I didn't tell him—I simply turned up at the touchline and shouted my support.

Despite the challenges I faced during my time in Dubai, each experience reaffirmed the importance of family and friendship in navigating the complexities of life. The memories of adventures shared with Rory, Ailsa, and Sean left lasting impressions on my heart, reminding me of the love and support that anchored me through every new challenge.

As I stood on my balcony, overlooking Dubai's impressive skyline, I felt a calm in my life like never before. Life was an ever-evolving journey, shaped by the connections forged and the experiences shared, and I was ready to embrace whatever came next with open arms and a grateful heart.

Noel, my friend from our days at Dubai World, was still living in the city when I returned from my stint in Jersey. We soon began discussing a practical solution to the financial strain of living alone in such an extravagant place. The idea was simple—Noel would move into my apartment, and we would share the rental costs.

As a property lawyer, Noel had always been sharp and insightful, possessing a level of professionalism and expertise that I greatly admired. By this point, he was in his fifties, a dedicated vegetarian, and an interesting character in his own right. Despite his many accolades, however, Noel's cooking skills were comparable to those of my mother, Dottie. To put it bluntly, I suspected he had never moved beyond his student cooking days, which often left me stepping into the role of chef in our shared home.

This unexpected arrangement became a delightful chapter of my life. I took on the culinary responsibilities, whipping up dinners and feasts, while Noel contributed his expertise in wine pairings and dietary nuances. We became something of a sitcom duo, embodying the classic trope of men behaving badly, with boisterous cocktail nights at home becoming our signature events. Our living room often transformed into a makeshift bar, where creativity flowed as freely as the drinks—each concoction a testament to our shared adventurous spirits. Oh, our poor livers! When Christmas would arrive, we would go into Dubai Mall and purchase the cheesiest of decoration and lights. We even had a large singing Santa in the living room.

One memorable weekend, we decided to take the Maserati GranTurismo for a drive. The sleek performance vehicle promised luxury and thrills, so we set off towards the Waldorf Astoria in Ras Al Khaimah (RAK). Our laughter echoed through the cabin as we sped down the highways, the powerful Ferrari-built engine roaring beneath us, adding to the excitement of the drive.

Upon our arrival at the Waldorf, Noel's mischievous nature took centre stage. As we parked, he stepped out of the passenger side, clutching a trendy man bag with flair, silently daring the world to take notice. He swayed his hips playfully, revelling in the moment. The valet approached, momentarily taken aback, as Noel strutted towards the entrance with an air of confidence that was both amusing and impressive. I couldn't help but shake my head and laugh, watching the spectacle unfold beside me.

Noel never failed to entertain, even in the simplest of moments. He was also a loyal friend—someone you could count on when life's challenges arose.

As the weeks turned into months, our friendship deepened, reflecting the joys of two individuals navigating life together in a city brimming with adventure. What had started as a practical arrangement of sharing living expenses had evolved into shared laughter, stories, and invaluable life lessons. We had not only created a comfortable home but had also built a solid friendship, rooted in mutual respect, humour, and the shared belief that life is meant to be enjoyed. When the children visited, Noel would either check into a hotel or return to the UK to spend time with his own family.

In the grand scheme of my life, this chapter reminded me of the importance of connection, the beauty of friendship, and the moments that bring joy amid the chaos. With friends like Noel by my side, I knew I could embrace whatever adventures awaited me on the horizon—one cocktail night and spontaneous drive at a time.

CHAPTER 40
Holidays with Rory and Ailsa

I would arrange summer holidays in various parts of Europe, as well as back in the UK with Rory and Ailsa. These trips became a cherished tradition for the three of us, allowing us to bond and create lasting memories in beautiful destinations. One adventure that stands out in my mind is our trip to Lanzarote, an island famed for its stunning landscapes, unique volcanic terrain, and vibrant culture. With the promise of sunshine and excitement ahead, I was eager to explore everything this island had to offer with my two enthusiastic children.

Determined to make the most of our time, I decided that hiring a car would be the perfect way to navigate the island. Ailsa, craving a touch of adventure, specifically requested a soft-top Beetle. Once booked, their excitement was plain to see, as we eagerly anticipated the joy of cruising along under the sun's warm embrace.

With no set itinerary, I proposed a spontaneous exploration plan: each day, we would randomly select a location via the sat nav and hit the road towards whatever our hearts desired. It was an exhilarating way to discover Lanzarote—no rigid schedules or tourist traps, just the freedom to stumble upon hidden gems along the way.

Each drive became an adventure, leading us off the beaten tourist track to experience old villages steeped in history. We wandered through quaint streets lined with charming, whitewashed houses adorned with colourful flowers and browsed local shops brimming with artisanal crafts. Every stop felt like uncovering a treasure trove of culture, history, and the warm spirit of the people who called Lanzarote home.

"Look, Dad! An aloe vera factory!" Ailsa shouted, so we pulled over to explore. Arms laden with every kind of skincare product imaginable, we piled back into the car, ready for our next discovery.

Lunch was another exciting exploration as we sampled delicious local dishes at restaurants tucked away from the usual tourist spots. Of course, every meal had to come with French fries—a staple for most of our adventures. From freshly caught seafood to traditional Canarian cuisine, each dish was an opportunity to indulge in new tastes and flavours. Some we loved; others were a little too adventurous for our liking. But the laughter shared over our culinary discoveries only brought us closer, strengthening our bond through shared experiences.

We also stumbled upon the occasional pizzeria—a particularly good one in Puerto del Carmen for a touch of Italian. After all, who doesn't love Italian food?

Naturally, we made sure to carve out relaxing days at the beach, soaking up the sun and enjoying the gentle ocean waves. We swam in both the inviting sea and our hotel pool, laughter ringing out as the children splashed and played. To add an extra touch of fun, I bought an assortment of floats, much to Rory and Ailsa's delight. They eagerly leapt into the water with their floaties, thrilled to experience the simple, carefree joy of sun-drenched days by the sea.

Reflecting on our holiday in Lanzarote, I realised it was more than just a trip. It was a collection of moments filled with joy, laughter, and exploration—an irreplaceable time that would forever be etched in our memories. The spontaneity of our adventures showed us the beauty of embracing the unknown, highlighting the importance of togetherness and the magic found in everyday explorations.

These treasured experiences would serve as reminders of the simple joys of life—of how travelling as a family can evolve into golden moments of laughter and learning. Although the trips with Ailsa were becoming less frequent, we still had fun whenever we were together, and I cherished every moment with my two wonderful children. Such moments reaffirmed my belief that even the most unexpected journeys can lead to the best adventures, and I knew that as a family, we would continue to explore and celebrate life, wherever it might take us.

The next holiday brought a flood of mixed feelings for me. By this time, Carol and I had gone through a very messy divorce, an experience fraught with upheaval and tension. Sadly, it had turned into a painful battle, with Carol trying to poison the children against me—an emotionally charged situation that weighed heavily on my heart. To be honest, the fallout had been building for years, and I had only delayed pursuing a separation for the sake of Rory and Ailsa, striving to create stability in their lives, even as my own was unravelling.

Amidst this turmoil, I had booked a holiday to Sorrento on the Amalfi Coast, one of the most breathtaking coastal regions in the world. This trip felt like an opportunity—a chance to escape the drama and create priceless memories with Rory. Ailsa had chosen not to join us, making the journey a special one-on-one adventure that I was determined to fill with joy.

As we boarded the plane, I felt a surge of anticipation, ready to embrace everything Sorrento had to offer. The flight was filled with laughter and excitement as Rory and I flipped through travel guides, eagerly discussing all the sights we planned to explore. I had secured a hotel perched on a clifftop, complete with a lift that descended to the beach, offering breathtaking views of the sparkling Mediterranean Sea.

Once in Sorrento, it was clear the place was magical. The picturesque streets were lined with vibrant shops, and the coastal landscape revealed its beauty at every turn. Rory and I set out to explore, indulging in gelato, fresh pastries, and the local cuisine. One unforgettable day took us to Pompeii, where history seemed to come alive through the ruins.

As we wandered through the ancient streets, we found ourselves repeatedly singing the theme song from the sitcom featuring Frankie Howerd—a comedian and actor from York who was a distant relative of my Auntie Jean. The playful absurdity of our singing stood in stark contrast to the solemn history of Pompeii, yet it filled our adventure with laughter and lightness. The intertwining of my past with our present created a bond that felt both meaningful and comforting.

We savoured some of the most exquisite Italian food during our travels, each meal bursting with flavour and authenticity. Naturally, we couldn't resist the chance to enjoy limoncello; it became our celebratory drink of choice, whether after a sumptuous meal or while basking in the sun on the terrace.

Our hotel boasted a lovely swimming pool, and although it was the end of summer, Rory was eager to take a dip. I remember him bounding towards the pool with uncontainable enthusiasm, his swimming gear at the ready. I, on the other hand, hesitated—the water looked a bit too brisk for my liking.

With a carefree spirit, Rory shot past me and leapt straight into the pool. To my amusement, I had never seen anyone exit water so quickly. It was as if he had transformed into a Polaris submarine missile, rocketing out of the pool in a flurry of splashes, wide-eyed with shock. Shivering and dripping, he wrapped himself in a towel before turning to me with an exaggerated expression of disbelief.

"Let's go, Dad, it's bloody freezing!"

I couldn't help but laugh all the way back to our room, the light-hearted moment easing my mind and grounding me amidst the challenges around me. By embracing the joy of our journey together, we created a beautiful memory to cherish.

Reflecting on this trip, I realised that despite the complexities of my life and the turbulent emotions surrounding my divorce, I still had the power to create joy for myself and Rory. The laughter we shared during our adventures in Sorrento reminded me that family bonds—built on love and connection—could withstand adversity and flourish in the moments of happiness we carved out for ourselves. Still, the pain of Ailsa not joining us on our holiday would add to a certain disappointment

In between family holidays, I seized the opportunity to recharge by taking advantage of national holidays to head to Thailand with my friend Phil and a group of fellow golfers. It became a cherished ritual—offering a break from the responsibilities of parenthood and a chance to reconnect with old friends over a few rounds of golf and plenty of cold beers.

Our trips to Thailand were infused with spirit of adventure. We often made our way down Bangla Road, my old stomping ground from my days in Singapore where the nightlife buzzed with energy. The laughter we shared at the vibrant bars echoed long into the night; it felt like stepping into a spontaneous landscape of revelry, reminiscent of our youthful days.

As for the golf courses, we were fortunate to play on some of the most spectacular links in the region. Red Mountain Golf Club, with its breathtaking layout, offered a challenging course that wound through stunning vistas and dramatic scenery. Each hole presented its own unique demands, testing our skills while immersing us in the beauty of the landscape. I revelled in the thrill of the game, each swing of the club lifting my spirits.

Blue Canyon, another of our favourites, exuded both prestige and character. The course was a well-manicured masterpiece, framed by lush greenery and striking mountains in the backdrop. The sheer beauty of the place, combined with the camaraderie of teeing off, made for unforgettable days on the green. We often debated who would emerge victorious after a round, but in the end, the real victory lay in the shared memories we created with friends.

After completing our rounds, we would often gather to clutch our trophies—beer bottles—and recount the day's events in exaggerated detail. Every miss and near hole-in-one became a story retold with increasing embellishment. The thrill of competition blended seamlessly with the joy of friendship, as if we were honouring a sense of brotherhood that transcended the game itself.

As we enjoyed the golf and friendship, I realised these trips were more than just holidays. They were vital respites that recharged me mentally and emotionally, allowing me to return to work with renewed vigour and perspective.

Looking back on those golf trips, I appreciate how they provided a balance between my responsibilities as a father and my need for recreation and connection. In that vibrant world of Thailand, surrounded by breathtaking landscapes and filled with the laughter of friends, I found moments of escape—temporary retreats where worries and stresses faded away, allowing me to embrace the pure joy of being alive

Phil and I effortlessly fell into a routine of enjoying weekend nights out in Dubai, often joined by our good friends Mark and Bruce. The city's vibrant nightlife always beckoned, drawing us into adventure, and we found plenty of spots to indulge our love of fun and music.

One standout venue was the Sea View Hotel, a popular spot renowned for its vibrant atmosphere and live music. Evenings there were electric, filled with the captivating sounds of Filipino bands—some of the finest musicians I've ever had the pleasure of hearing. They played tirelessly, gliding seamlessly between classic hits and contemporary favourites, their harmonies rich and soulful.

The connection between the performers and the audience was clear; we often found ourselves swept up in the rhythm, dancing and singing alongside strangers who quickly became friends. Each performance felt like a celebration, the warmth of the atmosphere radiating through the room, uniting everyone in shared joy.

Another favourite hangout was The Stables, a lively bar with a unique charm. The ambiance resembled a rustic pub but carried a distinct equestrian theme. Adorned with horse memorabilia, its warm décor created a welcoming and relaxed atmosphere. After a long day, we often gathered there, enjoying cold beers and hearty meals, balancing good food with lively conversations.

The Stables also featured a dedicated space for live music, where talented house bands reminded us how much we appreciated Dubai's vibrant music scene.

Joules, a trendy nightspot, was another staple in our regular circuit. With its chic interior and infectious energy, Joules delivered electrifying nights filled with live performances and a lively crowd. The atmosphere pulsed with excitement, and the dynamic mix of music created an exquisite blend of sounds that kept everyone on their feet. It was the kind of place where we often ended our nights, our voices hoarse from singing along to our favourite tunes, our faces sore from laughter.

To complete our triumvirate of treasured haunts, we often found ourselves at the York Hotel, a charming establishment that exuded comfort and hospitality. With its elegant furnishings and welcoming staff, the York provided the perfect setting for both casual gatherings and celebratory events.

The bar area carried an air of sophistication, offering a relaxed and inviting retreat after a long week of work. Here, we shared stories, made toasts, and enjoyed each other's company while soaking in the serene ambiance.

Each visit enriched our social lives and highlighted the unique fabric of Dubai's nightlife. These nights out were not just about the venues themselves but about the friendships strengthened over laughter, music, and unforgettable moments. We explored mew depths of friendship as shared the late-night chats, games of pool and the inevitable mischief that came with such outings.

Amidst the glitz and glamour of the city, I cherished these outings with Phil, Mark, and Bruce, realizing that each venue offered more than just entertainment—they provided a space for connection, personal growth, and countless memories I would carry forward. Through it all, the spirit of friendship thrived, reminding me that life's most cherished experiences often stem from the simplest moments shared with those we hold dear.

Even after Phil left the organisation, our friendship remained steadfast, transcending the corporate walls that had first brought us together. Dubai's vibrant social scene and endless opportunities for fun gave us plenty of reasons to keep meeting and savouring our time together. Our bond had been forged through shared experiences, and I was determined not to let his departure mark the end of our adventures.

Phil's departure from the organisation was one of those bittersweet moments; while we were sad to see him go, we understood that life often led us down different paths. He ventured into new endeavours elsewhere, carrying with him a sense of excitement for what lay ahead. I admired his willingness to embrace change and was determined to continue our friendship despite the shifting landscape of our lives.

We made a point of going out regularly, setting aside time in our busy schedules to reunite over beers or dinner. Sometimes, we gathered with our other friends, Mark and Bruce, often returning to our favourite venues like the Sea View Hotel or The Stables. Those nights were a blend of nostalgia and new memories, where laughter.

On various occasions, we explored new places, seeking out hidden gems in the city. There was a certain thrill in discovering quaint cafés, unassuming bars, and lively outdoor markets, each adding an element of surprise to our outings. Every experience together reminded me of the joy of friendship—how shared laughter and unfiltered conversations strengthened our bond.

Phil brought a unique energy to our gatherings, his humour and spirit infusing every meetup with warmth and delight. Whether we were exchanging light-hearted banter over a pint or diving into deep discussions about life, work, and our aspirations, our time together always felt meaningful. Those moments became a welcome reprieve from the fast-paced world we inhabited—a necessary reminder of the importance of connection and support in navigating the challenges of adult life.

CHAPTER 41
Back into the Fray, My Friends

Several months after the divorce, a dear friend approached me with a hopeful question: "Are you interested in dating again?" They had known that I'd been unhappy in my marriage for a number of years. It was a question I had both dreaded and anticipated. The thought of re-entering the dating scene sent a wave of mixed emotions through me. I reflected on my past experiences and the heartaches they had brought, making me hesitate.

Honestly, I responded with a resolute shake of my head. "I'm done with women and relationships," I said bluntly, the words spilling out before I could fully process their weight. The idea of putting myself back out there felt overwhelming. I wasn't ready to dive back into the complexities of emotional entanglement—especially while still navigating the aftermath of my marriage and the whirlwind of life as a father

It was, however, a curious thing—living in a city like Dubai, brimming with energy, vibrant social circles, and, inevitably, a fair share of working girls. It was something of a lottery. This made it difficult not to feel tempted by the idea of genuine connection. Yet, within me, there remained a barrier—a protective shield forged by past experiences that had left me wary of vulnerability.

My friend, seeing the resolve in my eyes, offered her understanding but didn't abandon the idea of companionship for me. "Life is short, Simon," she reminded me gently. "You deserve happiness and connection. You're a really nice guy—funny and friendly." Her sincerity lingered in my thoughts, igniting a spark of contemplation about what it truly meant to open myself up again.

As I sat with those thoughts, I noticed how my perspective gradually began to shift. I realised that while I had built defences to shield myself from further hurt, I was also denying myself the possibility of happiness and companionship. Love and connection had always been integral to life—something I had experienced deeply—even amidst the turmoil.

Days passed, and I found myself contemplating the idea of dating—not with trepidation, but with curiosity. Maybe, just maybe, it was time to consider letting someone in again. I began reflecting on what I truly wanted—a partner who could understand my journey, share in life's adventures, and perhaps even bring a little joy and laughter back into my world.

While I wasn't ready to jump headfirst into the dating scene, I acknowledged the possibility of new connections and began to embrace the idea of stepping out of my comfort zone. I started approaching it with an open heart, reflecting on the possibilities while still holding space for the lessons I had learned along the way.

Our conversations in the months that followed evolved into discussions about what dating looked like now—what connections to seek and the kind of person I wanted to welcome into my life. Meanwhile, I continued to focus on the priorities that mattered most: being a dedicated father, nurturing relationships, and ensuring that any decisions I made regarding dating stemmed from genuine interest rather than loneliness or fear.

After my initial reservations about dating again, my friend reassured me by mentioning that she knew a girl who would be perfect for me. Intrigued, I agreed to meet her, and that's how I found myself dating Winan, a lovely Thai woman who worked at a spa in one of Dubai's main hotels. Our first few dates were filled with laughter and connection, yet anticipation built as it took five dates before she would even kiss me—much to the hilarity of Phil and our other friends, who couldn't resist teasing me about the prolonged wait.

Despite the playful ribbing, I appreciated the slow pace at which our relationship blossomed. Winan carried an air of grace that intrigued me, and with each meeting, I found myself drawn closer to her charm, wit, and kind spirit. Winan was also a fiercely independent lady, never been married before and no children. She had her own money, land and property and although it didn't matter to me, it was reassuring.

Introducing Rory and Ailsa to Winan was a significant step in our relationship. The timing was crucial; too soon, and things might have gone wrong, too late, and the introduction would feel like a poorly kept secret. In hindsight, I waited a little too long. Looking back, my biggest regret is that I didn't introduce them sooner; I'd advise anyone in a similar situation to act sooner rather than later, avoiding the risk of your children learning about the new relationship from some kind soul, who could not wait to tell them!

Once everyone had met and spent some time together, we began planning a family holiday. Thailand, the "Land of Smiles," was the obvious destination to immerse Rory and

Ailsa in a new culture. We flew to Scotland to collect them before heading to Phuket. The next day found us all arriving in Thailand, excited and ready for adventure. Winan showed them around the island, visiting iconic landmarks like the Big Buddha and exploring less-touristed temples and cultural sites. Then, we journeyed to Bangkok, visiting the Emerald Palace and other significant landmarks, as well as the many shopping malls. Rory and Ailsa loved experiencing the Thai culture, and it was clear that Winan found immense joy in sharing her heritage with them. The trip concluded, and it was time to return home to Scotland. Ailsa, with a new found attachment, immersed herself in trying to learn the Thai language.

After about twelve months of dating, we reached a mutual decision—we wanted to get married. However, our approach was quite different from the traditional UK model. We preferred an uncomplicated arrangement, opting for a marriage certificate without the need for a formal ceremony, which would simplify visa processes rather than add complexities. It felt right for us, reflecting our unique journey. To make this happen, I arranged for a lawyer in Thailand to handle the paperwork.

Once the arrangements were made by our lawyers, we set off on a trip to Bangkok, eager to begin the process. Upon arriving at the British Embassy, we submitted our documentation, and a wave of anticipation and excitement washed over me. The process was straightforward, but I couldn't help but notice an older, flustered British man struggling to navigate the paperwork, a young Thai girl by his side. Watching him fumble through the forms was both amusing and slightly concerning, as the personnel behind the counter grew increasingly frustrated with his—shall we say—disorganised attempt.

Within ten minutes, our paperwork was handed back to us, and we were instructed to head to the Thai government building to complete our registration. Following the directions given, we entered the building and were met with a chaotic array of desks manned by officials, the atmosphere bustling with activity. We took a number—reminiscent of a deli counter at the grocery store—and patiently waited our turn.

As our number was called, excitement bubbled within me. In those moments leading up to our appointment, I felt the weight of anticipation and the significance of what we were about to undertake. I held Winan's hand tightly, a deep sense of unity and partnership settling between us.

We sat at the desk as the administrator meticulously reviewed everything, ensuring we fully understood the process. Next to me sat an older gentleman, European by the look of him, accompanied by a young woman. She was clearly a "bar girl," with numerous tattoos marking her skin. I couldn't help but be intrigued by what was happening beside us.

After about five minutes, the man suddenly jumped up, turned on his heel, and bolted out the door. Winan looked over before stepping in to console the young woman, who had begun to cry. It turned out the man had got cold feet and done a runner, leaving her behind. The saddest part? This was the third time it had happened to her. Clearly, marriage wasn't destined for her just yet.

Once our paperwork was finalised at the government building, we stepped outside, feeling triumphant. We had forged a legally binding commitment without the traditional fanfare.

Even though it was like buying a toaster, and nothing like a wedding, I had wished my children had been present, even though it was a long way to travel for what was around 5 mins in the sterile government building

We returned to Dubai and carried on with our lives. After several months, I was approached to join a world-leading airline, so once again, it was time to leave Dubai and move on. Six years had passed in the blink of an eye, and as we prepared for this new chapter, I realised that this next adventure would shape the course of our future together. The excitement of what lay ahead mingled with gratitude for the journey we had travelled. Through it all, I knew that the bond I had formed with Winan would sustain us as we embraced new beginnings in another part of the world, laying the foundation for a life filled with love and shared experiences.

Our move brought the promise of fresh opportunities, and I was determined to nurture our relationship, building a partnership that would withstand both the challenges and joys that life had in store. Together, we were ready to step into the unknown—hand in hand, with hearts full of hope and excitement for the future that awaited us.

CHAPTER 42
New Beginnings in Qatar

As we prepared for our move to Qatar, Winan decided to return to Thailand while I settled into our new life. She had invested time and energy into building our home there and wanted to ensure that all the construction work went according to plan. I admired her dedication. While she travelled back, I focused on making arrangements for my own relocation.

Upon my arrival in Qatar, I stayed in a hotel for a few weeks while waiting for my executive apartment to be ready. The accommodation was luxurious, situated on the 18th floor of a towering building on The Pearl—an exquisite development overlooking the ocean. The views were nothing short of breathtaking, with vistas stretching to the horizon and stunning sunsets painting the sky in vivid hues. Each room offered glimpses of the vibrant sea, a constant reminder of how fortunate I was to be embarking on this new chapter.

Once I was settled, Winan eventually arrived to join me, and together, we revelled in the excitement of exploring our new surroundings. Just as things were starting to feel like home again, Rory, having finished school, expressed a desire to come and live with us. We were overjoyed at the idea of having him join our new adventure, so we wasted no time in making the necessary arrangements.

When Rory flew out to Qatar, I was filled with anticipation. I remember the moment I saw him—he stepped off the plane sporting a haircut that made him look like a farmer's scarecrow: wild, untamed, and in desperate need of grooming. Winan, always the epitome of kindness and care, chuckled and said, "Don't worry, I'll take him to the barber tomorrow." I was relieved that she was so eager to help him adjust to this new environment.

The next day was transformative. Winan took Rory to the barber, and when they returned, I could scarcely recognise him. His new haircut was stylish and modern, seamlessly fitting into the vibrant lifestyle of Qatar. He looked handsome—no longer the dishevelled child I had seen just the day before, but a young man exuding the quiet confidence of youth as he embraced the changes unfolding around him.

Winan embraced her role in Rory's life with enthusiasm. She took him under her wing, thoughtfully introducing him to contemporary clothing styles and ensuring he had everything he needed to settle into his new home. But beyond fashion, she focused on imparting essential life skills that had somehow eluded him until then.

Rory began learning how to cook, manage laundry, and take care of himself under Winan's gentle guidance. I watched with pride as they settled into this new rhythm together; I could see a bond forming between them, built on mutual respect and care. Cooking lessons turned into shared laughter in the kitchen, and with each dish prepared, I saw my son grow more confident and self-reliant.

As we settled into our new life in Qatar, Winan adjusted to being a homemaker while I focused on my career. With Rory gradually adapting to his new environment and our family dynamics taking shape, Winan decided it was time to welcome a new member into our family. After much consideration, we agreed that a dog would be the perfect addition—one that would bring even more joy and energy into our home.

And so began our journey to find the right companion. We researched various breeds and decided on an Australian Labradoodle—a breed known for its friendly temperament, intelligence, and hypoallergenic qualities. After connecting with a reputable breeder in the UK, we eagerly prepared for her arrival. Over the course of several months, we waited in growing anticipation, excited to welcome Krapow into our lives—a name that captured our adventurous spirit and paid homage to the Thai cuisine we both loved.

Finally, the day of her arrival came, and I was bursting with excitement as we prepared our apartment for our new furry friend. We made sure everything was in place—her bed, toys, food bowls, and treats—all ready for her to explore and claim as her own.

When Krapow arrived, it was love at first sight. Her soft, curly fur and exuberant personality immediately captured our hearts. However, our joy took an unexpected turn when, in what can only be described as a classic case of first-day nerves, she bolted into the bedroom and left a massive poo right on the bed. It was a comically disastrous introduction that left us momentarily speechless before we burst into laughter at the sheer absurdity of the situation. "What a great start!" I exclaimed, shaking my head in disbelief.

Krapow, of course, seemed completely unfazed by our reactions, happily trotting around her new home as if to say, "I'm here, and I'm ready for adventure!" While we scrambled to clean up the mess—an unexpected welcome gift from our new family member—our hearts swelled with affection, nonetheless.

As the days passed, Krapow quickly settled into our family routines, joining us on outings and adventures. She became a constant source of joy and laughter, her playful spirit breathing new life into our household. Winan took on the role of primary caregiver, nurturing Krapow's training and embracing her mischievous antics, while Rory spent countless hours playing with her in the gardens and parks.

Krapow was not just a dog; she became an invaluable companion for the family, a source of comfort and a gentle presence in our lives. The bond formed was heartwarming—each wag of her tail and playful nudge offered endless affection and created rich memories. It was incredible to watch Rory and Ailsa grow even closer as they navigated the joys of having a pet and shared the responsibility of caring for Krapow.

In those moments, I marvelled at how a simple addition to our family could foster such profound connections. As laughter echoed through our apartment, I was reminded of life's beautiful unpredictability and how every experience we shared—be it the joy of welcoming Krapow or the occasional mishaps—continued to weave the narrative of our family.

While Qatar was not the most exhilarating place in the world, especially when compared to the vibrant pulse of Dubai, it offered a sense of tranquillity that we grew to appreciate. The atmosphere was quieter, and the pace of life slowed considerably. Yet, this change was refreshing—a sanctuary that felt safe and clean, qualities we valued highly against the backdrop of our busy lives.

There was plenty to do in Qatar, even if it wasn't the bustling paradise of our previous home. One of our favourite weekend activities was going to the cinema. The experience was far from ordinary; in Qatar, a trip to the movies was akin to indulging in a lavish night out. We often opted for large recliner seats, sinking into comfort as we wrapped ourselves in blankets and enjoyed a three-course meal—all while watching the latest films unfold on the big screen. It transformed the simple act of watching a movie into an extravaganza, a cherished ritual that allowed us to bond as a family.

In fact, we visited the cinema so often that our car's sat nav began to recognise our routine, frequently prompting us with the question, "Are you going to the Mall of Qatar?" This little quirk became a running joke among us, like a reliable friend reminding us of our weekend plans, and it soon became part of the fabric of our new life.

However, one of the aspects of living in Qatar that brought us immense joy was Krapow's daily adventures at Fur Camp. This pet daycare facility was a veritable paradise for dogs, offering a space where our furry friend could play with others, have fun, and be pampered like the princess she was. Each morning, we would drop her off, and the staff treated her with the utmost care, ensuring she had plenty of time to socialise and play.

In true Middle Eastern fashion, Fur Camp provided an environment brimming with joyous energy. They even sent us videos halfway through the day, capturing Krapow having the time of her life—running around and interacting with her canine friends. Each clip filled our hearts with joy and relief; it truly felt like a Royal daycare for dogs. Knowing she was happy and well cared for eased our minds as we went about our daily routines.

It was incredible to see how this community valued pets and prioritised their well-being. Every interaction Krapow had—with both staff and other pets—reflected the spirit of care that resonated throughout our lives in Qatar.

Though the pace felt slower and the energy less frenetic compared to Dubai, we embraced the opportunities for connection that Qatar offered. Each weekend became a chance to create cherished memories—whether it was a movie night, watching Krapow bask in her glory at Fur Camp, or exploring the local markets brimming with exquisite goods.

Life in Qatar, while quieter, began to weave its own charm—a narrative of contentment and simplicity that stood in delightful contrast to the fast pace we had once known. As we settled into this new existence, I realised that joy often lay in the little moments we shared: the laughter at the cinema, Krapow's playful antics, and the warmth of family life. Each day reinforced the notion that home is not just where you live but where you find comfort, connection, and love amidst the chaos of it all.

One of the most incredible perks of working at Qatar Airways was the affordable air tickets offered to employees—an opportunity that transformed weekend getaways into vibrant adventures. Every month, I found myself planning trips to Bangkok with my family, flying in business class and revelling in the comfort of spacious seats and exceptional service.

These frequent journeys not only gave us the chance to explore a city brimming with culture and vibrancy, but they also allowed Rory to forge a deeper connection with his stepmother's homeland and her family. Each visit unveiled new layers of Thai culture, from bustling markets to serene temples.

Rory's experiences in Bangkok flourished, and to my delight, his tolerance for spicy food grew impressively strong. He embraced the local cuisine with an adventurous spirit, eagerly sampling dishes that would have made my taste buds recoil. Simply put, Rory became far more tolerant of heat than I ever was. He dived into spicy curries and fiery noodles, laughing as I winced at the overwhelming flavours and heat.

I often watched in amusement as he animatedly recounted tales of the culinary delights he had discovered, sharing his experiences with his stepmother and relishing the opportunity to engage with her culture on a deeper level. Each dish he sampled was more than just food; it became a bridge that connected him to his heritage and his stepmother's family, enriching his understanding of their roots and the vast diversity of the world around him.

In between these culinary adventures and family visits, we often explored the sights of Bangkok, taking in everything from the Royal Palace to the picturesque temples, marvelling at the delightful chaos of the markets. The vibrant colours, bustling energy, and friendly faces painted a picture of a city alive with endless possibilities. One of my fondest memories from these trips was stumbling upon a street vendor selling fresh mango with sticky rice; Rory's face lit up with delight as he took his first bite of the sweet treat, utterly immersed in the experience—a moment forever etched in my mind.

These adventures highlighted the beauty of shared moments as a family-exploring foreign lands, tasting delicious food, and embracing hew traditions together Each trip to Thailand deepening connection to Rory's stepmother's culture, nurtured through our journeys to Bangkok, strengthened a unique bond within our family—one that transcended geographical boundaries. It was heartwarming to watch Rory flourish, his curiosity for bold flavours blossoming into a genuine love for Thai cuisine, while he simultaneously created cherished memories into his adulthood.

As life continued to unfold, our journeys became an anchor—grounding us with purpose while offering opportunities for connection, exploration, and a celebration of diversity that would forever shape our family's story.

Just as we were settling into our new life in Qatar, with our trips to Bangkok and the warmth of family ties, the world suddenly changed in early 2020 with the emergence of COVID-19. What initially seemed like distant news from Wuhan, China, quickly escalated into a global pandemic—one that would alter the course of everyday life. Borders closed, cities went into lockdown, and the health crisis sparked fears on a scale many had never experienced before.

In those early days, uncertainty hung in the air like a thick fog. Reports of rising infection rates and the virus's rapid spread dominated headlines across the world. The realities of COVID-19 crept into our lives, abruptly transforming bustling streets into silent corridors and lively gatherings into solitary confinement. Fear intensified as nations scrambled to respond, prompting governments to implement a myriad of measures—from public health campaigns to stringent travel restrictions.

Suddenly, our treasured freedom of movement was at the mercy of an unseen adversary. Qatar Airways, which had once been the fabric binding my family to the heights of travel and adventure, now faced its own significant challenges in the wake of the outbreak. Flights were grounded, schedules cancelled, and the airline industry teetered on the brink of collapse.

As we navigated life in Qatar, the realities of lockdown set in. Initially, it felt surreal; my family was forced to adapt to a a different routine and grappling with the complexities of daily life under new constraints. It was a stark contrast to the easy-going lifestyle we had embraced—our trips and adventures abruptly halted by the pandemic.

For many, including our family, the emotional toll was profound. The news cycles were filled with stories of loss and struggle—families separated by borders, frontline workers tirelessly battling the pandemic, and the relentless strain on healthcare systems worldwide. Despite the challenges we faced at home, we remained acutely aware of the suffering unfolding around us.

In those early months of the pandemic, video conferencing became our lifeline, replacing the vibrant face-to-face interactions we had once cherished. This virtual landscape allowed me to stay connected with colleagues, but it could never replicate the sense of community found in the shared physical spaces we once occupied. We relied on technology to maintain our bonds, yet each click to join a meeting served as a stark reminder of the distance between us.

As days turned into weeks, the world adapted in uncanny ways. Grocery shopping became a strategic mission, with social distancing measures in place and shelves often left bare due to supply shortages. Here in Qatar, we embraced new routines as the community adjusted to evolving protocols and guidelines. Masks became an everyday accessory—a symbol of our collective commitment to protecting one another—while a sense of resilience began to emerge amidst the disruptions.

Throughout this tumultuous phase, we faced challenges as a family. We missed the social interactions that we had been used to, while Winan's desire to connect with her Thai family felt strained as travel became an impossible dream.

In the absence of regular outings, we began exploring our own backyard, discovering parks, trails, and hidden paths where we could roam while maintaining social distance. These outdoor adventures fostered a newfound appreciation for our surroundings, offering a semblance of normalcy amidst the chaos.

Then came the stories of hope and community. Neighbours rallied to support one another—whether through food sharing, virtual gatherings, or simply checking in. As the world faced an unprecedented crisis, we came to realise the strength found in solidarity. It was a poignant reminder that even in the most trying times, the bonds forged through shared experiences could lift spirits, spreading warmth across the distance created by the pandemic.

As the months passed and the situation evolved, signs of resilience began to emerge. Vaccines were developed, and efforts to immunise populations took shape, allowing hope to slowly return to our lives. Plans for the future were made, and, little by little, the world began to reopen.

Reflecting on the impact of COVID-19, I realised that it reshaped my perspective on life, leadership, and relationships. It was a stark reminder of life's fragility and the need to prioritise what truly matters—family, connection, and compassion. While the pandemic brought immense challenges, it also illuminated the power of community and the resilience of the human spirit, which endures even in the darkest times.

Resilience became the hallmark of our family's journey through this unprecedented crisis. With every challenge we faced, we adapted, bound together by the shared goal of supporting one another through life's uncertainties. As we moved forward, I carried these lessons with me, ready to embrace whatever lay ahead, strengthened by the knowledge that we could weather any storm as long as we stood together.

CHAPTER 43

The journey home

After our return to the UK during the pandemic, life settled back into a rhythm following the chaos of that time, I found myself at a crossroads—a moment where my experiences and aspirations converged, leading me toward an exciting new chapter. Fuelled by the lessons I had learned over the years and the resilience forged through both personal and professional trials, I decided to embark on an entrepreneurial venture with my brother and close friend, Lewis.

Together, we launched a business centred around boxing fitness—a concept that had been steadily gaining traction. Our goal was to create an environment that encouraged people to get fit while learning the art of boxing. Recognising that many were searching for effective and enjoyable ways to stay active, we saw an opportunity to promote health and well-being while instilling the discipline and self-defence skills inherent to the sport. The idea was simple yet powerful: combine fitness with empowerment, shaping a unique experience for our clients.

The initial buzz surrounding our venture energised us, and we poured our passion and effort into making it a success. From promoting classes to designing our programmes, every step brought excitement. In those early days, I found immense satisfaction in working alongside my brother and Lewis, shaping a shared vision while reflecting on the journey that had brought us to this moment.

However, as fulfilling as the boxing fitness venture was, I soon felt the pull of the corporate world once more. After a period of consulting for various organisations, I accepted a position with a UK construction company determined to transform its HR department. The complexities of the construction industry presented an intriguing challenge, and I was eager to lend my expertise to help cultivate a more effective and supportive workplace culture.

Transitioning from our entrepreneurial pursuit back into a structured corporate environment was both daunting and exhilarating. The construction company, while full of potential for cultural improvement, presented its own unique challenges—an industry that could often be difficult to navigate, particularly when it came to understanding employee needs and enhancing engagement.

My mission was clear: to drive change from within, focusing on creating a more compassionate and dynamic workplace. Drawing on my experiences with various organisations, I developed strategies centred on employee involvement and engagement. I prioritised fostering open communication, promoting professional development opportunities, and cultivating an environment that recognised and celebrated success.

Reflecting on my time spent building a boxing fitness brand with my family, I realised that the spirit of unity and collaboration I had experienced there could be mirrored in the construction company's HR transformation. I engaged employees at all levels, listening to their insights and incorporating their feedback, laying the foundation for strategies that genuinely resonated with the workforce.

Throughout this journey, I carried with me the understanding that every challenge presented an opportunity. Each programme developed and every initiative implemented became a stepping stone towards a more engaged and satisfied workforce. As the changes took root, I found fulfilment in witnessing the organisation flourish, creating an environment where employees felt valued and empowered. The serious responsibilities of corporate management-I understood that each experience had forged me into a resilient leader devoted to fostering positive workforce culture.

As I continued to navigate this new chapter, I knew it would bring both challenges and opportunities. Yet, equipped with the lessons of my past—both the joy of developing my team, and the importance of trust-there was a profound sense of purpose guiding me forward. and the significance of trust— I felt a profound sense of purpose guiding me forward. Every step of the way, I remained dedicated to ensuring that wherever my journey led, I could help create environments where individuals not only worked but thrived—an ambition that would resonate throughout my career in the years to come.

As I completed this phase of my career, having achieved all I could within this organisation. The world of construction is going through a turbulent time, with many large organisations going bankrupt. My hope is that out of the embers rise a number of stronger, better equipped businesses that prosper, but this industry needs to change and update itself. I hope some of the people related initiatives I put in place, along with a solid business strategy, make sure this organisation goes from strength to strength!

CHAPTER 44
Life Lessons and Reflections

As I stand on the precipice of my journey, reflecting on the myriad experiences I've lived through, I've come to realise that life is a rollercoaster ride, with moments of joy, struggle, and profound lessons. Each chapter of my story, whether marked by the sorrow and laughter of my childhood, the challenges of parenthood, or the intricacies of corporate life, has imparted wisdom that has shaped who I am today.

Embrace Change and Adaptability

Life is inherently unpredictable, and being open to change is imperative. Whether it was moving to Singapore and adapting to a new culture or later transitioning from organisations in media to airlines, I learnt that embracing change, rather than fearing it, often leads to growth and invaluable experiences. For readers, it's essential to be flexible—to recognise that each transition presents an opportunity for learning and that adaptability can be your greatest asset.

The Power of Relationships

Throughout my life, the importance of relationships has continually echoed. From the bonds forged with my siblings and friends in my childhood, like those laughter-filled days at Hull Fair, to the connections made in my professional career, I realised that success is rarely a solitary journey. Building a network of supportive relationships can create a foundation for resilience. Surround yourself with people who uplift you, challenge you, and share in your journey. Don't waste time on negative people; they suck the life out of you.

Remember, humans are pretty much like socks in a dryer—no matter where you are in the world, you're bound to find a few that just don't match! You might think the issues you're dealing with are unique to your company, but chances are, they're as universal as the Monday morning blues. I've encountered the same quirky people problems all over the globe and in various sectors. That's why I like to say, "It's a different circus, but the same clowns!" So, when you're wrestling with a tough problem, don't hesitate to ask for help. Even the best jugglers need a hand sometimes!

The Value of Humour

Humour can be a powerful tool in navigating the complexities of life. Be it through the antics of Trevor the 'Slopa' or the unexpected laughter from a family situation, I learnt that laughter not only eases tension but fosters connection among people. Find laughter in every situation—it can create bridges, lighten heavy moments, and remind us that even in struggle, joy can be found.

Prioritize Trust and Integrity

As I delved deeper into management roles, best practices emerged: trust isn't simply given; it's earned through integrity and transparency. The tumultuous incidents involving colleagues highlighted the critical importance of fostering trust within teams. For readers, remember that trust creates a supportive environment where motivation thrives. Whether in professional settings or personal life, a commitment to integrity strengthens your relationships with others.

Resilience in Adversity

Life's trials shape our character and resilience. Recalling the moments faced during my father's passing, the challenges at work, or the complexities of my marriage, and subsequent divorce began to understand that adversity builds strength. Embracing challenges as growth opportunities, rather than setbacks, will empower you. Look back on how you've navigated difficulties and use those experiences to bolster your spirit in future challenges.

Create a Balance Between Work and Personal Life

The pursuit of career success must be balanced with personal well-being. My travels, whether to Thailand or engaging in boxing fitness, highlighted the significance of finding pleasure in both work and leisure. Carve out time for what you love, whether it's spending quality moments with family, pursuing hobbies, or indulging in a few rounds of golf with friends.

Throughout my career, I have been fortunate to hold senior positions in some of the world's leading organizations across various fields. I have also served on several boards for global multinationals, start-ups, and in the education sector. Overall, I have greatly enjoyed my professional journey and consider myself lucky at times. However, whenever I found myself not enjoying my work, I chose to move on. The lesson I've learned is that life is short, so we shouldn't waste it doing something we don't enjoy.

Life is a tapestry of experiences—make sure to weave in joy. The most important thing is that money can never buy additional time with loved ones. Don't always chase the high paycheck.

Empower Through Leadership

Being in a leadership position means embracing opportunities to uplift others. Drawing from my experiences with youth clubs as a child and executive roles later in life, I learnt the value of empowering those around me. As a leader, inspire trust, foster collaboration, and cultivate an environment where everyone's input is valued. Remember, great leaders develop other leaders.

Encourage growth, allow space for innovation, and watch your team flourish. Once you have trust, people will follow you as a leader.

Cherish the Simple Moments

It's essential to appreciate the small moments—the laughs over a shared meal, the joy of a child learning to swim, or the simplicity of a family gathering. Life isn't just about grand achievements or milestones; it's those simple, heartwarming moments that often bring the largest smiles.

Be present and allow yourself to soak in the joy of everyday life.

The Challenges of Parenthood and Navigating Divorce

Lastly, as I reflect on the lessons learned, one of the most profound aspects of my journey has been the experience of parenthood. The challenges that accompanied my divorce and its impact on my children have left lasting impressions on my heart. No one teaches you how to be a parent, and mistakes are inevitable. I sometimes grapple with the regret of how my actions may have affected Rory and Ailsa. I failed to recognise the complexities of their emotional landscape during a tumultuous time. For that, I am eternally sorry. While I strived to be a good parent, the pressures of adulthood and the fallout from the divorce complicated my efforts. The most important thing I can share is that no matter how much you might dislike one another in a divorce, you loved each other once, and you should always ensure the children come first, regardless of your own feelings. Through these experiences, I learned the importance of empathy and open communication with my children; they deserve to know that they are loved, supported, and understood, no matter the circumstances.

My childhood, a chaotic patchwork of laughter, unexpected surprises, and hardship, irrevocably shaped my understanding of family and relationships. Amidst the confusion, Margaret's presence and the arrival of new siblings taught me resilience, acceptance, and the profound beauty of forging bonds in the face of life's unpredictability. Those chaotic scenes, though painful at times, became stepping stones on my journey of self-discovery. Even within the familial complexities, moments of joy and connection laid the foundation for the person I am today. The enduring bonds with my siblings, a constant source of light through the darkest times, are something I will forever cherish.

I realised over time that my mum's behaviour stemmed from mental illness. I have no ill feelings towards her at all; I love her dearly, and she remains a key part of my life, for which I am deeply thankful. Once she married Ken, her entire life changed for the better. He was truly a calming influence on her. In a strange way, she taught me many life skills that I still hold on to, even if she hadn't intended it that way.

In sharing these life lessons, my hope is to inspire readers to reflect on their own journeys, the challenges they face, and the relationships they nurture. Embrace each chapter of life with an open heart and a willingness to learn. As you move forward, consider actions that can enrich your experiences—cultivating resilience, nurturing relationships, and embracing change. Life will bring its share of ups and downs, but with these tools and insights, you can navigate your journey more successfully and joyfully, turning every experience into an opportunity for growth and connection.

Remember, even amidst the challenges of parenthood, mistakes, and regrets, there is still endless potential for love, understanding, and healing as you forge ahead in your own unique story.

My future remains unwritten, but it is a future filled with hope—one I embrace with open arms and a heart overflowing with gratitude for all that has come before. The next chapter awaits, and I am ready.

www.ingramcontent.com/pod-product-compliance
Lightning Source LLC
Chambersburg PA
CBHW070418010526
44118CB00014B/1799